By the Court

LAW AND SOCIETY

Law and Society Series
W. Wesley Pue, Founding Editor

The Law and Society Series explores law as a socially embedded phenomenon. It is premised on the understanding that the conventional division of law from society creates false dichotomies in thinking, scholarship, educational practice, and social life. Books in the series treat law and society as mutually constitutive and seek to bridge scholarship emerging from interdisciplinary engagement of law with disciplines such as politics, social theory, history, political economy, and gender studies.

Recent books in the series:

Anna Jane Samis Lund, *Trustees at Work: Financial Pressures, Emotional Labour, and Canadian Bankruptcy Law* (2019)
Shauna Labman, *Crossing Law's Border: Canada's Refugee Resettlement Program* (2019)
Kate Puddister, *Seeking the Court's Advice: The Politics of the Canadian Reference Power* (2019)
Taryn Sirove, *Ruling Out Art: Media Art Meets Law in Ontario's Censor Wars* (2019)
Jennifer Tunnicliffe, *Resisting Rights: Canada and the International Bill of Rights, 1947–76* (2019)
Randy K. Lippert, *Condo Conquest: Urban Governance, Law, and Condoization in New York City and Toronto* (2019)
L. Jane McMillan, *Truth and Conviction: Donald Marshall Jr. and the Mi'kmaw Quest for Justice* (2018)
Sarah Grace Marsden, *Enforcing Exclusion: Precarious Migrants and the Law in Canada* (2018)
Jasminka Kalajdzic, *Class Actions in Canada: The Promise and Reality of Access to Justice* (2018)
David Moffette, *Governing Irregular Migration: Bordering Culture, Labour, and Security in Spain* (2018)
Constance Backhouse, *Claire L'Heureux-Dubé: A Life* (2017)
Christopher P. Manfredi and Antonia Maioni, *Health Care and the Charter: Legal Mobilization and Policy Change in Canada* (2017)
Julie Macfarlane, *The New Lawyer: How Clients Are Transforming the Practice of Law*, 2nd ed. (2017)

For a complete list of the titles in the series, see the UBC Press website, www.ubcpress.ca.

By the Court

Anonymous Judgments at the Supreme Court of Canada

PETER McCORMICK and MARC D. ZANONI

UBCPress · Vancouver · Toronto

28 27 26 25 24 23 22 21 20 19   5 4 3 2 1

Printed in Canada on FSC-certified ancient-forest-free paper (100% post-consumer recycled) that is processed chlorine- and acid-free.

Library and Archives Canada Cataloguing in Publication

Title: By the court : anonymous judgments at the Supreme Court of Canada / Peter McCormick and Marc D. Zanoni.

Names: McCormick, Peter James, author. | Zanoni, Marc D., author.

Series: Law and society series (Vancouver, B.C.)

Description: Series statement: Law and society series, 1496-4953 | Includes bibliographical references and index.

Identifiers: Canadiana (print) 20190119446 | Canadiana (ebook) 20190119489
ISBN 9780774861717 (hardcover) | ISBN 9780774861731 (PDF) |
ISBN 9780774861748 (EPUB) | ISBN 9780774861755 (Kindle)

Subjects: LCSH: Canada. Supreme Court – Decision making.

Classification: LCC KE8244. M33 2019 | LCC KF8764.ZA2 M33 2019 kfmod |
DDC 347/.71035 – dc23

Canada

UBC Press gratefully acknowledges the financial support for our publishing program of the Government of Canada (through the Canada Book Fund), the Canada Council for the Arts, and the British Columbia Arts Council.

This book has been published with the help of a grant from the Canadian Federation for the Humanities and Social Sciences, through the Awards to Scholarly Publications Program, using funds provided by the Social Sciences and Humanities Research Council of Canada.

Printed and bound in Canada by Friesens
Set in Myriad and Sabon by Artegraphica Design Co. Ltd.
Copy editor: Frank Chow
Proofreader: Judith Earnshaw
Indexer: Margaret de Boer
Cover designer: Martyn Schmoll

UBC Press
The University of British Columbia
2029 West Mall
Vancouver, BC V6T 1Z2
www.ubcpress.ca

TO OUR FAMILIES,

FOR THEIR PATIENCE AND SUPPORT.

Contents

Tables and Figures

Tables

Figures

Preface

This book represents an unusual co-authoring partnership, between a senior (and now emeritus) faculty member on the one hand and a graduate student on the other. Indeed, it is sufficiently unusual to call for an explanation.

Marc Zanoni came to the University of Lethbridge to work on a Master of Arts degree in political science, to be supervised by Peter McCormick. After some discussion of alternatives, it was decided that the thesis topic would involve an examination of the Supreme Court of Canada's *By the Court* decisions – those decisions that are not attributed to any specific individual but mysteriously and cryptically to *the Court*. The thesis project was originally conceived in terms of the chronology, inventory, and typology found in Chapters 8 and 9 of this book.

This plan quickly went off the tracks, however. A routine element of any thesis is the literature review, which situates the project in relation to the work that has already been done on the subject. The first sign that there would be nothing routine about this master's thesis was the discovery (which still surprises us every time we mention it) that there was simply no academic literature on the subject. Although most court-watching academics are well aware that such decisions appear from time to time, and that at least some of them have been extremely important, there were no books, no articles, no focused discussion of any kind of the genesis or the parameters or even the frequency of the phenomenon. So much for the literature review, which gave Zanoni nothing to go on save for passing references and occasional brief footnotes.

As an alternate starting point, then, Zanoni set to work checking out what has been generally accepted as the starting point for the practice that we refer to in this book as the "standard story" and the "Laskin thesis" – namely, the Laskin court's two language decisions of 1979 (*Blaikie* and *Forest*), often thought of as picking up on the *per curiam* practices of the United States Supreme Court.[1] The plan was for him to work through the relevant judicial biographies on the one hand and academic accounts of these two specific decisions on the other, to explore and document the background that everyone was taking for granted. This might or might not unfold in such a way as to become a useful part of a revised thesis proposal in itself.

This inquiry also went in an unexpected direction, however. This was partly because many of those academic accounts focused on the content and implications of the two decisions, one focused on Manitoba and the other on Quebec, without even mentioning the unusual anonymous delivery format, which gave Zanoni nothing to work with. A greater problem was that the assumptions built into the standard story were simply not borne out, as will be explained in Chapter 7. This was somewhat embarrassing because some of McCormick's earlier publications had become part of the footnote trail for that standard story. What had been initially contemplated as a straightforward introduction morphed into a genuinely original inquiry into the questions no one else had even considered: tracking down the "who" and "when" and "why" of the real first *By the Court* decisions. Readers are free to imagine how Zanoni felt as his literature review came up empty and his attempts to document "what everybody knew" fell through, after months of hard work with nothing much to show for it. Fortunately, this last reframing of the inquiry proved fruitful, although carrying it through required scouring through the *Supreme Court Reports* all the way back to 1875, and then following up with an exploration of the Supreme Court archives that was initially scheduled for several days but actually lasted several weeks.

The outcome was a revised thesis project that now appears in reduced form in Chapters 6 and 7, "Early History: The 'Minor Tradition'" and "Emergence: The Birth of the 'Grand Tradition.'" Chapter 7 began as a draft chapter for the thesis, was turned into a paper that Zanoni presented at the 2014 Canadian Political Science Association (CPSA) conference, and then became a co-authored article in the *Manitoba Law Journal.* Although that inquiry had already pushed *By the Court* back a dozen years earlier than the "standard story," Zanoni's scouring of the *Supreme Court Reports* suggested that such decisions were drawing on even earlier court practices, and the story of this extended early evolution became the new focus of the thesis. Chapter 6 reflects Zanoni's weeks of toil in the Supreme Court archives, working toward an understanding of what he called the "minor tradition" of *By the Court.* That accomplished, he headed off to a PhD program in public policy at the University of Guelph. Chapter 6 is a considerably shortened version of the MA thesis, and was initially presented by Zanoni as a paper at the 2016 CPSA conference. Chapter 4 also began life as an introductory segment in the 2014 CPSA conference paper.

However, Zanoni had uncovered enough to make the *By the Court* project something that was clearly much too large and ambitious for a master's thesis, leaving us with a much larger story still waiting to be told. For one thing, the chronology, inventory, and typology originally contemplated still needed to be tackled (Chapters 8 and 9). In addition, the academic responses to our conference papers and journal articles demonstrated the necessity of defending the originality and the uniqueness of the Canadian practice (Chapters 4 and 5), since both were often challenged. It was also obvious that we needed to defend our assumption, perhaps not entirely self-evident, that the decision presentation format itself really matters in the first place (Chapter 3). Finally, we had to establish the conceptual frame within which to locate this new development, which after a couple of false starts is now identified in terms of the "third phase" of Supreme Court judgment delivery. These were the elements of the larger project that McCormick was best qualified to tackle on the basis of three decades of research into appellate courts in general and the Supreme Court in particular.

The book is therefore not the product of collaboration in the usual sense of two authors working through circulated drafts to generate a single unified voice; rather, it consists of separate segments with different lead authors. The pivotal Chapters 6 and 7 are essentially Zanoni's; the others are McCormick's, with a more collaborative conclusion. Presenting the book as a co-authorship is the only fair way to reflect the basic reality that without the prompting of Zanoni's project, without his discovery that accepted truths were not truths at all, without his persistence in chasing down unanticipated aspects of the practice, and without his diligence in sifting through the archives and decoding those records to correct our simplistic assumptions about the every-case journey from argued hearing to reported outcome, the core discoveries of Chapters 6 and 7 would never have been made and this book could never have been written. Without Chapters 6 and 7 to anchor them, the other chapters would have lacked the central link that made them useful parts of a single larger story. Co-authorship was the only honest presentation of this product; relegating the graduate student to an enthusiastic footnote appended to two chapter titles would have been both unfair and misleading. The unusual origins of this book project undoubtedly still show through to some extent in terms of a different writing style in these two central chapters.

A number of people have contributed to this project in significant ways, including the colleagues who cheerfully responded to email inquiries, the people who commented on our conference presentations, and the external reviewers who dealt with our various journal submissions. More specifically, we would like to single out three individuals. Professor Philip Girard of Osgoode Hall Law School, Bora Laskin's biographer in his magnificent *Bringing Law to Life* and also Justice Willard Estey's law clerk in 1979–80, gave useful pointers and steered us away from some dead ends. Professor DeLloyd Guth of the University of Manitoba Law School not only commented on but also painstakingly copy-edited an early version of the *Manitoba Law Journal* piece. Finally, Alicia Loo of the Library and Information Management Branch of the Supreme Court of Canada was unstintingly generous in the assistance she provided to Zanoni as he spent several weeks working through the archives, and as he struggled to correct on the fly our naive expectations of how the

Supreme Court operated in its earlier decades. The necessary assistance was considerably greater than might be expected because the records are kept in the form of that wonderful information storage technology of the 1980s, microfilm. Our fellow researchers will appreciate the now-problematic implications of that then-virtuous technological choice – oh, for hyperlinks and search engines, to say nothing of the convenience of remote access! We are also grateful to the anonymous readers who worked through a longer and more ponderous early version of the manuscript to make helpful suggestions that provoked some major revisions, and to Randy Schmidt of UBC Press, who cheered – and prodded – us on. Responsibility for any mistakes that remain (and we do not doubt that there are some) is fully our own.

Our greatest thanks are to the members of our respective families, who were for months on end frequently obliged to share at considerable length both our enthusiasm over unexpected new findings and our frustration over false starts and dead ends, and who have been kind enough not to make too obvious their relief that this particular intellectual journey is finally over.

PART 1
Introduction

What Are *By the Court* Decisions? 1

The last half-century has been a time of dramatic political and constitutional change in Canada. One of the most important elements of such change has been the emergence of the Supreme Court of Canada as a major national player. Far more than in earlier decades, the court now plays a significant and highly visible part in almost every major political and constitutional event, acting as the final authority such that no story about law or policy is complete until it has spoken. No one can write a history of Canada's last fifty years without devoting a major chapter to the Supreme Court (or perhaps even one to each of its last four chief justices, easily the four most visible holders of that office in the history of the institution). No one can provide a satisfactory account of political current events without mentioning the shadow of the court. This rise to such prominence is the big judicial story of the last fifty years, and this chapter will expand on and validate this assessment. We will describe it in terms of the emergence of the Supreme Court as a constitutional court – a slight overstatement, since the court has always played a constitutional role, but the scope of that role has expanded so dramatically, with such significant consequences, that this mild hyperbole is justified.

But within that large development is another story, one more important than anyone seems to have realized – the emergence of a highly unusual and uniquely Canadian style of delivering judgments for a select but impressive list of its major decisions, specifically for decisions in important constitutional cases. That judgment delivery style is the anonymous, and almost always unanimous, *By the Court* style. We consider it unusual because for Canada, as for all the comparable countries in the common law tradition, decisions of the court are typically attributed to a single specific judge – "the judgment was delivered by Justice X" – whether the decision itself is unanimous or delivered on behalf of a majority of the panel. Our own Supreme Court, however, has invented, repeatedly used, and (perhaps) recently begun to regularize a unique style for an important subset of its decisions, under the format "the judgment was delivered by THE COURT." "Invented" and "unique" are strong claims, but we will substantiate them.

Whereas the "judicial power" story is so obvious that none would question it, the *By the Court* story has been completely overlooked. Remarkably, there has never been an academic exploration of this phenomenon, not even to the simple preliminary extent of generating an inventory of the examples. Before our own recent publications, not a single journal article, let alone a book, focused specifically on the subject.[1] Even when academics write about *By the Court* decisions, they often do not even mention this unusual feature; and when they do mention it, they do so as a passing acknowledgment without speculating on the reason for, or the meaning of, this departure from the norm. Our own journal submissions exploring various aspects of the development were sometimes treated dismissively by the anonymous external reviewers – not because these unusual-format decisions did not exist but simply because "anonymity doesn't matter," "there aren't enough of these to worry about," "the delivery format makes no difference," or (our favourite) "perhaps it is the Court's way of saying that these decisions aren't particularly important."[2]

This book will refute each of these objections. We will demonstrate that anonymity does matter, because it cuts against the practices that have characterized the history of the Supreme Court of Canada and that characterize to this day the national high courts of other comparable countries. By establishing an inventory of several dozen such decisions, we will demonstrate that there are more of these cases than most people realize. Similarly, we will demonstrate that this inventory is by no means limited to not "particularly important" cases, first, because it is strongly focused on constitutional cases, and second, because it includes some of the court's most salient and high-profile decisions. Most specifically, *By the Court* decisions have clearly emerged as the Supreme Court's preferred format for dealing with another important and uniquely Canadian practice, the federal constitutional reference.

In sum, then, we will be examining a judgment delivery style for Supreme Court of Canada decisions that is characterized by an impressive list of unusual features:

- It is *a striking departure* from normal practices, specifically the common law convention that specific judges assume signed responsibility for the reasons for judicial decisions.
- It is *original* to the Supreme Court of Canada, not an imitation of the practices of any other relevant court.
- It is *recent,* having emerged only a few decades ago (although, as will be discussed below, we would say five decades rather than the "less than four" of what we call the "conventional" story).
- It is *unique,* a practice that is still not followed by any other comparable court.
- It is *infrequent but persistent,* averaging one per year for five decades, and its use is growing even as the Supreme Court caseload shrinks.
- It is *narrowly focused* on constitutional decisions (especially, but by no means only, the important subcategory of federal reference cases).
- It has been used for some of the Supreme Court's most *politically salient and high-profile* constitutional cases, perhaps most notably the *Quebec Secession Reference.*[3]

It is striking that the Supreme Court itself has never provided any discussion of the practice – has never addressed the "when and why" questions regarding its use for some cases but not for others. The court has been candid (in the public speeches that Supreme Court justices now frequently give, the journal articles that several of them write, or in some of the judgments themselves) about other changes in practice, such as the strong move toward larger panels, the "circulate and revise" practice for the writing of judgments, and the discouragement of fragmented panels in favour of more unanimity. But this special kind of unanimity remains as mysterious as when it first emerged. Although the identity of the author has always been one of the most routine and regular pieces of information provided for its judicial decisions, the court has decided, without any explanation whatsoever, to keep this fact secret for several dozen of its constitutional cases.

The obvious question is how such an unusual, original, distinctive, and self-highlighting practice could have escaped wider notice. How could this country accumulate four dozen major constitutional judgments over half a century of Supreme Court practice, precisely when the Supreme Court itself was very much in the public spotlight, without anyone focusing on this striking new way of doing business? How is it, when so many academics are assiduously tracking the evolving story of what specific judges have to say about specific aspects of the law, that no one has attached any importance to these cases where no specific judge is claiming or being given credit for these ideas?[4] Why has academic and professional curiosity been so muted? Perhaps the answer lies in the rather subtle distinction between "The judgment of the Court was delivered by [Justice X]" and "The judgment was delivered by THE COURT." Perhaps it is partly due to the degree of confusion created by the fact that the Supreme Court has had a practice of using a *per curiam* (Latin for "by the court") label that long predates the more recent *By the Court* style. This confusion is then compounded by the *per curiam* practices of the United States Supreme Court, which are in fact different from both the Canadian *per curiam* and *By the Court.*[5] Perhaps it is because the Supreme Court of Canada often deals with its oral from-the-bench decisions on minor appeals in single paragraphs (sometimes single sentences) that are delivered "By the Court." Beyond these suggestions, we really cannot explain why this practice has managed to fly under the radar for so long, but we will attempt to tell the story that no one seems to have noticed and give this unique practice due attention.

We will attempt to unfold the *By the Court* story in the rest of this book. In the process, we will justify our claims that judicial delivery formats matter, that this particular style of judgment delivery has emerged only recently, that it was invented in and by the Canadian Supreme Court, that it is neither an imitation of other courts nor a standard variant of appeal court decisions, that no other common law country has a comparable practice, and that the court seems to be stepping up the frequency of such decisions. Our approach is resolutely institutionalist, focusing on how the Supreme Court as an institution has reshaped both itself and the way it presents itself through its formal judgments to deal with new challenges, rather than on the specific content of its responses. That said, we will to some extent be "naming names" and identifying the chief justices who presided over the important steps in this evolution. We give notice now that the most important of those names will not be Laskin or Dickson but McLachlin, and the first will be Cartwright. This book is intended to be a contribution to the history of the institution of the Supreme Court as it transformed itself into a court whose main business is constitutional law, but it is also a consideration of current events as a prominent chief justice has led the court through uniquely challenging times. For Chief Justice Beverley McLachlin, more than for any of her predecessors, *By the Court* was part of this process.

Let us begin with a brief description of *By the Court.* In the *Supreme Court Reports,* there is a standard format for organizing the reasons for judgment in the court's decisions. This format has evolved considerably, as will be discussed in Chapter 3, but the current format has been in place, with some modifications, for several decades.[6] It begins with the name of the case (formally, the "style of cause") that identifies the immediate parties to the case and lists any interveners (third parties, not directly involved but presenting legal arguments as to the optimal resolution of the case). This is followed by a list of judges serving on the panel; the dates for the oral argument and the delivery of the decision; the headnotes (short phrases identifying the various issues that are touched on in the reasons, generally grouped in some sort of order of centrality or importance); a short description of the case and a "Held" paragraph that gives the outcomes and identifies dissenting reasons (if any); and a summary of the various sets of reasons that members of the panel have delivered. Finally, there is a list of cases judicially noted and of legislative/constitutional and academic materials referred to; a short statement of the provenance of the case (citations for the initial trial judgment and intervening appeal court decisions); and a list of the lawyers involved representing the immediate parties and any interveners. After all this information, which often takes up a substantial number of pages, we get the reasons for judgment written by the judges themselves (with some unknown but presumably not negligible assistance from their clerks).

If the decision was unanimous, it is introduced with the phrase "The judgment of the Court was delivered by [a specific judge]." If it was a majority decision of a divided panel, the phrase is "The judgment of [names of the judges signing on to the majority reasons] was delivered by [a specific judge]." This format suggests that the other judges involved may have done more than simply sign on to someone else's work (the judgment delivery formats of some comparable national high courts emphasize the lead author in a way that carries no such implication, although it seems unlikely that there was not some degree of interaction). The other judges will have participated to the extent of commenting on earlier drafts of the judgment in the expectation that some accommodation will be made to those comments, and judges have indicated in speeches and articles that they take this circulation seriously and that the exchanges over revisions are much more than superficial. However, the normal practice involves attribution to a specific individual who has taken the lead in writing the reasons and who accordingly draws the praise or criticism with which the decision is received.[7] The Supreme Court has declared that the giving of reasons is an important aspect of its accountability to the Canadian public.[8] The convention of specific attribution adds a further dimension to this accountability by making those reasons, as well as their rigour and persuasive power, part of the reputation of an individual judge.

Sometimes, however, the introductory phrase is different, declaring simply that "The judgment was delivered by THE COURT." There is no attribution, no indication of a lead author (although, curiously, the

Supreme Court Reports usually tell us the language in which the judgment was actually written, which narrows the range of possibilities). Unanimous judgments are not infrequent in our Supreme Court, but the general rule has long been that the substantive reasons for such judgments are attributed to a specific individual. To be sure, whether or not a specific author is identified, we can assume that all the judges must have agreed to those reasons or they would not be signing on to them (which the judges literally and physically do). We also presume that they did so only after the circulate-and-revise process has enabled them to comment on the earlier drafts and possibly to receive accommodations; there is a collegial, and to some extent even a negotiated, aspect to Supreme Court decisions.

Sometimes the court goes further in the direction of collegiality. Not only does it "circulate and revise" an initial draft but it also chooses not to identify the lead author or authors, without giving any indication of the reason for this. It may be that this signals a set of reasons for judgment where the collegiality and negotiation have been unusually pronounced – a genuine committee decision for which identifying a lead author would be misleading. We are skeptical about this, however. At the very least, it is curious that these "so extensively collegial that solo attribution would be misleading" decisions never seem to occur except in constitutional cases.

In Canadian practice, and excluding the from-the-bench decisions noted above, *By the Court* promises a single extended anonymous set of reasons directed toward explaining the outcome of a significant (and almost invariably constitutional) case. By "extended" we mean that it is thousands of words long, as opposed to a sentence or a paragraph of boilerplate text or a routine resolution of a minor case. We therefore need to distinguish what we shall call the modern practice (the "grand tradition") from an older and continuing "minor tradition." By "a single set" we mean that this set of *By the Court* reasons is all that is provided, without any further elaboration by a specific judge or any expressed reservation or disagreement in the form of dissents or separate concurrences by one or more of the other judges.[9] By "anonymous" we mean that there is no indication whatsoever as to which justice or justices on the panel may have taken a lead role in the drafting of the reasons.

The application of this very particular form of decision presentation constitutes the Canadian practice of *By the Court.*

One complicating factor in our delineation of *By the Court* is the fact that the Supreme Court has been using this label to serve two distinct purposes. On the one hand, there is a very long-standing practice (which we call the "minor tradition" and will describe in more detail in Chapter 6) that involves brief (and usually *very* brief) presentations of routine decisions in an anonymous form. Recent examples include *Aitkens* and *Peers,* which show that minor-tradition decisions can be as brief as a single cryptic paragraph or even a single sentence.[10] Of such decisions, we would suggest (echoing Robbins's comment about most of the US Supreme Court's *per curiam* judgments, a subject we will explore in Chapter 4) that it does not matter who wrote the words because those words contained nothing of any wider legal significance.[11] On the other hand, there is a more recent practice (which we think of as the "grand tradition") that uses an anonymous format to present extended discursive reasons in major, and almost exclusively constitutional, cases. It is the emergence and deployment of the latter that is the focus of our analysis and that directs our use of terms: rather than refer to "*By the Court* (grand tradition)" and "*By the Court* (minor tradition)," we will speak of *By the Court* on the one hand and "the minor tradition" on the other.

But if the extremes – some of the least significant and some of the most significant of the court's decisions (*Aitkens* and the like on the one hand, the *Quebec Secession Reference* on the other) – define themselves, the problem is deciding where to draw the dividing line. The point of our investigation is to examine when and how the Supreme Court presents its reasons anonymously in cases that really matter. For us, such cases are characterized by being assigned to a larger panel, by drawing interveners, by being reserved for a reasonable length of time, by drawing discursive reasons of at least modest length, and by being cited in later decisions of the Supreme Court.[12] As might be expected, there is a high degree of correlation between these factors. Turning these elements into a five-item "index" to be applied to borderline cases gives a solid cut-off point that is both objective and reasonable. The most obvious element of that cut-off point is reasons for judgment that are not less than 2,000 words in length, or about five pages of text. A lower cut-off point risks allowing the modern practice to be swamped by routine cases (minimum panels, cryptic reasons, no interveners, or never cited). A higher cut-off point of, say, 4,000 words would have excluded only half a dozen cases from our grand-tradition set, but it would have been awkward as one of them was the 1979 *Forest* case, one of the pair of companion cases that, prior to our research, has generally been regarded as the starting point of the phenomenon.[13]

This anonymity is highly unusual for courts such as the Supreme Court of Canada. For major decisions, especially those dealing with constitutional issues, it is even more unusual and (as we shall demonstrate) absolutely unique to Canada, and even more so for the way that the examples continue to accumulate. This is an age in which judges of the national high courts of various countries are more aware of each other, interact with each other, and consider each other to be part of a supranational community of some sort to a greater extent than ever before – an age when the practices of one court may be expected to generate imitations or echoes in the courts of other countries.[14] However, the Canadian practice of *By the Court* was not copied from any other country, nor has it influenced the regular practices of any other country to date.[15] The constitutional *By the Court* style is a recent Canadian invention that continues to be unique in the common law world, a claim that we will substantiate in the chapters that follow.

We reject the suggestion of some commentators that *By the Court* is a way for the court to tell us that a decision is not particularly important. The "greatest hits" list of these decisions makes the argument for us. The *Quebec Secession Reference* is clearly the poster-child example of the device. It was the court's response to the ongoing drama following Canada's constitutional near-death experience in the 1995 Quebec referendum, rendered more provocative by the court's transformation of the question from "Under the Canadian constitution or international law, does Quebec have the right to secede?" to "Under what circumstances and through what sort of procedure could Quebec secede?" This was not the court's first foray into this territory, however. That distinction belongs to the 1982 decision, also *By the Court*, on the idea of a Quebec veto on constitutional change.[16] The *Securities Act Reference* somewhat surprisingly stymied Ottawa's move in the aftermath of the global financial crisis to establish a national securities regulator.[17] Major decisions about language rights in Quebec in the face of the provincial government's measures to promote the use of French (such as *Ford* and *Devine*) signalled that the Supreme Court was once again being drawn into the conflict over Quebec's possible separation.[18] Directly engaging the abortion issue, *Daigle v Tremblay* was the Supreme Court's sympathetic treatment of an abortion case that rejected a Quebec Court of Appeal decision suggesting a constitutional "right to life."[19] *United States v Burns* provided the opportunity for the court to speak out on the question of capital punishment; at the very least, this decision effectively rewrote an extradition treaty with the United States and may also have precluded the reintroduction of the death penalty in Canadian criminal law.[20] *Marshall 2*, the court's salvage attempt after ambiguities in *Marshall 1* inflamed relations between First Nations communities and their neighbours, was also a *By the Court* judgment (although *Marshall 1* itself was not).[21] The list is nicely bookended by two extended discursive interventions in the constitutional amendment debate: the *Reference re Upper House* of 1980 and the *Reference re Senate Reform* of 2014.[22] The court's handful of "not quite *By the Court*" judgments (which we argue are nonetheless part of the general phenomenon) are comparably important: the *Patriation Reference* of 1981 (even more unusual for having two different sets of joint judgment reasons attributed to no specific individual judge, each of which is confronted by joint dissenting reasons similarly unattributed), the *Exported Natural Gas Tax* case of 1982, and the *Nadon* case on appointments to the Supreme Court of 2014.[23] The court's 2016 decision on the federal government's motion to extend the deadline on the suspended invalidation of the *Criminal Code* regarding assisted suicide is an intriguing echo, with a decision that is a joint judgment of five listed names confronted by a (partial) dissent that is a joint judgment of four listed names – there is not a specific solo attribution to be seen.[24] This is, we submit, a very impressive set of cases – and not at all amenable to being described as not "particularly important."

We also reject the suggestion that there are not enough of these decisions to be concerned about, not enough to justify a focused look. There have been several dozen constitutional decisions of significant length by the Supreme Court that have taken this form, a reasonable proportion of which have been headline-grabbing blockbusters. Not all *By the Court* cases are major decisions, and not all major constitutional decisions (even unanimous ones) have taken this form, but enough of them have done so, repeatedly for several decades, under several successive chief justices, and for important enough cases, that we cannot dismiss them as curious and idiosyncratic aberrations. This book attempts to set the record straight and stimulate the continuing closer look that this style of judgment deserves.

We reject the notion that the high courts of any comparable common law jurisdictions employ the same practice, or that the Canadian device has been copied from or inspired by any other country (including, especially, the United States, which critics often suggest is the real originator of *By the Court,* albeit under a slightly different label). We have sorted through hundreds of decisions on more than a dozen court websites, and have not found anything that approaches the phenomenon that is the subject of this book (this scrutiny will be described in a later chapter).

Finally, we dismiss the casual assumption within the discipline (which we ourselves shared until evidence pointed elsewhere) that *By the Court* was an innovation dreamed up by Chief Justices Bora Laskin and Brian Dickson, briefly important but subsequently fading from its initial promise. Not only does this get the historical genesis of the practice wrong, as we will explain in a later chapter, but it completely misstates the relative frequency of the use of the practice by recent chief justices. The McLachlin court has been far and away the most frequent and the steadiest user of *By the Court* judgments from the very first days of McLachlin's tenure as chief justice. *By the Court* is not something that was important for a little while several decades ago; it is a practice that has continued to be used in important constitutional cases, more so in the 2010s than in the 1970s.

Original, unique, recent, important, and both reasonably and increasingly frequent – this is the *By the Court* phenomenon that has never before enjoyed the spotlight that we shine on it in these pages.

We assume that the use of the *By the Court* device in the modern grand tradition is not something casual or whimsical but rather a conscious choice by the judges on the panel with strategic overtones. Unanimity (all judges agreeing on an outcome) and univocality (all judges agreeing on the reasons leading to that outcome) are important attributes of modern Supreme Court decision making, but we assume that *By the Court* signals something more, a greater degree of solidarity that implicitly invites a greater degree of attention. We assume that it is something more than happenstance that it has been targeted so directly on constitutional cases, a major component of the modern court's significant caseload. And we utterly reject the notion that one finds in some of the American literature that it is a way of reducing the workload by allowing judges to produce work that is shoddier than they would ever want to put their individual names to. These rebuttable assumptions frame our inquiry.

In Chapter 2, we will defend our assertion that about fifty years ago – not earlier – the Supreme Court of Canada became primarily a constitutional court, and we will spell out the change in the role of the Supreme Court that is implied by this shift, and the way the court has moved to accommodate it.

In Chapter 3, we will defend the idea that presentation style matters, and matters enough to merit study. Specifically, we argue that presentation style is part of a battery of choices made by courts that reflect evolving conceptions of the judicial role in general as well as the role of the individual judge within the institutional setting of a final court of appeal. So framed, this is a choice that sends signals; to fully understand the evolving judicial role, we must know how to decode these signals.

In Chapter 4, we will defend the notion that the Canadian Supreme Court's use of *By the Court* is original by refuting the standard explanations of its emergence, which see it as either following English examples or echoing developments in the United States Supreme Court.

In Chapter 5, we will defend the notion that the Canadian Supreme Court's use of *By the Court* is unique within the common law world by undertaking a survey of the most directly comparable common law courts, canvassing the variety of modes through which judicial decisions are delivered. In the process, we will demonstrate that none of these courts has a practice remotely similar to that of the Supreme Court of Canada.

In Chapters 6 and 7, we will describe the institutional background of the practice. Chapter 6 will provide an "early history" of *By the Court* that has never before been described or examined. We will call this the minor tradition and will track it through eight decades and three distinct phases. In Chapter 7, we will feature the transitional moment when the minor tradition was transformed into the modern practice (the grand tradition). The year was *not* 1979, and the judge responsible was *not* Laskin.

In Chapter 8, we will provide an inventory and chronology of the grand tradition, highlighting the major examples and tracing its evolution through the tenures of successive chief justices.

In Chapter 9, we will generate a typology of *By the Court* judgments, with each of four types having its own history and rationale. This typology will in itself provide at least a partial explanation of why the Supreme Court is using the device, why those were the cases for which it was used, and what signal or signals the use of *By the Court* is sending. Generating such a typology is made more problematic because the Supreme Court has never given any solid explanation of the device – not in any of the decisions themselves, nor in any formal statement of practice, nor in any speech or writing by any of the judges on the court.

In Chapter 10, we will move beyond typology to explanation: Why *these* cases? We will present four possible explanations, rejecting the first and focusing on the fourth and more recent consideration that is transforming the practice by making it part of a new and broader development.

In Chapter 11, we will connect our findings to the comparative literature on national judiciaries. In the process, we will indulge in some speculation about the future of the practice now that McLachlin, who presided over the most extensive use of *By the Court,* has been replaced by a new chief justice.

The Supreme Court of Canada Takes to the Constitutional Stage

2

By the Court is a phenomenon of the modern Supreme Court of Canada. One important element of this modernity is the fact that the court has become a constitutional court in the fullest sense of the term. Situating the emergence of *By the Court* at the point of transition to this new role is very important to our argument.

On the face of it, our notion of the Supreme Courts becoming a constitutional court may raise some eyebrows. From the very beginning, with its establishment in 1875, the court's jurisdiction has included constitutional matters, whether those were raised by private litigants, arose from direct confrontation between federal and provincial governments, or were presented to the court through constitutional reference questions from the national government. Such cases as *Severn v The Queen, City of Fredericton v The Queen,* and *Citizens' and The Queen Insurance Cos. v Parsons* – all decisions about the federal-provincial division of powers and decided within the Supreme Court's first five years – make this point very clearly.[1] At first glance and in an important sense, therefore, the Supreme Court has always been a constitutional court. However, as we shall see in this chapter, there are three respects in which an important transition to a distinctly modern period can be discerned, a transition that we will be situating in the late 1960s and early 1970s.

Oversimplifying only slightly, the modern Supreme Court is a fully constitutional court in a way that in its earlier decades it was not.

The Not-Yet-Supreme Court

The first constraint on the Supreme Court's constitutional role was the fact that it was supreme in name only – it was not in fact a national final court of appeal. Its decisions could be appealed to the Judicial Committee of the Privy Council in London, a "quasi-court" largely staffed by judges, most of them English Law Lords.[2] It was not part of the English judicial hierarchy, and did not hear English appeals from the regular English courts; as the "Privy Council" part of its title suggests, its legal status was instead that of an advisory body to the monarch.[3] In practice, it functioned very much like a court, hearing legal arguments and delivering judgments that relied heavily on its own judicial precedents. Instead of following the *seriatim* style of the House of Lords, however, it restricted itself to delivering a single set of reasons, following from its obligation to present focused advice to the monarch.[4] Decisions of the Supreme Court of Canada could be, and not infrequently were, appealed to the Judicial Committee; the total number of such appeals was just over 250 in 75 years, or just over 3 per year. The Judicial Committee was not at all reluctant to reverse the decision of the Canadian court or to enunciate rather different principles in explaining it. Indeed, on one noteworthy occasion, the Supreme Court concluded its delivery of a decision on a constitutional case with the peevish comment that it was not going to be providing reasons for judgment because the case was certainly going to be appealed further and there was no indication that the Judicial Committee took the Supreme Court's reasons seriously.[5]

Further attenuating the Supreme Court's role, it was possible (with the consent of both parties) for an appeal from a decision of a provincial court of appeal to be carried directly to the Judicial Committee, bypassing the Supreme Court altogether. This *per saltum* procedure accounted for more than 400 of the Canadian appeals to the Judicial Committee before these appeals were ended in 1949. The Judicial Committee decision in such cases was still binding precedent for the Supreme Court, despite the court having been completely bypassed and unable to contribute to the Judicial Committee's consideration of the matter.

The Canadian federal system as we know it is very much a creature of the decisions of the Judicial Committee. Consider a handful of important examples: *Citizen's Insurance v Parsons* in 1881 became the definitive word on the interplay within the *British North America Act, 1867* (now the *Constitution Act, 1867*) between section 91.2 (the federal Parliament's jurisdiction over "trade and commerce") and section 92.13 (the provincial legislatures' jurisdiction over "property and civil rights within the province").[6] It sharply constrained the former in favour of the latter and created the famous "two branches" of the federal trade and commerce power that were not fully realized until Dickson's 1989 decision in *General Motors of Canada v City National Leasing*.[7] *Russell v The Queen* in 1882 was a first (and somewhat problematic) exploration of what the phrase "peace, order and good government" in section 91 of the *Constitution Act, 1867* added to the specific list of matters assigned to the legislative authority of the federal Parliament.[8] *Bank of Toronto v Lambe* in 1887 began to sort out both the relative taxation powers of the federal ("any mode or system of taxation") and provincial ("direct taxation within the province") governments, and provided an early elaboration of the "pith and substance"/"double aspect" doctrines that softened the potential rigidities of the federal-provincial distribution of legislative authority.[9] The *Local Prohibition Reference* of 1896 was one of a string of Privy Council cases that articulated the need to interpret "peace, order and good government" narrowly, on the grounds that doing otherwise would destroy the autonomy of the provinces.[10] All these decisions bound the Supreme Court of Canada, and all remain important to an understanding of the constitutional aspects of Canadian federalism.

Just as important were the decisions of the Judicial Committee in a string of cases involving challenges to the federal government's legislative authority as it attempted to deal with the Great Depression.[11] This was in some ways a northern replay of the New Deal skirmishes between President Franklin Delano Roosevelt and the United States Supreme Court, except that where Roosevelt largely prevailed, the Bennett government's initiatives were largely found to be unconstitutional.[12] Given the timing – the Great Depression coincided with the English Statute of Westminster, which acknowledged the war contributions of the "white" Empire by relinquishing statutory control over countries such as Canada, Australia, and New Zealand – this also involved the question of the extent to which Canada's new status interacted with some of the imperial carryovers in the constitutional document. The most notable example was whether the Imperial Treaty Power clearly stated in section 132 of the *Constitution Act, 1867* had morphed into a new national treaty power; despite a hint in the *Radio Reference* that it had ("this amounts to the same thing"), the Judicial Committee of the Privy Council clearly decided in the *Labour Conventions Reference* that it had not.[13] Academic and professional dissatisfaction with the implications of these federally constraining decisions was one of the elements in the move to end appeals to the Judicial Committee.

The Supreme Court of Canada was largely a bystander (or, perhaps more accurately, a passenger) on this constitutional journey. Only in 1949 did its appellate subordination to the Judicial Committee end, with an amendment to the *Supreme Court Act* such that the court now exercised "ultimate appellate jurisdiction" within and for Canada, and the judgment of the court "is, in all cases, final and conclusive."[14] That said, however, the court's judicial emancipation was gradual rather than immediate, as it continued to treat the Judicial Committee's decisions as binding precedent, much to the disappointment of academics such as Bora Laskin, who decried this self-imposed "English captivity."[15]

The Constitutional Caseload

The second transformational element involves a pair of simple questions: how many and how often? For much of the court's history, constitutional cases were a very small part of the caseload. Before a take-off point that we are about to identify, the Supreme Court heard about twenty constitutional cases per decade. Only twice in those earlier years – in 1936 and 1960 – did it decide as many as half a dozen constitutional cases in a single year, and there were many years when the court heard no constitutional cases at all. For the modern court, constitutional cases are a major part of the total caseload every year. This is reflected in Figure 2.1, where of the two lines showing an annual count,

Figure 2.1 Constitutional law case count in the Supreme Court of Canada caseload

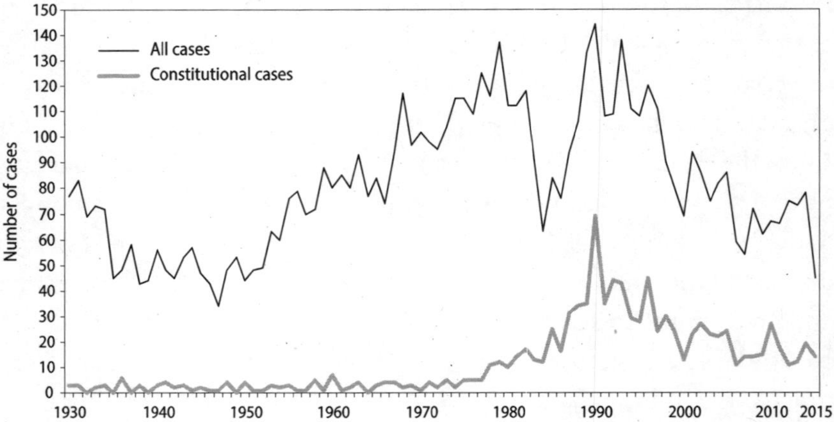

the higher line is the total number of reported decisions and the lower line is the number of cases identified in those reports as constitutional decisions.[16] Unsurprisingly, the *Canadian Charter of Rights and Freedoms* has been an important part of this sea change, but only as a part of a larger story: note that the upturn seen in Figure 2.1 was already clearly established before the 1982 entrenchment. The year 1978 was the first that the number of constitutional cases reached double digits. In the single peak year of 1990, the court decided more constitutional cases than it had in the three decades after the Second World War. Thus Figure 2.1 validates our suggestion that only recently has the Supreme Court really become a constitutional court.

Our argument may appear to be undermined by the fact that the constitutional case count has declined fairly steadily from its peak in 1990, but this is offset by the fact that the court's total caseload has been falling as well. Perhaps a more useful way to make the point is to show constitutional cases as a percentage of the annual caseload (Figure 2.2). In Figure 2.2, the smoother line running through the middle is the five-year running average, which allows longer-term tendencies to emerge from the year-to-year fluctuations.

Figure 2.2 Constitutional law cases as a percentage of the Supreme Court of Canada caseload

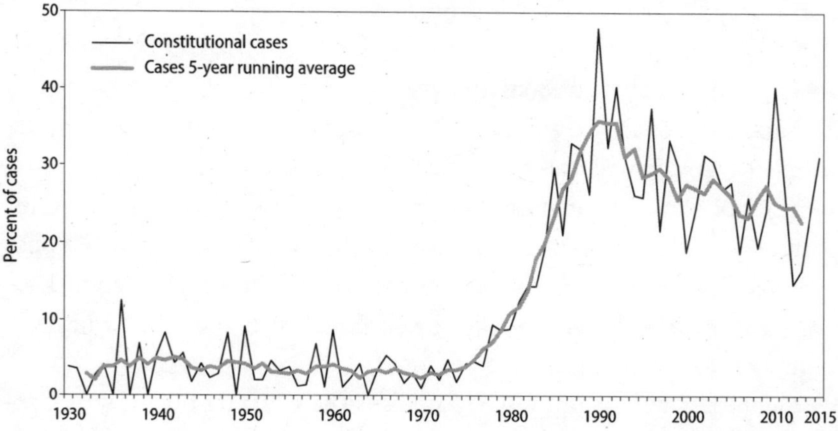

This makes our point even more emphatically. For several decades, constitutional cases were a fairly steady proportion of the caseload, running just below 5 percent.[17] Early in the 1970s, however, the line takes a sharp upward turn, despite the new 1970s practice of reporting every single decision. The sharp rise peaks in 1990, just under 50 percent for the single year and just over 35 percent for the five-year running average, before sliding downward to a new plateau around 25 percent.

In practical terms, this makes a big difference. Before the 1970s, constitutional cases were sufficiently infrequent that the average member of the court would see only one or two each year, a tendency reinforced by the widespread use of small panels. Since the 1980s, the court has been looking at several such cases every month, and the swing toward larger panels means that the average member of the court would be sitting for almost all of them. Even more to the point, the notional one-ninth share of the judgment-writing assignments would mean that the average judge would have two or three such decisions to write every year.[18] One criticism of academic studies of national high courts is that they tend to be unrealistically focused on the high drama of the major constitutional cases, when in fact most of the work of those courts is directed to other subjects. For the Supreme Court of Canada, this is clearly much less true than it used to be, and the modern court is constantly engaged in constitutional cases.

An Expanding Constitutional Agenda

The abolition of appeals to the Judicial Committee of the Privy Council in 1949 transformed the Supreme Court, and the steadily increasing number of constitutional cases reinforced the importance of that transformation. Today there are new dimensions to the constitutional issues that such cases are bringing before the court. The modern court's expanding constitutional role has flowed down several distinct but comparably important channels.

The most obvious of these channels is the ongoing business of Canadian constitutional law: federalism. Although the basic frame of federalism was established by the decisions of the Judicial Committee, many of them in the nineteenth century, federalism issues have continued to make up a steady part of the caseload in recent years. For example, the *Insite* case (ultimately a Charter decision but raising federalism issues as well), the *Securities Act Reference* (which invalidated proposed federal legislation establishing a national securities regulator), and the *Senate Reform Reference* (which sharply curtailed the federal legislative potential for unilateral changes in favour of the formal amending process) are perhaps the most high-profile of these decisions.[19] More generally, however, the Supreme Court has been carving out its own theory of Canadian federalism. Although it uses the label "cooperative federalism," this is not at all what political scientists have in mind when they use the label.[20] Rather, the Supreme Court is describing a deliberate policy of strictly constraining the doctrines of federal paramountcy and interjurisdictional immunity in order to permit a considerable degree of duplication and overlap between federal and provincial legislation.[21] This led to a serious mismatch between the court's "cooperative federalism" and the Harper government's espousal of an "open federalism" built around a clearer demarcation of federal and provincial jurisdictions with a minimum of entanglement.

The second channel, and the one that has held the spotlight for some time, is the Charter. Since 1982, the court has had the responsibility of interpreting and applying an entrenched *Charter of Rights and Freedoms* that included (in section 52) a clear power of judicial review – an explicit power to find offending legislation, federal and provincial alike, "null and void and of no force or effect" – as well as the even more ambitious, open-ended potential of section 24(1), which empowers the courts to provide any "such remedy as the court consider appropriate and just in the circumstances." The *Morgentaler* decision, which struck down the *Criminal Code* sections making abortion illegal outside certain limiting procedures, was the first clear indication that the court was willing to wade into the most controversial issues of the day in ways that would provoke direct confrontations with government policy.[22] And the very first of the equality rights decisions – *Andrews* – signalled that the court was going to take seriously the notion of "analogous rights" under section 15, reaching beyond the seven so-called enumerated rights to accommodate a variety of other inequalities that trigger constitutionally unacceptable discrimination.[23] This role has continued to expand since, perhaps most controversially to include sexual orientation (*Egan, Vriend*).[24] The court has also reversed its earlier position (in *Rodriguez*) to find a constitutional right to assisted suicide (in *Carter*).[25] It would be difficult to find three more socially divisive issues than abortion, gay rights, and assisted suicide, but the Supreme Court has grasped the nettle on all three.

In the process, it has enhanced its impact on the public policy process with a growing variety of remedial strategies. The initial result of a finding of unconstitutionality under the Charter was the obvious one, following from section 52 of the *Constitution Act, 1982:* any statute that is incompatible with the Constitution is null and void to the extent of that incompatibility, which means that the legislation is struck down in whole or in part.[26] This was the Charter strategy of the Dickson court during the first years of the Charter, with the striking down of the *Lord's Day Act* in *Big M Drug Mart* as the most obvious and clear-cut early example.[27] But more imaginative responses were soon developed. In *Vriend,* the Supreme Court solved the problem of Alberta's omission of sexual orientation from its *Individual Rights Protection Act* by "reading in" the omitted words, essentially instructing lower courts that they should deal with future cases by applying the statute as if it included words that the Alberta legislature had deliberately omitted. During the 1990s, it developed the idea of suspended invalidation, which involves a finding of invalidity (in whole or in part) but a suspension of the effect of that finding for a stated period (usually between six and eighteen months) to allow the offending legislature to make the appropriate corrections.[28] This has become the Charter remedy of choice for the Supreme Court and its use has grown steadily.[29] Finally, the court has toyed with the idea of a "constitutional exemption," a notion first bruited (but not applied) in *Latimer.*[30] At one point, the court appeared to have abandoned the idea entirely, only to embrace it in very special circumstances in the recent *Carter* decision.[31]

The important "first wave" of Charter cases may now be over, with at least first approximations to a resolution of almost all the major issues, but the boundaries of the general principles will continue to need clarification for some time to come.[32] The "Charter count" in the Supreme Court caseload may be down from its peak in the early 1990s but it is far from vanishing.

The final channel involves Aboriginal rights, put on the constitutional agenda by the Supreme Court itself in the *Calder* case in 1973 and then entrenched ("existing Aboriginal and treaty rights") in section 35 of the *Constitution Act, 1982.*[33] That entrenchment did not provide a specific definition, however, and it has fallen to the Supreme Court to both define Aboriginal right (and the related notion of "Aboriginal title") and establish the circumstances that must be proven by the specific Aboriginal community in order to claim something as an Aboriginal right. The *van der Peet* trilogy is perhaps the central decision in this process, although the important issue of the relevance of oral tradition evidence was dealt with in *Delgamuukw.*[34] In both respects, this has been a set of doctrines that continues to evolve. In the context of contemporary resource development, the establishment of an Aboriginal right (or even the existence of a land claim that has not yet been resolved) triggers issues of the "honour of the Crown" (a modern phrase that has recently emerged in this context) and a governmental duty of consultation and accommodation, most recently in *Tsilhqot'in.*[35] The related issue that the court seems to have deliberately steered clear of to date is the question of Aboriginal self-government, which was put on the constitutional agenda in the failed Charlottetown Accord of 1992 and has remained prominent in First Nations expectations ever since; this seems to be on the way to being accomplished more through the new treaty process than through Supreme Court discovery and explication.[36] That particular journey has not been without its detours and difficulties, most notably the *Marshall 1* decision of 1999.[37] This was, the court subsequently determined, interpreted over-generously by so many First Nations communities that it was necessary for the court to revisit the decision (in what was self-described as neither a rehearing nor a formal clarification) in *Marshall 2* to narrow its implications, an implicit retreat that was deeply resented by the Aboriginal community.[38] The steady flow of First Nations cases continues, for example, with the important decision in *Daniels* that clarified the meaning of "Indians" in section 91.24 of the *Constitution Act, 1867* rather more generously than the federal government would have preferred.[39]

Along the way, the court has dealt with other things as well. It completely redefined judicial independence in the *Remuneration Reference.*[40] It identified a right to secession within the Canadian Constitution and suggested an appropriate procedure in the *Quebec Secession Reference.*[41] It clarified the status and content of parliamentary privilege in *Vaid.*[42] It has, in *Nadon,* brushed aside ambiguities in the amending procedures of the *Constitution Act, 1982* and entrenched itself in the Canadian Constitution in a way that makes any changes to itself as an institution extremely difficult.[43] And it has effectively rewritten the Canada-US extradition treaty in *Burns.*[44]

Summary

The purpose of this chapter has been to validate our claim that we can identify a recent period in which the role of the Supreme Court as a constitutional court expanded dramatically and quickly. It is reasonable to expect that any such major change in judicial role will in some way be reflected in its procedures – how you do something depends on what you see yourself as doing. The modern challenge of "interpreting and applying the constitution on an ongoing basis" is quite different from the role of the court in its earlier decades, when private law cases predominated, or in the immediate postwar period, when the age of positive government ramped up the frequency of public law cases and the emergence of a criminal appellate bar increased the volume and importance of criminal cases. In the next chapter, we will make the case that these changes in procedure, particularly changes in the way the court presents its published reasons, matter.

Why Decision Presentation Formats Matter

3

It is hardly controversial to say that Supreme Court decisions matter, that the reasons given by the court for a particular outcome provide leadership for the lower courts and therefore send implicit signals to potential litigants. Supreme Court decisions matter first and most importantly for their content, which involves something more than the headline-drawing question of who won the day in the dichotomous (appeal allowed/appeal dismissed) world of the appellate courts. The reasons for judgment are equally important because they provide the statements of legal principles and constitutional interpretation that are the substance of precedent – a lower court can (and is expected to) "follow" the Supreme Court's reasons, but it cannot in any useful sense "follow" an outcome.

Our position is that the way that Supreme Court decisions are presented and packaged matters very much as well. This may make us sound like little children at Christmas who want to play with the boxes the presents came in rather than the expensive, currently fashionable items that the giver worked so hard to find. Examined more closely, however, this metaphor actually makes the point for us, because people often do make an effort to match the packaging to the recipient, the occasion, and any implicit message; as the importance of the recipient, the occasion, and the message increases, so does the attempt to find the most appropriate packaging. Anyone who doubts this can try giving this year's very special present to his or her significant other unwrapped, with nothing but the bag the sales clerk put it in at the store. Good luck with this!

Given that the court is (in the conventional American phrase) without the power of purse or sword, it is only the words in its judgments that convey and reinforce its message, which makes the packaging and presentation of those words something considerably more than a peripheral matter. As Garoupa and Ginsburg put it, "Armed only with pens, judges can only be effective if they are persuasive and authoritative to the parties before them, the legal community, and the public as a whole."[1] Judicial power is very much a question of rational persuasion, buttressed by professional reputation, preserved and enhanced by appropriate presentation. At its core, the courts have just as much power (no more and no less) as a general public consensus feels they should have – a consideration that Gibson, Caldeira, and Baird refer to as "diffuse support."[2] Packaging is therefore not a secondary or peripheral aspect of what they do, but a major part of the self-presentation that both reflects and reinforces the current public understanding and acceptance of their role. To make the point by an extreme example: we would be highly surprised if the Supreme Court were ever to deliver a decision in verse or as rap.[3] More to the point, the court would erode its own prestige by indulging in such frivolous behaviour.[4] "Diffuse support" is a marvelous asset for the exercise of influence but it can be squandered, and once lost, it is difficult to recover.

To use an obvious metaphor: just as the four tires on your car are all that give you any chance of influencing the speed or direction of the vehicle, so the words in judicial reasons are the only points at which a court has any opportunity to influence or direct the actions of the various actors and legal officials whose performance gives the court its apparent power. The mode of presentation of the reasons for a decision is therefore something that must be carefully crafted to maintain the gravitas of the institution and to conform to the expectations of its publics so as to reinforce rather than undermine its impact. One of the most important strategies for accomplishing this is, of course, simple continuity – tradition is one of the most effective elements of the Supreme Court's influence repertoire – although in circumstances of broader social, political, and legal change, careful alterations may be called for. It is in this context that we are presenting the unusual fact of conscious judicial innovation, and its unusual product in the form of the *By the Court* judgment.

At first glance, this may seem to be an unpromising angle of attack, because the current standard form of presentation for judicial decisions appears self-evident, an appearance that is constantly and deliberately reinforced by its simple continuity.[5] The Supreme Court's decisions, one might think, look the way they do because that is simply how judicial decisions in the common law tradition look. Presumably, they must look much the same in other common law countries, and presumably they must have looked much the same throughout the history of the Supreme Court itself.

Neither of these presumptions can be sustained, however. In Chapters 4 and 5, we will provide a quick global survey of common law judicial practices with respect to the presentation of national supreme court judgments, and the patterns that we will describe are far from uniform. In this chapter, however, it is the second presumption that we will refute, using the evolution of the Supreme Court's own practices to do so. We can indeed talk about a "standard format" for Supreme Court decisions within a particular time period, and it is well worth noting that for any time period there is indeed a "standard format" subject to minor variations and gradual evolution. That format can change significantly from one time period to another, however. In the language of the social sciences, we are looking at the phenomenon of "punctuated equilibrium" – there is a general rule of continuity, of things remaining largely the same over a span of many years, but from time to time this is dramatically interrupted as a new format emerges. The new format then becomes the new standard so that the rule of continuity again prevails; the new format becomes so routine as to be virtually invisible once again.[6]

Why does this change in presentation matter?

First, it matters because it embodies a theory of law. Does the court declare the law, or does the law speak through the court? The modern style is to think of the decision itself as the law (to take the most powerful example: the modern formula is that Supreme Court decisions about the Constitution are themselves part of that constitution), which means that the court declares the law or, yet more controversially, makes the law. But at one time the law was envisaged as something that was progressively unfolded through a judicial conversation – between different judges on any given panel, between judges on different levels of courts, between yesterday's courts and today's courts – such that any specific set of judicial reasons was no more than a contribution to that understanding. As Gerhardt puts it, "There was, in effect, no precedent until a later majority declared what it was."[7]

Second, it matters because it displays a theory of the role of courts in general and the Supreme Court in particular – is it answering a single focused question, or is it painting on a broader canvas? The Supreme Court always has a choice between a minimalist decision that explains the immediate decision in constrained and grounded terms, a generalist decision that contains reflections on immediately tangential aspects and issues, and a maximalist decision that uses this as the occasion for a grander statement about the law or the Constitution.[8]

Third, it matters because it tells us whom the court is addressing. Is it speaking to the legal profession or to the broader public? Is it assuming that its readers will have a solid knowledge of background and an ability to decode professional jargon? Or is it spelling things out for the benefit of a broader audience, carefully explaining many things that lawyers and judges already know? Simply scanning a handful of decisions at random from sequential decades of the *Supreme Court Reports* makes it clear that the Supreme Court was once engaged in a technical and coded conversation with the legal profession but is now targeting a broader educated lay public.

Fourth, it matters because it tells us how the Supreme Court thinks of itself, whether as nine individuals speaking out and casually grouping and ungrouping, or as a committee in search of a solid centre of gravity to be expressed in a majority judgment, or as a coherent institution that speaks as often as possible with a single voice displaying consistency over time. This is only partly a matter of competing or cooperating personalities, or of a particularly assertive chief justice; it is also a reflection of a broader sense of role on the part of all the members of the court, and also of broader professional expectations. In da Silva's language, is the court merely collegiate (meaning that decisions are made by a group) or is it also collegial (meaning that that group works together to speak as an institution)?[9]

Fifth, it matters because it reveals something about the interactions within the court, most specifically about the nature of the office of chief justice (that strangely underexplored position in what is widely recognized as a global age of judicial power). "Who writes" always matters (a consideration that we will expand on below), so the derivative question is how often, and on what types of cases, it is the chief justice who is writing – and, to anticipate a question that will occupy an entire chapter, whether the chief justice always does so explicitly and under his or her own name.

Nor is it fanciful to suggest that serious and explicit consideration is given to whether the presentation format matches the court's status, especially when that status is undergoing some change. In the early 1950s, when the end of appeals to the Judicial Committee of the Privy Council finally made the Supreme Court of Canada truly supreme in fact as well as in name, there was a public discussion of whether the court should alter the way it presented its decisions to mark this new status. Debates were held within professional organizations such as the Canadian Bar Association, and Chief Justice Thibaudeau Rinfret joined in to indicate that he favoured adopting the "single attributed judgment" style of the Judicial Committee itself. Ultimately, nothing came of these proposals (then-professor Bora Laskin was one of the strongest critics of the idea), but they resonate with our suggestion that presentation formats matter enough to receive direct and explicit attention at moments of major change.[10]

We will follow through on our premise that judgment formats matter by tracing the evolution of judgment presentation by the Supreme Court of Canada, an evolution with two clear major stages to date as well as (a suggestion we will defend at length in a later chapter) clear signs of an emerging third stage (see Table 3.1).

To anticipate the argument that we will make more fully in our concluding chapter: *By the Court* is the early, and in some sense the initial, form of modern co-authorship practice, a practice that rose to prominence

Table 3.1 Evolution of judgment presentation in the Supreme Court of Canada

Decision style	*Evolutionary developments*
The *seriatim* era	Pure *seriatim* Clustered *seriatim* Transitional: occasional notice of "majority"
The judgment era	Emergence of "judgment" and "reasons" Failed transition: "the majority" and "the minority"[1] Two languages and more accessible reasons A new standard format
The co-authorship era	Anonymity for selected major decisions Anonymous majority/minority for divided major cases Shared two- and three-judge authorship of many judgments

Note:
1 This might actually be an example of an emulation of a court in another country, namely, the Judicial Committee of the Privy Council, which in 1966 amended its procedures to allow a single set of concurring or dissenting reasons, but not any additional minority reasons.

during the McLachlin court, with implications profound enough that it deserves to be treated as a new phase in the history of the court.[11] Although *By the Court* came first, by three decades, co-authorship by two or three judges now occurs several times as often. It would be a mistake, however, to think of co-authorship as entirely displacing the earlier form, because *By the Court* itself has become more frequent at the same time. A "one, several, all" evolution of judgment authorship might make more intuitive sense than a "one, all, several" sequence, but it is the latter rather than the former that emerges from the historical record. This broadening development reinforces our argument that *By the Court* deserves closer attention: first, for its very novelty; second, for the focus of the practice and the number of high-profile examples; and third, for the more recent broader departure from single authorship to which it seems to be linked.

The *Seriatim* Era

A *seriatim* decision (meaning "individually, one after another") is one that involves every member of a multi-judge panel writing full separate free-standing reasons to support their preferred outcome for the immediate case; these preferences are accumulated at the time of their presentation (but not before) as votes that generate a result – namely, an appeal that is allowed or denied. In its purest form, each set of reasons is a complete treatment of every element of the immediate case, and none makes any reference to any of the other sets of reasons, either by responding positively or negatively to an argument or a conclusion, or by "piggybacking" (explicitly adopting some element, even the most routine, of another set of reasons) rather than presenting its own free-standing account.

In its purest form, the writing of these separate reasons is so independent that although an outcome will be reached by counting each set of reasons as a "vote" to allow or dismiss, this counting takes place only at the time the judges assemble to deliver the decision. Should a judge happen not to vote with a majority of the panel members, his or her reasons would be considered a "dissent," but the judge did not write those reasons with any knowledge of this, because there was no set of reasons that had in advance a status such that the judge could either dissent from or comment on it. Conversely, none of the reasons written by judges in what turns out to be the majority are "concurring" judgments in the modern sense, first because none of the opinions had a status to which the others were responding, and, second, because none of the contents of any of the "winning side" opinions were known in advance.

To the modern eye, this process has not one but three disadvantages and, taken together, they are so transparently dysfunctional that some readers will have trouble taking the description seriously.

First and most obvious, there is what seems to be a massive waste of judicial time and energy. Much (even most) of the time, the various sets of reasons delivered in this way are largely duplicative – they are of comparable length, they follow roughly similar sequences of arguments and ideas, and they cite much the same set of judicial precedents before reaching the same general conclusion. Why do something five times when you need to do it only once?[12] And why have every judge invest the time to write for every case when they could be both more prompt and more thorough by negotiating minor differences and then taking turns doing the writing, with the judges concentrating their research and writing efforts on a smaller fraction of the caseload?

Second, to the extent that the multiple reasons are largely but not perfectly duplicative, it is difficult for readers to determine whether any of those differences are significant. It is necessary to read every paragraph of every set of reasons, only to discover that much of the time they are so similar that you did not need to read them all. If you do not read them all, however, you risk missing the page or so of one judge's analysis that will be the most directly useful to you in some future case. If writing all those reasons seems to waste the judges' time, then reading all of them seems a comparable waste of time for lawyers and lower court judges.[13] But there is no shortcut available because each set of reasons has the same formal status – all are equally "judgments," none is self-described or pointed to by the others as having a special lead status. Instead of the modern presentation format for divided panels (judgment first, separate concurrences second, dissents third), the plural reasons of *seriatim* decisions are always presented in order of the seniority of their author, but this is no guarantee of their relative importance to the evolution of precedential authority.

Third, on those occasions when the plural sets of reasons are not duplicative but follow different explanatory routes or draw on different precedential sequences or use different interpretations of relevant documents, the consequence will often be that "the opinions gave an incoherent view of the law."[14] This leaves the law in a state of confusion, all the more because the fully independent production of the multiple sets of reasons has precluded any meaningful dialogue between the judges, any direct confrontation between conflicting viewpoints, any movement working from persuasion or negotiation toward a synthesis or compromise – and no single set of reasons can be identified as the authoritative reasons to be followed in the future. All are "judgments" in the terminology of the times; as a result, none is "the judgment" in the modern sense. Extracting the core precedential nugget or nuggets is a process that must now take place gradually; as Gerhardt puts it, the "real" meaning of such a decision is not given by the immediate court, but must be worked out over time by subsequent courts that draw on the variety of positions to create (not just passively receive) binding authority.[15]

One lasting legacy of this early Supreme Court tradition is the way that multiple sets of reasons were long presented in the *Supreme Court Reports.* If everyone was going to be writing, and if no set of reasons was institutionally designated as a "lead" judgment, then the most logical sequencing was seniority – chief justice first, then all the others in the order of their appointment. This meant that even if the chief justice or some other reasonably senior colleague dissented (which initially simply meant supporting a different outcome from a majority of the other sets of reasons), theirs were still published as the first set of reasons. Only in 2005, decades after the tradition of "all sets of reasons have equal status" had been replaced by new practices, did the court switch to the more logical sequencing of judgment first, concurrences next, and dissents last.

A second lasting legacy is the curiously conditional language with which the conclusions of even a unanimous court were presented – always a carefully couched "I would dismiss/allow the appeal" rather than an emphatic "The appeal is dismissed/allowed." Today, when we are looking at a unanimous judgment, assigned at the post-hearing conference and written from the first draft in the firm knowledge of that unanimity, this self-deprecatory style seems curiously engaging. However, it made perfect sense at a time when judges wrote independently without knowing how their colleagues were going to line up: "I would dismiss, but at time of writing I don't know if enough of my colleagues would do so to make that the actual outcome."

There are several reasons, however, why *seriatim* might have seemed a logical way of pursuing an appellate court judgment.

First, it respects the complexity and nuance of the law, without any tendency to negotiate away reservations and nuances in favour of a mutually acceptable common ground. Strings of almost-but-not-quite precisely similar sets of reasons retain these qualifications and reservations, for the information and guidance of future practitioners and judges (an argument that is still often made in defence of minority reasons more generally). By the same token, by precisely informing lower court judges, lawyers, and litigants of those divisions and reservations, it provides a warning of the possibility of future changes in the law that might otherwise come as a complete surprise.[16]

Second, and especially if the panel has been unanimous as to outcome and heavily duplicative as to reasons, it demonstrates that an objectively correct outcome has been reached; its "precedent is particularly weighty, because it represents a consensus independently reached."[17] We might think of it as something similar to a medical second opinion, except that there are five or seven or nine separate opinions, and they are rendered simultaneously rather than sequentially. Replicability is a hallmark of a scientific finding – we can rely on the conclusions because we know that anyone who conscientiously repeats the experiment will get the same results. By a parallel logic, it is the very repetitiveness of the parallel arguments and conclusions that provides a reassurance of objective and replicable legal analysis, of a process that generates the same result no matter which legal professional is conducting the inquiry.

Third, to make the same argument in a more pointed way (as Thomas Jefferson did when he criticized Chief Justice John Marshall for doing away with the United States Supreme Court's *seriatim* practices): it avoids the appearance that a dominant clique (or individual) within the panel court is willfully imposing its own preferences and silencing minority voices. There are judgment presentation styles that indeed involve the stifling and silencing of dissenting minority voices – for example, the pre-1966 practices of the Judicial Committee of the Privy Council – and even a strong *de facto* institutional preference for majority decisions can have, or can be perceived by outsiders as having, some of the same implications. Only *seriatim* ensures that every justice will speak his or her own mind, leaving it for the broader legal community to work out the "real" message of the decision over time.

In sum, then, the *seriatim* system "has the advantage of giving a more fine-grained information about each judge's view of the law" and is justified "for reasons of transparency and judicial accountability."[18] The point we are making is that the *seriatim* style was not some bizarre departure from common sense that was rightly (and not prematurely) discarded, but that it served in a fully functional way a concept of the law and of the judicial role that differs significantly from our own.

Seriatim judgments were so frequent as to be the norm for the newly established Supreme Court, but the practice was already declining by the early years of the twentieth century and largely disappeared during the interwar period.[19] Interestingly, however, they continued to be used almost exclusively for judicial responses to federal reference cases, right up to the very day they were replaced by the *By the Court* style. As we will discuss in a later chapter, the English House of Lords continued for a long time to report many of its decisions in the *seriatim* style, and the Australian High Court does so to this day.

In "pure" *seriatim* style, each judge writes and there is no appearance of any interaction or sharing of views before the decision is formally delivered, but it seems unreasonable to take this absolutely literally. Certainly there were no conferences of panel members after oral arguments, but there must have been some exchanges between at least some of the judges, especially after 1939, when they had their own building and their own chambers in that building. Over time, it became increasingly common for several judges on the panel to write, with one or more of them doing so on behalf of a colleague as well ("The judgment of A and B was delivered by B").[20] Peter Hogg suggests that in the late 1920s, Chief Justice Francis Anglin encouraged the writing of a single majority judgment whenever possible, but there were still many fragmented judgments in the *seriatim* style.[21]

Throughout this period, there were also a certain number of decisions where a majority of the panel combined behind a single set of reasons. Contemporary readers might find it hard to resist thinking of this as "really" a majority judgment whose authority eclipses the solo reasons that accompany it, but it is important to realize that in the *seriatim* tradition this assumption simply does not apply. It is only in the "majority tradition" that in some countries or for some purposes has replaced the *seriatim* tradition that this is true. More generally, "in the seriatim tradition, these opinions do not carry additional weight," and it is possible for the solo reasons of other judges on the panel to have a greater impact on precedent.[22]

This claim may seem rather extreme. It is difficult from a modern standpoint not to look at an earlier decision, find the largest bloc of judges who supported the actual outcome, and think of this as a modern (definitive, law-stating, and law-setting) majority judgment that was or at least should have been treated as such by subsequent and lower courts. We should instead be thinking of the long-standing common law principle that any specific judgment is final and decisive only as to the outcome; the statement of the reasons is a contribution, and not necessarily a decisive one, to an understanding of a law that the judgment seeks to fulfill. It follows that any set of reasons, even solo reasons and even reasons supporting the outcome the others rejected, may be discovered by a later court to have made the most useful contribution. Consider, for example, the 1954 case of *Johnson v A.G. Alberta*, dealing with the validity of provincial regulations on slot machines, with five sets of reasons from a seven-judge panel.[23] When this case was cited twenty years later, by Chief Justice Brian Dickson in *MacDonald v Vapor Canada Ltd.*, it was taken as establishing that the provinces cannot acquire greater legislative jurisdiction through the device of supplementing the federal *Criminal Code*.[24] However, although this was presented as "the case means" rather than as "Rand suggests," it was only the solo reasons of Justice Ivan Rand in 1954 that had even raised this aspect of the question, let alone used the "supplementing" language to resolve it.

A transition from this to the next phase was hinted at by a practice that began in the late 1950s: it was sometimes explicitly noted in the *Supreme Court Reports* that a particular set of reasons was supported by more than half the judges, the typical format being "the judgment of A, B and C, in the majority, were given by A." This was done sporadically rather than systematically, however, and without any clear indication that it carried precedential consequences, which is why we treat it as "change pending" rather than "change accomplished."

The "Single Judgment, Single Author" Era

The critical shift in the presentation format for Supreme Court decisions in Canada occurred in the late 1960s and the early 1970s. It first appeared under Chief Justice John Robert Cartwright (1967–70) and became so routine under Chief Justice Laskin (1973–84) as to have become invisible once again. What happened was that the *Supreme Court Reports* began to assign the label of "judgment" uniquely to that set of reasons that was signed by at least a majority (or, more rarely, a plurality) of the panel; all other sets of reasons, separately concurring or dissenting, were labelled as "reasons." At the same time, the proportion of reserved decisions delivered by such a clearly highlighted majority climbed steadily.

This change is considerably more portentous than might first appear. The two critical elements of the *seriatim* style are 1) that every judge (or almost every judge) on the panel simultaneously and independently writes his or her own set of reasons, and 2) that every one of those sets of reasons enjoys the equal status of a "judgment." This means that the phrase "dissenting judgment" was once a perfectly sensible and commonly used term in Supreme Court judgments – a search for the term on the LEXUM website yields hundreds of results – but it has almost entirely vanished since the mid-1970s, except when the reference is to an earlier decision of the court from a time before the new protocol emerged.[25]

This change in the Supreme Court's own terminology reinforces our conviction that what underlies a major and persistent change in presentation format is a corresponding shift in the routine understanding of the nature of modern law and the role of the modern Supreme Court. The *seriatim* style of the "old" Supreme Court presented an outcome supported by a string of opinions about the law, none of which is transparently privileged in relation to the others, and all of which are therefore "in play" in the subsequent development of precedent. But the modern "majority style" dramatically privileges one of those sets of reasons – the "judgment" – which is, strictly speaking, the only one of the sets of reasons that carries pre-emptive precedential value, and that set of reasons is as much an institutional as an individual product.[26]

This change in decision presentation could have come about only after an equally important change in the decision procedures themselves. Specifically, there could be a single judge delivering the reasons on behalf of a majority of the panel only if the entire panel had met after oral argument to share their thoughts on how to proceed, such that both the existence and the composition of that majority could be clearly identified. Precisely how that speaking-for-the-majority writing assignment was made remains somewhat opaque to this day, but for present purposes what matters is that a procedure was developed for identifying the majority, for assigning the responsibility for writing the reasons on behalf of that majority, and for highlighting the elevated status of those reasons in the official reports.[27] It was only in the late 1960s that Chief Justice Cartwright initiated the process of regular post-hearing conferences, and therefore it was during his tenure that the "judgment/reasons" distinction began to appear in the *Supreme Court Reports.*[28]

This practice has since absolutely solidified – post-hearing conferences are part of the regular procedure of decision making, and all decisions (save for a problematic handful) are reported with a single "judgment"; should there be dissents or separate concurrences, they are always labelled as "reasons."[29] Since 2005, this has also been reflected in the sequence in which those sets of reasons are presented in the *Reports:* judgments first, concurrences next, dissents at the end.[30]

It is also striking that the *Supreme Court Reports* underwent a number of dramatic changes in the 1970s:

- The new rule was that all decisions of the Supreme Court were reported, without the selection process that had earlier omitted cases deemed of lesser importance.
- All decisions were reported in both official languages (with an official translation into the official language other than the one used by the judge).
- The reasons in those decisions became considerably more discursive and explanatory, transparently targeted to a wider audience than the legal professionals to whom the reasons had been directed in earlier years.

The end result was vastly more approachable than the style it replaced.

A further consequence of the practice of conferencing and the identification of a spokesperson for the majority position has been the emergence of a strict protocol that the majority reasons should be drafted first; judges who have found themselves in a minority position are expected to wait until the majority reasons have been circulated before drafting their response.[31] This is the reason for the standard phrase at the beginning of almost all minority reasons on the Supreme Court of Canada: "I have read the reasons (of the majority)."[32] Indeed, the Supreme Court of Canada has recently developed a very specific and distinctive judgment delivery format in which minority reasons are focused, polite responses to clearly identified and complete majority reasons; even more recently, the majority sometimes responds directly (and also politely) to those concerns.[33] This makes a coherent package of the reasons of even divided panels in a way that has no counterpart in the practice of comparable national high courts.

In da Silva's delightfully succinct summation, the *seriatim* court is one that decides without deliberating.[34] By contrast, the conferencing court – with an assigned spokesperson for the majority who circulates reasons and responds to the suggestions of colleagues – decides only after deliberating. Both the *seriatim* and the conferencing court are "collegiate" bodies in the sense that decisions are made by a group of persons, but only the conferencing court is "collegial" in the sense that the members of the group cooperate in the decision-making process and seek to speak as an institution rather than as an aggregate. The new decision presentation format both reflects and promotes this new reality.

Briefly, in the early 1980s, the *Supreme Court Reports* packaged the material in the decisions slightly differently, labelling one set of reasons and its supporting material as "the majority" and the other as "the minority." Clearly, this is a style that works if, and only if, there are just two sets of reasons. Certainly for the clear communication of the differences that have divided the court, this is in many ways a highly desirable way to present the relevant material. Indeed, there is a contemporary judicial body – the Judicial Committee of the Privy Council – that formalized just such a process when it altered its rules in 1966 to permit minority reasons, albeit only one such set of reasons for any specific decision. Alder has criticized such a formal practice – which simultaneously permits and yet partially suppresses the articulation of minority views – as "the worst of all possible worlds."[35] It is reading a great deal into a brief and transient practice of the *Supreme Court Reports* to present it as a movement in this direction, but the labelling is suggestive.[36] At any rate, the practice was neither systematic nor continued.

Rebecca Gill highlights the essential difference between the "*seriatim* practice" and the "majority practice" that has replaced it in some but by no means all national high courts.[37] The critical element of the *seriatim* practice is the fact (once the preponderance of judgments has produced an outcome) that as many judges as are so inclined have provided their own explanation of how that outcome relates to established law, and elements from any of these reasons may evolve into precedent. The critical element of majority practice is a strong institutional preference for a majority or even unanimous decision, with a solid bloc of judges uniting behind a single set of reasons that declares the law and therefore provides precedent for the future. The changes involve an important double shift:

1 The decision of the Supreme Court takes the form of a single explicitly identified set of reasons that constitutes a clear statement of the law for the guidance of the lower courts.
2 That decision emerged from the interactive deliberation of all the members of the panel as a collective institutional product, greatly enhancing the status and importance of the first shift.

For our purposes, the important point is that the court's decision-delivery formats reflect both the contemporary understanding of the law and the contemporary understanding of both the role of the court and the nature of the interactions among its members. There is nothing ephemeral or casual or whimsical about these presentation styles; they emerge in the context of professional interactions in an evolving world, and no one is more aware than the court itself of the importance of finding the optimal packaging.

For those not fully convinced, we suggest a thought experiment. Suppose that tomorrow the Supreme Court of Canada were to revert, deliberately and systematically and with a formal declaration to that effect, to the pure *seriatim* style of the court's early decades – that is, every member of what is now usually a nine-judge panel will work completely independently to generate full sets of reasons comparable to what we now expect from a majority judgment; every such set of reasons will be treated identically, as an equal contender for providing the best guidance as to precedent, with the choice between those equal contenders left to other judges and other courts in the future. This suggestion cannot be treated as completely fanciful (unlike our earlier suggestion of reasons delivered in a rap style) for the simple reason that the Supreme Court did follow precisely this practice for about one-half of its institutional history. We can safely predict that both the legal profession and the general public (and the media that is the access point for the general public) would react with complete consternation, wondering whether the learned members of the court had completely lost their minds –and we think that such a reaction would be fully justified. The *seriatim* format reflected a view of the law, of the relationship of the courts to the law, and of the members of a panel court to each other that has on all three counts been replaced by a modern understanding that is quite different. The *seriatim* style accurately reflected the "old" Supreme Court just as the majority style reflects the "modern" Supreme Court. There is an architectural adage that form follows function; applying the same notion to the judiciary, we would reformulate this as evolving presentation format follows evolving purpose and context.

Beyond "Single Judgment, Single Author"?

There is no reason to assume that the evolution of judgment presentation formats has reached an end point, which means that there is no reason to think that we will not at some time have a Supreme Court that has moved beyond the "single judgment, single author" style that emerged in the late 1960s. We are not suggesting that *By the Court* in itself represents such a shift, although we do consider it important that the Supreme Court has been flirting with a judgment presentation style for an significant segment of its caseload that is as different from the "single judgment, single author" style as that was from the *seriatim* style. In our concluding chapters, we will present evidence that the court is undergoing a genuine shift to a third era of judgment presentation; *By the Court* is part of that process, having in some sense foreshadowed it and in another sense having been folded into it. But raising the question at this point allows us to take the general question of whether decision presentation formats matter and turn it into a much more specific question: Why would the adoption of this presentation format for this kind of case matter?

We would frame this in terms of the inherent paradox of any appellate court, namely, the unavoidable trade-off between individual and institution. The *seriatim* tradition is the most individualist way of dealing with this dilemma; the institutionally generated product is the outcome, but the all-important reasons that explain that outcome are multiple and completely individual. The majority judgment tradition represents a strong shift toward the institutionalist side of the spectrum, in that interactive deliberation precedes the declaration of an outcome, and that deliberation is reflected in a set of reasons that is itself an institutional product by virtue of the "circulate and revise" procedure.[38] *By the Court* is an even more dramatic step in the institutionalist direction.

The current "one judgment, one author" format is significant because this type of authorship reflects the relative impact of specific individuals within the jurisprudential positioning of the court at any given time.[39] "Circulate and revise" gives other judges a say, but the acknowledged author presumably has a larger say, including the option of resisting some proposed changes and absorbing the lost signature this may imply for the judgment. Particularly on a Supreme Court like our own that (unlike its American counterpart) has no general practice of anything approaching an equal sharing of the writing of judgments, this capacity for identifying effective leadership is both possible and useful.[40] It is the attribution of judgments that tells us which judges matter more in which specific areas of law.[41]

But the importance of this practice of attributed authorship goes much deeper. It is a central and persistent element of the common law tradition that specific judges take personal responsibility for their reasons for judgment. The Canadian "circulate and revise" practice slightly softens the edges of this principle, but not to the extent that specific single-judge attribution no longer constitutes a public "stand up and take (primary) responsibility" declaration. Lasser, in his powerful comparison of the common law and civil law traditions, identifies this personal acceptance of responsibility as a central element of common law practice, and a major part of the reason decisions within common law judicial systems enjoy a much wider scope than their continental European counterparts, to the extent of including judicial reflections on policy issues or philosophical ideas.[42]

It has also been suggested that the functional reason for the attribution of a judgment to a specific individual is not only the desire for the acclaim that accompanies the writing of good judgments but also (and even more so) the "threat of searing professional criticism" that serves as an effective check on less than sterling efforts.[43] Specific attribution "puts the judge's conscience and reputation on the line"[44] in the writing of the reasons, whereas more anonymous or shared formats "reduce personal responsibility" in a way that can lead to "opinions of lower quality."[45] A common put-down of *per curiam* judgments by American state courts (which are most common in Texas and Georgia) is that they serve as cover for opinions so weak that none of the judges are willing to sign them alone. This personal reputation factor is greatest for *seriatim* decisions, with each judge's reasons published directly alongside those of each of the other members of the panel. It is attenuated by the "circulate and revise" process of the modern Supreme Court of Canada, which makes the acknowledged author the lead rather than the genuinely sole author of the published reasons, and of course it disappears almost entirely for the anonymous product of *By the Court* judgments.

In this vein, we think it striking how often the academic discussion of specific *By the Court* judgments has not attempted to understand the label in its own right, but rather has attempted to penetrate the veil of anonymity to identify the "real" author. Sometimes, as in biographies, this is done by using access to a deceased or retired judge's papers to find the internal court communications and the first drafts of the reasons that were ultimately presented *By the Court;* more commonly, it takes the form of attempts to identify stylistic tendencies or turns of phrase as trails that lead reliably to the actual writer.[46] Both approaches deny *By the Court* decisions their own unique place within the judgment delivery repertoire, and seek instead to assimilate them into the normal attributed authorship practices of the court.

In Chapter 5, we will demonstrate how deeply ingrained this principle of attributed authorship is in other national high courts in the common law tradition, and therefore how unusual the *By the Court* solution is. The purpose of that chapter is to demonstrate that *By the Court* is a dramatic departure from one of the central elements of the English common law tradition, a road down which only the Supreme Court of Canada has taken even tentative steps. This does not make it illegitimate, but it does call for both explanation and justification. As Sirota has suggested, a conscious decision on the part of an official institution to withhold information that has normally and routinely been made available is not necessarily indefensible, but it does call for a serious and explicit explanation of why *this* information is being withheld at *this* time.[47] The more repetitive or even systematic the new practice becomes, the more important it is for that institution to provide a clear explanation for it, but we have had no such explanation from the Supreme Court – no policy statement, no major speech, no practice note that would provide its rationale and its parameters. This book is an exploration from the outside to make up for the unfortunate lack of candour from the inside.

But if the practice is in fact so unusual, and if courts tend for strong functional reasons to be more interested in continuity than innovation, then where could the idea of *By the Court* have come from? We shall tackle this question in the next chapter.

PART 2

The Road to *By the Court* Decisions

Originality: Nothing to Copy 4

We have suggested that courts are not particularly given to innovation. There are obvious functional reasons for this. Continuity and tradition are important elements of a court's prestige and an important reason why its decisions are likely to be accepted as legitimate. A court that improvises too freely and innovates too often is liable to be perceived, in Paul Weiler's pithy phrase, as "just making it up as they go along," a corrosive complaint when applied to judicial authority.[1] At the same time, courts periodically confront the need to make adjustments that respond to the changing expectations of the legal profession and other relevant publics. Squaring this particular circle is a challenge.

One obvious way to give change an acceptable face is to present it as building on the experiences of other respected institutions – in the case of the Supreme Court of Canada, arguably those of the high courts of other nations. In large part, this is a very modern idea – it is only in recent decades that we have begun to think of a global community of judges, interacting personally and observing closely how their counterparts in other judiciaries perform.[2] Turn the clock back a few decades and judiciaries were considerably more closeted. In the 1990s, for example, McCormick took part in a three-year cycle of Canadian Judicial Appellate Court Seminars and was surprised to discover that many long-serving judges even in neighbouring provinces had never met, let alone exchanged ideas formally or informally. If this was true within a single country, and true of judges occupying equivalent positions, it was even more so between countries, even those that shared a language or a border or a shared initial modelling on English practices.

From earlier chapters, it is clear that we consider *By the Court* decisions to be the Supreme Court's own complete invention, drawing only on its own past practices and emulating no one. In this chapter, we will consider the opposing argument – that such a practice has been adopted and adapted from the practices of some other court – by examining the most likely sources of the idea, and we will explain why we find our own premise of creative originality more convincing than any of these suggestions.

The Judicial Committee of the Privy Council

The first, and logically the strongest, candidate for emulation is the Judicial Committee of the Privy Council, for the simple reason that it was until 1949 the highest court of appeal for Canada, and its decisions were binding on Canadian courts, including the Supreme Court of Canada itself. As we have recounted earlier, it was seriously proposed (although the idea was ultimately abandoned) that the Supreme Court after 1949 should take up its new role as the final court of appeal by changing its practices to follow the "single attributed judgment" style of the Judicial Committee.

The Judicial Committee was the final court of appeal for Canada from 1867 to 1949; moreover, appeals could also be taken directly (*per saltum*) to the Judicial Committee from the highest court in a province on the application of both parties. During this period, there were 934 appeals, mostly *per saltum*. Although Canadian appeals ended in 1949, the Judicial Committee had a wider remit and still exists to this day. It had jurisdiction over Australian appeals until 1986 and over appeals from New Zealand until 2003; it still functions as the highest court for a number of "current and former Commonwealth countries, United Kingdom overseas territories, crown dependencies, and military sovereign base areas," and hears "occasional appeals" from a number of ancient and ecclesiastical courts and specialized bodies, such as the High Court of Chivalry.[3]

Technically, the Judicial Committee was not a court but rather a board of the Privy Council – that is, part of the executive branch of government with an advisory role to the monarch. To this day, the standard format that it uses for the conclusion of a case is not "The appeal is dismissed" but rather "The Board humbly advises Her Majesty." However, most of the members of the committee were Law Lords (members of the Appellate Committee of the House of Lords), and for several decades there was a provision for the service of judges from various high courts within the British Empire (including Canada). The result was that the Committee performed very much like a court, including relying strongly on precedent. One consequence of the quasi-court status was that for the entire period during which it had a Canadian jurisdiction, it confined itself to a single official set of reasons without dissent or separate concurrence, on the grounds that this was the form that advice to a monarch should take. Only in 1966 were the rules amended to permit a member of the Judicial Committee to publish a dissenting judgment.[4] As noted above, this was initially only a partial retreat from the "single voice" position, as only one set of minority reasons was permitted. We are not sure how it would have been handled had two different members wished to dissent for distinctly different reasons.

Decisions were attributed to a specific member of the board.[5] That the attribution was genuine rather than merely formal is indicated by the fact that it was not always (or even usually) the most senior member of the panel who was the designated author. This explains why accounts of the early evolution of Canadian constitutional law focus so heavily on specific members of the Judicial Committee who wrote a string of the most significant decisions, most notably Lord Watson and Viscount Haldane.[6]

As noted in Chapter 3, after appeals from the Supreme Court to the Judicial Committee ended in 1949, there was some public discussion within the profession about having the Supreme Court mark its new "final appeal" status by adopting the "single judgment" style of the Judicial Committee, but this would also have been an attributed single judgment by one specific member of the panel (not necessarily the senior member). It would not have been the *By the Court* style.

We have identified only a single example of a Judicial Committee decision that is presented in a "judgment of the Board" format – a single unanimous set of extended (15,000 words) reasons that is not attributed to any specific individual. The reason for this anonymity is candidly explained in the opening sentence: "This is a judgment to which all members of the Board have made substantial contributions."[7] (A follow-up application to vary the terms of relief from forfeiture was also resolved through a 4,500-word "judgment of the Board."[8]) The explanatory comment in the opening paragraph makes the point that this is an unusual response to unusual circumstances rather than a regular practice of the Judicial Committee (and "regular practice" is a significant element of our claim regarding the Supreme Court of Canada's *By the Court* device). At any rate, it long postdates the Canadian practice, and is in no sense an inspiration for it.

The British House of Lords

Until recently, the British House of Lords (or, more precisely, the "Appellate" or "Judicial" Committee of that body; accounts on this terminology differ) was the highest judicial authority for the United Kingdom. In 2009, it was replaced by the Supreme Court of the United Kingdom, with all the Law Lords being reappointed to the new body. It was one of the most highly regarded courts in the world, and although no appeals went directly to it from any Canadian court, it was in a real sense the "supreme court" of the English common law, which Canada had adopted as the basis of its own legal order. As late as the 1960s, the Supreme Court of Canada was citing the English courts more often than all other sources combined, and several times more often than it cited its own decisions.[9] For many decades, Canadian judges prided themselves on how closely they followed and how quickly they could incorporate House of Lords decisions.

But the House of Lords could not conceivably have been the model for the Supreme Court's adoption of *By the Court*, for the simple reason that its practices were strongly tilted toward the opposite end of the judgment presentation continuum. The House of Lords was the standard bearer for the *seriatim* style, and most of its decisions were accompanied by reasons (always labelled "speeches" although given their length we find it unlikely they were actually read out loud in their entirety) by all or most of the Law Lords on the particular panel. They were clearly and explicitly the model for the Australian *seriatim* practice, and presumably played a similar role in the early practices of the Supreme Court of Canada and even the United States Supreme Court, which delivered *seriatim* judgments until the reforms of Chief Justice John Marshall early in the nineteenth century. Although this style has recently become more controversial and contested, and the Supreme Court of the United Kingdom that replaced the House of Lords now tends toward a single unanimous judgment attributed to a specific member of the panel, it still has its defenders and was the preferred judgment presentation format of the House of Lords right up to its replacement as the highest court for the United Kingdom.

The United States Supreme Court

A number of academics have suggested the United States Supreme Court as a source of the *By the Court* practice, but we do not find this persuasive. Precisely because the sparse literature makes it the most credible candidate, however, we will deal with this suggestion at the greatest length.

Our identification of the 1960s as the starting point for *By the Court* makes emulation of an American court less likely as a source of this practice. Despite their geographical proximity, there was no historical tendency for the Canadian legal profession to look to American practices, or for the Canadian courts to follow American decisions (taking "follow" in the simple sense of "read regularly" as well as in the strong sense of "treat as a precedent to be adopted"). As Bushnell has pointed out, for many years the Supreme Court of Canada did not, for budgetary reasons, even stock the major American law reports in its library.[10] An unsigned note in the 1940 *Canadian Bar Review* went further, suggesting that there was a strong "prejudice" against the use of American authorities and sources, which MacIntyre links to the overt hostility to American authorities expressed by the more highly respected English courts and judges.[11] Certainly American case law of any sort was rarely cited, outnumbered sixty to one by the English citations that constituted by far the largest part of judicial authority. La Forest describes the citation of American cases as "infrequent, sometimes shallow, and definitely overshadowed" by the much more favoured English precedents.[12] To this day, the United States Supreme Court is cited less often than the House of Lords and the Supreme Court of the United Kingdom that recently replaced it. This would make direct emulation of an American practice unlikely.

This historical background notwithstanding, the example of the United States Supreme Court has been suggested by several academics as the obvious inspiration for *By the Court.* L'Heureux-Dubé makes the attribution specific: as a response to concerns about multiple opinions, she says, the court "borrowed from the Americans, who had developed the format of the unanimous and anonymous decisions 'of the Court' for certain important cases."[13] Somewhat more cautiously, Ted Morton finds it "tempting to speculate" that the Canadian Supreme Court "may have consciously borrowed the U.S. Supreme Court's tactic in the School Desegregation case of a 'united front,'" although the "united front" of that specific case[14] was in fact a unanimous judgment delivered by the chief justice, and not an anonymous judgment at all.

The American practice that L'Heureux-Dubé and Morton find suggestive is the *per curiam* judgment, hardly surprising given that *By the Court* is simply the English translation of that Latin phrase. From time to time, the US Supreme Court hands down a *per curiam* judgment in some dramatic high-profile case; the most recent and instantly familiar major example is *Bush v Gore* after the 2000 US presidential election.[15] Under the "standard story," which situates the emergence of *By the Court* in the Laskin court's 1979 language decisions, the plausibility of this suggestion is enhanced by the fact that both Bora Laskin and Willard Estey had graduate law degrees from American universities. In any event, whether *By the Court* started in 1979 or our own date of 1967, the suggestion does not survive close scrutiny.

US Supreme Court *per curiam* decisions fall into two general categories. The first, and by far the largest, the oldest, and the most clearly established, consists of short anonymous judgments dealing with appeals that can be resolved without addressing any significant legal issue.[16] As John Council puts it, these are "short opinions on well-settled law that have little precedential value," and, according to Robbins, they are frequently limited to "formulaic, boilerplate language" without any trace of individuality.[17] Simply put, for these decisions it does not matter which judge said it because so little is being said. To be sure, this is a fuzzy boundary that does not always confine as much as it might, but it places the centre of gravity for the US Supreme Court *per curiam* set well within the "minor, routine" side of the continuum as it deals with its potentially enormous caseload. It is frequently used to deal with "DIGs" ("dismissal of certiorari as improvidently granted") and "GVRs" ("granting certiorari, vacating the judgment, and remanding in the light of a recently decided case"). As Robbins notes, "attribution of these orders or opinions would have little value, because the language would not usually address any particular aspects of the case."[18] These are an ongoing element of the US Supreme Court's workload and have been for well over a century. From the statistics collected annually by SCOTUSblog, there would seem to be at least half a dozen or so of these every year.[19]

An unusual set of *per curiam* decisions along this line occurred during the 1950s. After the landmark case of *Brown v Board of Education,* the Warren court dealt with a string of further cases – Motley suggests that there were seven of them – through staccato *per curiam* judgments (often of "eleven words or less") that extended the impact of *Brown* but without any discursive explanation of how or why this expansion flowed from the specifics of *Brown*.[20] The academic and professional opinion that had been generally welcoming of *Brown* turned icy. For example, Bickel and Wellington wrote sternly: "This is not to say that the *per curiam* orders were wrong. Nor is it to say that they could not be found in reason, only that the court made no effort to do so."[21] The negative reaction perhaps explains why this particular use of the practice was neither extended nor repeated. Simply juxtaposing these cryptic declarations with the extended justificatory text of the Supreme Court of Canada's *By the Court* decisions makes our point: most US Supreme Court *per curiam* decisions are anonymous but not substantive, and as Wasby and colleagues document, they are often not unanimous either, as about half of them are accompanied by authored dissents or separate concurrences.[22]

If these American cases do have a Canadian parallel, it is the oral from-the-bench decisions that cryptically dismiss (or, much more rarely but equally briefly, allow) appeals by right. These usually employ similar boilerplate language, of which the most common and most reductionist version is "the appeal is denied for the reasons given in the court below" (this being the entirety of the reasons for judgment, not an introduction or conclusion to a more substantive comment).

Besides this post-*Brown* string of cases, there are a small number of US Supreme Court *per curiam* decisions. At first glance, this seems more promising because there are more extended and substantive reasons, and because they often deal with important issues in a way that reverberates through later jurisprudence. As far as we can determine, the following are the strongest candidates for a list of "major" decisions delivered *per curiam:*

- *Cooper v Aaron,* 358 US 1 (1958) – scope of US Supreme Court's institutional powers
- *Brandenburg v Ohio,* 395 US 444 (1969) – freedom of provocative speech
- *New York Times v. United States,* 403 US 713 (1971) [*Pentagon Papers*] – free speech/publication ban
- *Furman v Georgia,* 408 US 238 (1972) – death penalty
- *Buckley v Valeo,* 424 US 1 (1976) – free speech/commercial speech
- *Bush v Gore,* 531 US 98 (2000) – presidential election.

This is an impressive list and the issues addressed are significant, although the list is remarkably short and largely centred on the cases of the 1970s. As Ray notes, "*New York Times* [*Pentagon Papers*], *Furman* and *Buckley,* the great trilogy of the 1970s, represents the high water mark of the per curiam, its grandest and most substantial use by the Court."[23] A closer look dramatically undermines the view of them as the practice on which the Canadian *By the Court* might have been based. When Canadian scholars mention *Bush v Gore* as a counterpart to the Canadian practice, they usually qualify this by saying that it is "unusual" and "not typical" of the American practice because of the string of five dissenting and concurring reasons attached to it. In fact, this fragmented plurality of reasons is so common as to be a defining characteristic of the American practice, and *Bush v Gore* is not even the most extreme example. The *per curiam* judgment in *Furman v Georgia* was accompanied by five solo separate concurrences and four solo dissents – every single member of the panel wrote separate reasons of considerable length. Similarly, *Pentagon Papers* drew six solo concurrences and three solo dissents – again, every single judge wrote separate reasons considerably longer than the *per curiam* itself. *Buckley v Valeo* accomplishes the apparently impossible by featuring a nine-judge panel with five sets of dissenting reasons (five solo reasons, each "concurring in part and dissenting in part") – the only reason this left a majority judgment to be dissented from was the fact that the dissents were from different parts of the judgment. The institutional solidarity that is the central feature of the Supreme Court of Canada's *By the Court* decisions is completely missing, and the *per curiam* text is a thin introductory gloss over a badly fragmented court. Only *Brandenburg* is unanimous, albeit in embarrassing circumstances: the reasons for judgment were written by Justice Arthur Goldberg, but the decision was not handed down until he had resigned from the bench because of scandals involving monies received from litigant organizations, which would have made it extremely awkward to have his name permanently attached to this important decision.[24]

Even when the decision itself is such as to deserve serious and expansive attention from the dissenting and concurring members of the panel, the *per curiam* reasons themselves are cryptic and short. In *Furman v Georgia*, the *per curiam* opinion is only 200 words long; in *Pentagon Papers* it is 250 words. Only in *Buckley v Valeo* is it longer than 4,000 words, or about ten pages of text. Thus, the US *per curiam* practice could not be further away from the Canadian *By the Court* practice. In the major examples discussed above, the *per curiam* opinion serves only as a terse introduction to extended reasons from a badly divided panel – exactly the opposite of the discursive unanimity that characterizes the Canadian practice of *By the Court*.

The most unusual one of the set, and the one that is closest to Canadian practice, is *Cooper v Aaron*, which has been described as "the purest example of Supreme Court joint authorship."[25] It is not as straightforward as the Canadian *By the Court,* however. It consists of a *per curiam* order and an opinion jointly authored by all nine justices, but is undermined by an extended separate concurrence by Justice Felix Frankfurter (who, curiously, was the person who suggested the "joint authorship" option in the first place).[26] Rather than introducing a new protocol for selected cases, this proved to be a simple "one-off." "Whatever the implications of *Cooper*'s joint authorship model, the Court has never again employed it."[27]

At the time of writing, an additional subset of *per curiam* decisions is making its appearance. The death of Justice Antonin Scalia in 2016 and the firm resolve of the Republican-dominated Senate not to consider a nomination from a Democratic president when the Republicans hoped to win the 2016 election left the US Supreme Court an eight-judge court with a tendency to split four-four in the most controversial cases.[28] Thus, a number of decisions were handed down in 2016 with offsetting full sets of reasons published under a short *per curiam* declaring that the "The [lower court] judgment is affirmed by an equally divided court." This, too, is a phenomenon that is completely unlike the Canadian practice.

Curiously, there is a long-standing Canadian counterpart to the American *per curiam* practice – not *By the Court,* but rather the Supreme Court of Canada's own *per curiam* practice. In Canada, it is the English rather than the American practice that is followed. The Canadian and English *per curiam* is not an "opinion" but rather a labelled element within the headnotes, usually appended to the "held" paragraph in those notes.[29] The Canadian Supreme Court has accumulated more than 100 examples, dating back to 1891, although the practice has declined in recent years, with only a single *per curiam* notation from each of the Lamer and McLachlin courts.[30]

The Canadian *per curiam* has often served as a cryptically brief summary of the central legal finding for a badly divided panel. Seventeen of them introduced *seriatim* decisions, twelve were plurality decisions where no set of reasons drew the support of a majority of the panel, and half a dozen others involve what we might call "complex" decisions, where the reasons of divided panels were complicated by the fact that several judges signed on to more than one set of reasons. Perhaps the most unusual and significant example involves an otherwise badly divided panel firmly uniting on a secondary issue: in *Morgentaler,* the panel split 2-2-2-1 on whether and how much the abortion provisions of the *Criminal Code* offended the *Canadian Charter of Rights and Freedoms,* but all agreed emphatically that the doctrine of jury nullification had no place in Canada, and this is the substance of the brief *per curiam* note in the headnotes.[31] All the Canadian examples are very short, typically less than 100 words.

A French Connection?

Canada is unusual being not only bilingual but also bijural, combining the civil law traditions of Quebec with the common law traditions of the rest of the country. It follows, then, that the French civil law system might be considered available for possible emulation. In particular, one of the most obvious features of the French judicial system is the fact that the decisions of judicial panels are always required to be both anonymous and unanimous. Might *By the Court* be a North American reflection of this continental European practice? For a number of reasons, we think not.

For one thing, it would involve the Supreme Court's very selective adoption of a French practice that is not selective at all. All panel decisions in the French system – including not only appeal courts but also the upper echelons of the trial courts – must always be unanimous; minority opinions, whether in the form of dissents from the outcome or concurring opinions that differ on the reasons, are never permitted. Even more unlikely, it would be an application of the French example narrowly and specifically to the one type of case that French courts absolutely never deal with: constitutional cases. The notion of judicial review, involving the power of a regular court to overrule an action of the National Assembly, is inconsistent with French ideas about the essential nature of the judicial role. In the late 1960s, France did have a Constitutional Council (established only a decade earlier), but its role at the time was strictly limited to commenting on the constitutionality of proposed legislation before its passage, and doing so only at the request of the government itself. Thus, it served as an executive check on the legislature rather than as a judicial check on the executive.

Second, the role of judges within the French legal system is completely different from their role in Canada. To the North American eye, French judicial decisions are so brief and cryptic as to lack credibility for the common law reader. Decisions, even of the higher appeal courts, take the form of a formal syllogism that is usually less than a page long. The general style is something along the following lines:

- WHEREAS [a brief single-sentence summary of the core facts], and
- WHEREAS [a summary or quotation of the relevant section from the relevant code]
- THEREFORE [a finding of guilt or innocence, or liability, or something else], and
- THEREFORE [consequences in terms of imprisonment or fines or damages or something else].

This is not simply an introduction to the decision: *it is the decision itself in its entirety,* magnificent for its boilerplate blandness. Turn the page and you find yourself looking at another case altogether that is handled with identical brevity.

Where, we North Americans would ask, is any sense of the legal issues involved, and what the litigants thought was at stake, and the principled arguments that are used to deal with answers that are not as straightforward as the syllogism makes things appear, and the policy considerations that sometimes complicate the formal legal logic? Part of the answer is that there are other documents – drawn up by another judge (the *juge debout* as distinct from the panel's *juges assis*) who is not a member of the panel but drawn from the same level of the same judicial hierarchy – that lay out in more expanded form the issues and alternatives that are to be addressed in reaching a decision. The other part of the answer is that when the issue is considered sufficiently important, an academic will be asked to write a case commentary that is published along with the decision itself. In France, it is academics, and not judges, who are the major vehicle for the evolution of legal ideas.[32]

Third, to the extent that we can use judicial citation practices as an indication of which courts the Supreme Court justices over any period of time were following, it is absolutely clear that through the 1960s it was the English courts (and, to a much more limited extent, other Commonwealth courts) that were followed, to the exclusion of any other elements whatsoever, including American courts. For that matter, there was always something paradoxical about the citation of French decisions as judicial authority. Judicial citation is not a major element of French decisions, certainly not to the extent of treating earlier judicial decisions as judicial authority in their own right. In France, much greater respect and deference are shown to the venerated legal textbooks or the academic commentaries on recent decisions than to the individual decisions themselves.

Finally, one might wonder about the extent to which the courts of Quebec, from which a portion of the members of the Supreme Court are drawn, might have been a roundabout vehicle for the transmission of the *By the Court* practice. An empirical investigation almost seems to confirm this – the decisions of the court of Queen's Bench (renamed the Court of Appeal of Quebec in 1974) for this time period do begin with an "*Arrêt*" that precisely mirrors the standard French syllogism described above. However, this is only a preliminary introduction to the decisions, which take the form of one or more sets of discursive reasons attributed to specific individuals – in other words, except for the *Arrêt* itself, they look like the decisions of the other provincial courts of appeal save for the fact that they are usually in French; they also cite judicial authority in much the same way as their counterparts in the common law provinces.

We therefore do not find that the obligatory and across-the-board French practice of unanimity and anonymity provides a credible springboard for the highly focused Canadian practice. Nor, given the particular timing and the particular personnel involved, can we find a credible conduit for the introduction of these ideas. As we will describe at some length in Chapter 7, Chief Justice Robert Taschereau's participation at the critical time was both constrained and problematic, Thibaudeau Rinfret declined to continue the practice when he became chief justice a few years later, and the third of the three Quebec justices was Douglas Abbott, the last Anglophone to fill a Quebec seat on the court and who had had no experience as a Quebec trial or appeal judge. We cannot imagine how a suggestion to "look at how the French do it" could have been injected into the court's deliberations leading up to the first *By the Court* decisions. For this reason, we find the notion of a French origin for the *By the Court* decision style unpersuasive.

In sum, *By the Court* is an original Canadian phenomenon, emulating neither English nor American nor French practices. The casual suggestion in the literature of parallels to the US Supreme Court is a dead end. In the next chapter, we will provide a short survey of the national supreme courts of a various common law countries to vindicate our further claim that the Canadian practice is unique.

Uniqueness: A Global Common Law Survey

5

We have said that the distinctiveness of the Supreme Court of Canada's *By the Court* decisions derives from its originality and uniqueness. Chapter 4 addressed the question of originality; in this chapter, we will back up our claim of uniqueness by looking at the "obvious suspects" among the high courts of the common law world.

Such a claim might at first seem unlikely for several reasons. First, Canada's non-revolutionary development from its English colonial past suggests pervasive and enduring English influences, reinforced by a heavy reliance on English precedent, a context that is fully shared with a number of Commonwealth countries.[1] Second, the existence of a much larger same-language common law neighbour with a highly regarded Supreme Court suggests a possible diffusion effect. Third, in an age of judicial conferences and exchanges, each country's courts are much more aware than in the past of how their counterparts in other countries are doing things, and are in a much better position to discuss those practices with the individuals directly involved. Finally, the number of common law systems with extensive histories makes it seem unlikely that nobody else would have stumbled on the same idea. We will demonstrate, however, that although those other courts display a remarkable variety of judgment delivery styles despite their shared historical origins, none has developed a practice like Canada's *By the Court.*

Of necessity, this chapter will be something of a Cook's tour of the common law world, with relatively brief stops in each of the countries considered. If you are willing to take our word for the fact that no other common law country has a national supreme court that does anything comparable, then by all means jump to Chapters 6 and 7 for an account of the emergence of the practice in Canada.

Because our claim is for uniqueness within the common law tradition, we will start with the usual suspects – the United States and England/Great Britain – and then move more briefly through a string of other countries within the common law tradition: Australia, New Zealand, and South Africa.

The United States Supreme Court

More than any of the other national high courts that we shall cover below, the firm practice of the US Supreme Court is to sit the full court of nine judges unless this is precluded either by an unfilled vacancy or by a judge's recusal because of prior involvement in some aspect of the case. The most common panel by far consists of the full nine judges. The further implication is that if a single judge is not available for some reason (such as the death of Justice Antonin Scalia and the political deadlock that delayed the appointment of his replacement), then the court will sit with a panel of eight. The even number is unusual and is typically avoided by appeal courts because of the possibility of a tie vote, in which case the appeal will fail (the lower court decision will stand) but without any precedent being established. The Canadian custom of a chief justice deciding which judges will comprise the panel for which specific case is definitely not part of American practice, as a routine or even an unusual matter.

Like the Supreme Court of Canada, but unlike a number of other national high courts, the US Supreme Court always meets in conference after oral arguments on a case, to determine the extent to which the judges are agreed on how the case should be handled or, more often, how the judges are divided. The writing of reasons is then assigned. The senior judge (and by definition the chief justice is always the most senior for this purpose) within the majority group decides which member of that group will be responsible for drafting preliminary reasons for judgment for circulation to the panel. Considerable formality has developed around this procedure. Judges meet alone in the conference room with no staff members present (with the least senior judge sitting closest to the door and dealing with any interruption), and they speak to the issue in order of seniority before the assignment is made. The assignment within the majority group has been the subject of a considerable amount of academic research to generate pragmatic generalizations and even mathematical models to explain it. The emphasis on a specifically identified "opinion of the Court" is of long standing. In its very early years, the court issued *seriatim* judgments along traditional English lines, but under the leadership of iconic Chief Justice John Marshall this was replaced by a practice of unanimous authored decisions (initially mostly authored by the chief justice himself), which over time gradually came to accommodate minority reasons. During the 1940s, minority reasons proliferated and a parallel practice grew whereby the senior judge in the minority often assumed or assigned responsibility for writing the minority reasons. For our purposes, the important point is that the assignment is given to a specific individual judge, whose name is attached to those reasons.

But this understates the uniqueness of the judgment presentation style of the US Supreme Court, which is unlike that of any other comparable court.[2] The opinion of the court is divided into "parts" (and, more recently, subparts and sub-subparts), corresponding to major elements in the reasons for the majority judgment; these are identified by Roman numerals for the major parts and Arabic numerals for the subparts but without titles or headings. The other judges on the panel can then identify themselves in terms of not only whether they agree or disagree with the decision itself or with the reasons in their entirety but also whether they agree or disagree with each of the parts. According to Delson, this format first appeared in the 1920s and gradually solidified to become the normal and routine practice by the 1940s.[3] Along with it came the "syllabus," the one-page summary that now precedes every judgment in the court's official records and indicates each individual judge's position with regard to each of the parts and subparts of the opinion of the court. Delson provides an example of the complexity this generates, in a recent decision dealing with anti-terrorism legislation:

> STEVENS, J., announced the judgment of the Court and delivered the opinion of the Court with respect to Parts I, III and IV, in which O'CONNOR, KENNEDY, SOUTER, GINSBURG and BREYER, JJ. joined, and an opinion with respect to Parts II and V, in which SOUTER, GINSBURG and BREYER, JJ., joined. O'CONNOR, J., delivered the opinion of the Court with respect to Part II (except as to the footnote), in which REHNQUIST, C.J. and KENNEDY and THOMAS, JJ. joined, and in which SCALIA, J. joined, except as to the footnote, and an opinion concurring in part and concurring in the judgment, in which KENNEDY, J. joined.[4]

As Delson points out, this can create enormously elaborate patterns by raising questions as to which parts of the leading reasons actually have the support of a majority of the panel. Minority reasons are also similarly formatted, but not in a way that makes any attempt to match up to the divisions in the majority opinion.

For our purposes, there are two things to emphasize about this procedure. The first is that there is a procedural encouragement for each of the individual judges to clarify their position with some specificity – not just whether they joined the ultimate decision and reasons but how they positioned themselves with respect to each of the major issues dealt with in that decision. The second is that the decision of the court (the outcome) and the opinion of the court (the reasons for that outcome) are attributed to a specific individual who is "joined" (or not) by other members of the court, a less explicitly collegial and collaborative description than the Supreme Court of Canada's "the judgment of A, B, C and D was delivered by A."[5]

We have been talking about the judgments of the US Supreme Court as if the court is always divided, but this is of course not the case. As Corley, Steigerwalt, and Ward observe, about one-third of the court's decisions over the last fifty years have been "opinion unanimous" (only a single set of reasons for the outcome), and that proportion rises to about one-half if we broaden the consideration to cases that were "outcome unanimous" (one or more separate concurrences but no dissents).[6] But the very title of their book, *The Puzzle of Unanimity* (why should unanimity be thought of as a puzzle?), as well as their basic argument that unanimity responds to the "legal certainty" of a case (for which purpose they generate a "legal certainty" index to identify those cases in which there is no or little legal issue for the court to resolve), concede the point that the court is highly likely to divide on its important cases.

As discussed in the previous chapter, the US Supreme Court does have two different *per curiam* practices. However, despite the fact that *per curiam* is simply the Latin equivalent of "by the court," neither of these practices bears any similarity to the Canadian *By the Court*. The first is a way of providing brief "boilerplate" opinions on routine cases, the latter a way of providing a short capsule summary for unusually divided decisions.

The Judicial Committee of the Privy Council

As discussed in the previous chapter, the Judicial Committee of the Privy Council was the final court of appeal for Canada from 1867 to 1949, with a frequently used provision for an appeal *per saltum*, directly to the Judicial Committee from the highest court in the province on the application of both parties. Although Canadian appeals ended in 1949, the Judicial Committee had a wider remit and still exists to this day.

The Judicial Committee reports about forty cases per year. The following comments on its current practices are based on a survey of its decisions over the seven-year period from 2009 to 2015 inclusive. The normal panel size is five, with about two three-judge panels per year and only a single seven-judge panel in the seven years for which our data were collected. By far the most common form of judgment is a unanimous decision delivered by a single named member of the panel. This accounts for 90 percent of all reported cases, a figure that rises to 93 percent if we include the half-dozen unanimous decisions co-authored by two of the judges. Fourteen cases in seven years involved dissents, and three were *seriatim* judgments with every judge writing separate and reasonably extensive reasons. Before 1966, the Committee's invariant practice was to generate a single set of explanatory reasons attributed to a specific member of the panel. Only in 1966 were its procedures altered to allow a single minority opinion (which obviously happens, although infrequently), and the three *seriatim* judgments suggest that Alder's comments about the "one only" minority reasons have been superseded by further procedural adjustments.[7] There was also a single "Judgment by the Board" decision, explained in the very first sentence of the reasons by the comment: "This is a judgment to which all members of the Board have made substantial contributions."[8] (A follow-up application was similarly resolved through a 4,500-word "judgment of the Board."[9])

The normal format of attributed reasons for judgment simply identifies the attributed author with no specific collaborative role suggested for the other (sometimes) two or (usually) four or (infrequently) six judges on the panel. This differs from the standard format for the Supreme Court of Canada ("the judgment of Justices A, B, C, D and E was delivered by Justice D") in being silent as to whether the bracketed named judges had the opportunity to respond to an initial draft, possibly to negotiate wording changes. The Canadian format, on the other hand, signifies that it is the judgment of all the listed judges, of whom one is designated as lead (but not solo) author. For a handful of recent decisions, the attributed solo judgment is described as "giving the judgment of the Board," which, especially because of its non-routine appearance, might reasonably be taken as suggesting a higher degree of collaboration.

The Supreme Court of the United Kingdom

The Supreme Court of the United Kingdom was established on October 1, 2009. It replaced the Appellate Committee of the House of Lords and inherited the latter's jurisdiction as well as authority over devolution issues, which had previously been assigned to the Judicial Committee. It also inherited the Appellate Committee's members, all of whom became members of the new court (most have since retired).

The House of Lords had been well known for its *seriatim* tradition. Most decisions were accompanied by reasons by all or most of the Law Lords on a particular panel. Given the continuity in membership between the two bodies, the early expectation was that this practice would simply carry over to the Supreme Court of the United Kingdom. Sure enough, a European Parliament report found in 2012 that "the (U.K.) Supreme Court follows the tradition of *seriatim* decisions," even when the cases were based on the 1998 *Human Rights Act*, which incorporated into UK law the rights contained in the European Convention on Human Rights, which is perhaps the closest thing to formal constitutional review in British practice.[10]

These first impressions notwithstanding, the more recent performance of the Supreme Court of the United Kingdom is turning out rather differently. Over its first three years, fully 30 percent of its decisions took the *seriatim* form, but since January 2013 the proportion has dropped sharply to about 5 percent. Conversely, unanimous single-authored (or, more rarely, co-authored by two judges) judgments are up from 30 percent to 55 percent. If clearly majority decisions (single authored or co-authored) are added, this rises still further to 85 percent. It would be premature to declare the *seriatim* style dead, but it is certainly in serious decline.

The general form of these unanimous or majority judgments is that they are attributed to "Justice X (with whom Justices Y and Z agree)."[11] This carries less of a suggestion of collaboration than the Canadian style ("the judgment of A and B and C and D and E was delivered by Justice D"), an interpretation borne out by a format that the Supreme Court of the United Kingdom has used on a number of occasions. On thirty-four occasions, a unanimous decision was delivered by a single judge (not necessarily the senior judge) with the specific comment "This is a judgment of the Court" – suggesting both a degree of collaboration that was greater than the norm and the desirability of pointing this out to the legal public. This perhaps corresponds to the routine format for unanimous authored decisions in the Supreme Court of Canada: "The judgment of the Court was delivered by Justice X." However, these thirty-four examples occurred in the early years of the transition and we found only four examples since the beginning of 2013.

It is interesting that the judgment delivery practices of these two English high courts have largely converged. Fifty years ago, the Judicial Committee was noted for issuing a single judgment attributed to one of its members, taking no note of dissents or reservations (although we know from anecdotal accounts that there were disagreements within the panel from time to time).[12] Right up to its replacement about a decade ago, the House of Lords was noted for its frequent *seriatim* or near-*seriatim* decisions, which initially seemed to carry over into the early years of the new Supreme Court. For our purposes, however, the point is that neither the Supreme Court of the United Kingdom nor its predecessor, the Appellate Committee of the House of Lords, had any practice even remotely similar to the Supreme Court of Canada's *By the Court* format.

The UK Supreme Court's 2017 Brexit decision is a remarkable recent exception, the way that the decision was handled being unusual in three important respects.[13] First, it is a constitutional case in the strictest sense of the term – with a court telling the government itself what it must or cannot do – and this is a very new development for a country with no tradition of constitutional judicial review.[14] Second, it was resolved by a panel consisting for the first time of the full court of eleven members, whereas our seven-year database for the court shows that five judges is by far the most common panel size, with fewer than a dozen cases entailing a panel as large as nine. Third was the judgment delivery format itself. The court divided eight to three on the question of whether parliamentary approval was required for Britain's formal notice of withdrawal from the European Union. The three dissenters each wrote solo reasons, but the majority delivered a joint judgment, not under that label but rather by presenting all eight of the judges in the majority as co-authors. This format is directly comparable to, for example, the Supreme Court of Canada's decision in *Nadon,* and this presentation style itself was a first for the UK Supreme Court.[15] Alone among the decisions of all comparable national supreme courts, this single recent case touches on our uniqueness claim – but not in the sense of Canada emulating England. If anything, it is the reverse, especially since the Supreme Court of the United Kingdom quoted directly (in paragraphs 141 and 142) from a Supreme Court of Canada decision (the *Patriation Reference*) that similarly used a judgment jointly attributed to all the members of the majority to confront the dissenters.[16] This suggests a "diffusion effect," whereby practices from one common law high court could influence the innovative practices of other such courts through direct imitation. This type of effect could undermine our claims of uniqueness for *By the Court*, but this single case (the Brexit decision) shows how unusual such imitation seems to be.

The High Court of Australia

In many ways, Australia's High Court is more like Canada's Supreme Court than any of the others. Both are final courts of appeal for federal countries, which gives them an ongoing role in deciding constitutional issues. Unlike Canada, Australia does not have a constitutionally entrenched bill of rights, but in recent decades its High Court has developed a modest but significant jurisprudence grounding certain rights in the text of the Australian Constitution, making this difference less categorical than it might have been. The High Court of Australia is roughly the same age as the Supreme Court of Canada – 1901 versus 1875 – and about the same size, with seven judges (the same number as the Canadian court between 1928 and 1949). Again like Canada, the decisions of the High Court could for many years be appealed to the Judicial Committee of the Privy Council; this ended only in 1986, compared with 1949 for Canada. Unlike Canada, however, the Australian High Court does not have a reference jurisdiction under which it can give advisory opinions on constitutional issues.[17]

Despite these similarities, the judgment delivery practices of the High Court have been and continue to be completely unlike those of Canada, or indeed of any other comparable country. The High Court's practices have included the solo attribution of majority or unanimous judgments, *seriatim* decisions, and even occasional anonymity, with changing proportions of these over time so that any generalization would apply only to specific time periods. In none of these periods, however, has the High Court had anything directly comparable to the Supreme Court of Canada's *By the Court* decisions.

This is true even though at one time the High Court did hand down decisions under a "By the Court" rubric. In the 1950s, this was the most common type of decision, accounting for over 40 percent of the caseload, but it declined slightly in the 1960s and 1970s and disappeared entirely in the 1980s.[18] Both the function served by these decisions and the reason for their disappearance are signalled by the latter date. During the 1980s, there were two major changes to the jurisdiction of the High Court of Australia. The most obvious was the ending of appeals to the Judicial Committee of the Privy Council in 1986, which made the High Court the final court of appeal for Australia rather than an intermediate court of appeal within a larger judicial framework. The second was the abolition of absolute rights to appeal in 1984, which enabled the High Court to choose not to hear the more routine cases: "It is midway through the Gibbs court that significant institutional changes gave the High Court control over its docket and the last say in all matters. As a result, by the mid-1980s, the Gibbs court was freed from the routine mandatory jurisdiction cases of the past, and could concentrate on more difficult and important cases."[19] One consequence of this was the disappearance of short boilerplate "By the Court" decisions in the more routine cases. This means, however, that the High Court's practice was more like the Canadian "minor tradition," which the Supreme Court of Canada still uses for short from-the-bench dismissals, than the *By the Court* practice that we claim is unique to Canada.

In recent decades, the most common style of decision presentation in the High Court of Australia has been the "joint reasons" format: decisions are attributed not to a specific author, or even (Canadian-style) to a lead author of a collegial product, but rather to the full bloc of judges, either the majority on a divided panel or the entire panel on a unanimous decision. This product can emerge in several ways. One is a post-hearing conference at which judges share their views and identify an emerging majority or unanimous position that is then assigned to a particular judge, but the conference process has never really taken hold in Australia despite the efforts of several chief justices. The strongest claim one can make is that occasionally there are informal post-hearing conferences that can sometimes result in a single judge's assumption of responsibility for writing. Alternatively, several judges (or even all judges) on a panel can write and circulate initial drafts, only to discover that one of those draft judgments is considerably more satisfactory, at which time the others abandon their own efforts to join that better author.[20] Once they join, however, they are all listed in order of seniority, with no indication of who the initial author might have been. This practice has two implications. First, it is impossible to assign with confidence, for praise or blame, any particular line of jurisprudence in majority reasons to a specific judge on the court (which does not, of course, preclude the development of a feeling within the profession as to which judges are leading which tendencies).[21] The second is the "freeloader" problem, whereby individuals can join a judgment without making any contribution to it or without having worked on their own initial draft. Nonetheless, joint reasons have emerged as the dominant decision-delivery style. In recent years, fully half of the decisions of the High Court of Australia have taken the form of joint reasons by a majority of the panel, and one-third have been joint reasons by a unanimous panel. Whereas we consider *By the Court* a sort of deliberate and intentional "unanimity-plus" decision style for the Supreme Court of Canada, unanimous joint authorship does not carry the same message for the High Court of Australia, because it emerges in such a different way, without any sign of being focused on constitutional cases or major cases.

For many years, the High Court also handed down a certain number of *seriatim* judgments; in the 1970s, they accounted for fully one-third of the output. This is still the prevailing generalization about the High Court of Australia, resulting in it being lumped together in this respect with the House of Lords and the pre–John Marshall US Supreme Court. As recently as 2012, Robinson could confidently declare that the High Court "operates under a *seriatim* system, whereby justices generally write separate opinions in each decision."[22] Similarly, Lynch writes about a High Court "which has tended to follow the English tradition of seriatim opinion delivery," Gill says that the High Court "never strayed from the British *seriatim* tradition," and Dixon and Ginsburg refer to the "High Court's opinion practice," which contributes to a "multi-valenced approach to constitutional interpretation."[23] The description is no longer accurate; indeed, in recent years, the High Court has delivered only about one *seriatim* decision per year. As Gill reminds us, however, it is still worth recalling that the High Court remains within the *seriatim* tradition in the sense that where there are multiple reasons, all of them enjoy a comparable status and there is no special singling out of a single "judgment" for precedential purposes.

Both Robinson and Lynch describe not so much a general decision-delivery practice as one that is focused on constitutional decisions in particular. This would make the Australian High Court's practice intriguingly opposite to the practice we are suggesting for the Supreme Court of Canada: the Supreme Court has an anonymous joint style that seems to be used only for significant constitutional cases, whereas the High Court uses a comparable anonymous style as a general practice except for constitutional cases, where it switches to an English-style *seriatim* judgment. This would indeed be an intriguing idea, but alas it is not sustainable. The High Court's *seriatim* style was never as centred on constitutional cases as this suggests, and over the last six years the use of different decision presentation styles for constitutional cases has simply mirrored that of the total caseload. The High Court has used an impersonal and effectively anonymous style for judgment delivery, under a "THE COURT" rubric before the 1980s and under a joint judgment style subsequently, but the first was used for minor and more routine cases, while the latter is a not-particularly-frequent general style that is not at all targeted to major cases or constitutional cases. The latter does not signal unanimity either, since it is also employed for majority decisions or for minority reasons by more than one judge.

The New Zealand Supreme Court

The New Zealand Supreme Court came into being on January 1, 2004, when the right of appeal to the Judicial Committee of the Privy Council also ended.[24] The court consists of five justices (one of whom is styled the chief justice of New Zealand) and has dealt with a modest caseload, amounting to 248 appellate decisions in its first dozen years.[25] Just over half these decisions were unanimous and attributed to a specific named member of the court; just under 40 percent were divided, with both the judgment and the minority reasons always being attributed to specific judges as well. A small number (17, or 7 percent) were *seriatim* judgments where all five judges wrote at some length.

There have been a handful of unattributed unanimous judgments, simply labelled as "reasons," but over the first dozen years, there were only four of these and they were something of a mixed bag. One dealt with the "inherent power" of the (lower) High Court, one explained an appeal that had been allowed by consent of the parties, and one was an extended explanation of the concept and use of "counter-intuitive evidence." One was a challenge by the Maoris, invoking their rights under the Treaty of Waitangi – that is, something that was as close to a constitutional issue as a high court in a unitary country is likely to get. No cases under the *New Zealand Bill of Rights* – not a constitutionally entrenched charter like Canada's but rather an example of what some scholars call a "Commonwealth model" of rights protection – have been treated in this way.[26]

It is worth noting that the New Zealand Supreme Court's judgment-delivery style in no way follows the example of Australia (although perhaps many New Zealanders would be offended by the suggestion that it might or should). It is also worth noting that neither the unanimity practices of the Judicial Committee of the Privy Council before 1966 nor the *seriatim* practices of the House of Lords have carried over to the New Zealand Supreme Court either. Majority or unanimous decisions with single-judge attribution is by far the prevailing style.

The South African Supreme Court of Appeal

Unusually for a judicial system in the common law tradition, South Africa has two high courts – a Supreme Court of Appeal and a Constitutional Court. In the context of the post-apartheid regime, this device enabled the country to have it both ways: the Supreme Court of Appeal represented professional continuity with the existing judiciary, whereas the Constitutional Court was a new and high-profile institution that had no connection with the apartheid past; "The new constitution needed as its protector a new court – one untainted by the past."[27] The Supreme Court of Appeal was initially established in 1910 (as the Appellate Division of a "Supreme Court" consisting of the highest courts of the various colonies) and was renamed in 1997. This effectively gave South Africa two apex courts, one of which was supreme on constitutional matters and the other supreme on all other matters, but the relationship was altered in favour of the Constitutional Court in 2013 when a constitutional amendment gave it general jurisdiction to hear any matter should it be in the interests of justice to do so, effectively making it the country's single apex court.

The Supreme Court of Appeal consists of twenty-four judges (a president, a deputy president, and twenty-two other judges) who sit in panels of three or five judges to hear appeals from lower courts. In practice, they decide more than 200 cases per year, and five-judge panels are much more frequent (by a factor of five to one) than three-judge panels. By far the normal practice is a unanimous decision attributed to a single specific member of the panel. Co-authorship by two judges is rare (less than ten times per year), and divided panels even rarer, with only three examples in a calendar year. There were no examples of any kind of anonymity practice for these decisions.

The South African Constitutional Court

Established by the Interim Constitution of 1993 and continued under the Constitution of 1996, the Constitutional Court is the country's highest court on constitutional matters, and after the changes of 2013 it can be considered the single genuinely apex court in the country.[28] The chief justice of the Constitutional Court is the chief justice of the country, and unlike his counterpart on the Supreme Court of Appeal (who is styled the president of the court, and who receives the designation because of strict seniority), he is formally appointed to that position on the basis of merit.

The eleven judges on the Constitutional Court are appointed for nonrenewable twelve-year terms, and it is normally expected that all eleven will sit on every case (barring recusal or temporary absence for good reason). The court's website simply declares that "all eleven judges hear every case."[29] In practice, it does not quite work out this way: roughly one-third of the cases decided in the last ten years were handled by panels of eleven, one-third by panels of ten, and one-third by panels of nine or eight (with eight being the legal quorum).

The formal procedure followed by the court is unusually complex. Once a case has been set down, the chief justice asks a specific judge to do special preparation and presumptively to write the judgment, with a sharing of the workload being a significant factor in the assignment. After written arguments and often but not always oral argument, the judges meet to decide the probable outcome of the case, after which the writing judge submits a memo to all the others. Any disagreements over the decision or the reasons are expressed through written concurrences or dissents. The judges then meet to share comments or suggest changes, at which point they indicate which judgment they will follow and why.

About half the decisions handed down in recent years have been unanimous decisions attributed to a single justice – obviously the "writing judge" first selected by the chief justice. About one-third have been organized in a considerably more complex fashion that is not easy to interpret at first glance. The first set of reasons is always that of the writer, and the primacy of this is acknowledged through the "I have read the reasons" declaration that starts off most of the additional reasons. However, there can be a number of additional reasons, concurring or dissenting, and the signatures of the other members of the panel can be distributed in such a way that the lead reasons of the writer may or may not carry the signatures of a majority of the panel – indeed, sometimes the writer is the only person to sign them. Further complications are caused by the fact that judges can sign on to more than one set of reasons, although most of the time they do not do so. Solo attribution of reasons is the norm; there are only 16 examples in 321 cases where co-authorship of two judges is identified for any set of reasons.

For our purposes, what is of interest is a set of decisions attributed to "THE COURT." Almost all of these are short, routine responses to applications (applications for leave to appeal, applications for extension of deadlines, applications for "condonation," applications for "direct access," applications for costs or for the variance of costs).[30] Most are brief and are dealt with without oral argument; when there is oral argument, the decision is rendered the same day. However, this generalization includes a number of decisions on applications with broader implications. One deals with an application for leave involving a complaint against a provincial High Court chief justice alleging an improper attempt to influence a decision of the Constitutional Court.[31] A second deals with an application for direct access (first judicial hearing rather than on appeal) to challenge a decision by the president of South Africa to extend the term of the chief justice of the Constitutional Court.[32]

There is a single case that is not an application but a decision on an appeal.[33] It takes the form of a statement by "THE COURT" that the panel has divided between five different sets of reasons but all five ultimately reach the same conclusion, and the purpose of the statement is to outline briefly the shared elements that justify this conclusion – which makes it look very much like the *per curiam* format of the United States Supreme Court. Although the high profile of the issue is worth noting, this decision does not replicate the Canadian practice of a format that is focused on constitutional cases, nor does it present the solid unanimity of *By the Court.*

Conclusion

This survey could have been extended – to India and Pakistan, and even to African countries like Nigeria and Ghana – but for our purposes, suffice it to say that wider inquiries at an earlier stage of writing did nothing to undermine our claim. The role of these apex courts differs from one country to another, even though all are final courts of appeal in common law judicial systems within the English tradition. Some function always or almost always as "full courts," with every one of the judges involved in every appeal. The United States Supreme Court is the purest example of this, with Canada, Australia, New Zealand, and the South African Constitutional Court not far behind. The South African Supreme Court of Appeal functions as a "fragment court," however, with an extensive contingent of judges sitting in panels that are only small parts of the much larger total bench, and never engaging all together on the resolution of any judicial appellate function.[34] Some are deliberative courts, engaging every member of the panel in the discussion of outcome and reasons. The South African Constitutional Court is the purest example of this, with the conference and draft judgment circulation procedures of the US Supreme Court and the Supreme Court of Canada not far behind. Others are much more insular and solitary. For example, the *seriatim* judgment tradition was until recently fairly common practice on the High Court of Australia (reinforced by the failure of that court to establish regular conferencing after oral argument), and the literature suggests that the Supreme Court of the United Kingdom has only recently taken steps to provide for the circulation of draft judgments. Finally, some specifically identify which set of reasons carries the institutional stamp – the "judgment" of the Supreme Court of Canada, or the "opinion" of the US Supreme Court, or the "leading reasons" of the South African Constitutional Court – but most others do not, leaving the various sets of reasons as competing influences on the future direction of the court. Gill reminds us that this is not a simple oversight but rather a continuation of the *seriatim* tradition that has not yet been firmly replaced by the alternative "majority tradition," with its unambiguously labelled single judgment of the court.

Our concern in this chapter has been narrow: it is the question of what an apex court decision looks like in different common law countries. The answer is very simple – for all the variation in other aspects of the performance of the final appellate judicial function, they overwhelmingly tend toward the delivery of reasons attributed to the authorship or lead authorship of a single specific member of the panel. Only for Canada – in the *By the Court* phenomenon that we are examining – and for Australia's joint reasons is there any alternative practice in regular use, and since Australia's joint reasons do not signal major or constitutional cases, or even a unanimous decision, that practice does not refute our basic position that *By the Court* is a uniquely Canadian phenomenon.

In one of the first attempts to fit the unanimous-anonymous style into a broader framework, Bzdera declared that it was a standard device frequently used by apex courts in federal countries as part of the mechanism through which constitutional interpretation ratcheted up the predominance of central governments over regional governments.[35] Given the focus on federalism issues and advisory opinions that we will describe later in this book, this is not an implausible starting point for a study of the Canadian practice. What we are emphasizing here, however, is that the generalization cannot be extended outside the Canadian setting.

It is logically possible to imagine that the common law countries surveyed could, because of their shared roots in the Anglo-American tradition and because of a certain level of inter-citation, have worked from their shared origins to develop practices that evolved in generally similar ways through an emulation effect. The fact that courts are institutions that are heavily invested in continuity and tradition could have allowed these similarities to persist despite different local contexts. On the other hand, it is also logically possible that, these common roots notwithstanding, the different high courts could have evolved in quite different directions, responding to different cultures, different historical developments, different transformative events, and different styles of political and judicial leadership. In any event, the latter possibility is what is supported by the evidence of a remarkable range of practices.

This common law global survey has empirically validated our claim of the uniqueness of Canada's *By the Court* practices. No comparable common law country has anything like it – the practice is simultaneously important, unique, original, and recent, and the coexistence of these four elements demands closer scrutiny.

Early History: The "Minor Tradition" 6

We have acknowledged that courts are, for good functional reasons, inherently traditional institutions, not given to innovation. We doubled down on this argument by showing that Canada's *By the Court* practice was original, not copied from the practices of other countries. However, this ratchets up our explanatory challenge: if courts are not normally innovative, and if there is no hint of an emulation of a respected other, then where could *By the Court* have come from? In this chapter, we will demonstrate that *By the Court* builds on a long-standing practice of the Supreme Court of Canada that had previously been devoted to more routine matters. The originality of *By the Court* lay in the transformation of this low-profile practice, said transformation occurring in the context of an unprecedented level of controversy and embarrassment. In the next chapter, we will describe this embarrassing episode; here, we will describe the earlier practice – the "story before the story" of *By the Court.*

The analysis that follows is informed by three different elements.[1] The first is a careful perusal of the *Supreme Court Reports* starting with the first reported decisions in 1877, to ensure that we are working from a complete set of cases where the reasons for judgment were attributed to "THE COURT" rather than to any specific member of the panel. The second is an investigation of the archives of the Supreme Court in

Ottawa, to give us a better sense of how the decision-making and reporting process was being handled, especially in earlier decades. And the third is a consideration of the literature as it bears on the early evolution of the court and its decision-making practices. Although that literature never focuses directly on the phenomenon of unattributed reasons (the virtual invisibility of *By the Court* is of long standing), they provide the context in which the practice emerged and persisted. Building from these three elements, we will describe the evolution of the practice leading up to the emergence of the modern substantive and constitutionally focused *By the Court* decisions.

As early as 1886, the Supreme Court of Canada began attributing some of its decisions simply to "THE COURT," without identifying any specific member of the panel.[2] Between then and the emergence of the substantive constitutional *By the Court* format in 1967, these accounted for several hundred decisions in total. Figure 6.1 tracks the use of the device in the Supreme Court's reported decisions. The overall numbers are not particularly large, save for an unusual bulge toward the end of the second decade of the twentieth century, and there are a number of years in which there were no such cases. However, the practice clearly persisted for decades, and only in the 1940s does it seem to have been almost discontinued.

This early precursor of the *By the Court* practice can best be understood as having evolved through three reasonably distinct periods. Each is characterized by a distinct major function, with some accompanying changes to the form the device assumed. We describe these periods as "reasonably distinct" to acknowledge that what we had was not an abrupt across-the-board change but rather an emerging new practice that gradually displaced an earlier one, with a certain amount of overlap. The three periods saw 1) an administrative salvage effort, 2) a simplifying reporting convenience, and 3) a deliberate judicial choice with a tantalizing hint of more substantive reasons. This evolution set the stage for the modern practice.

The earliest *By the Court* decisions differed from modern examples not least in never being used for the more consequential judicial decisions. Initially, *By the Court* was not invented or controlled by the judges

Figure 6.1 ***By the Court*** **cases, all types, 1885–1970**

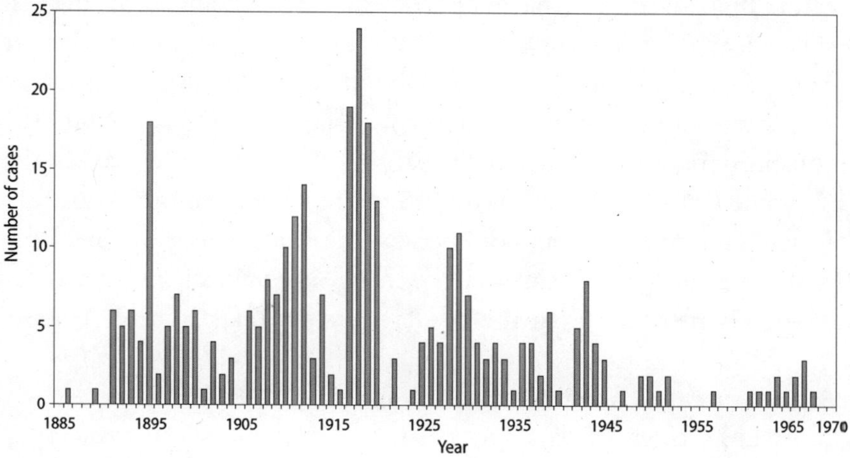

themselves but rather used by the registrar's office to fulfill its obligations in the face of certain procedural difficulties. Put simply, the earliest appearances of *By the Court* were an administrative salvage attempt to get around judicial underperformance. They were therefore an administrative rather than judicial development, emerging from the court's periphery rather than from within the court itself.

After 1905, a new practice emerged that displaced the earlier one. Importantly, however, it was still used for routine or procedural matters rather than for significant cases, and it still represented an administrative device to facilitate the reporting process. If the first stage involved an attempt to deal with an absence of written judicial reasons, the second stage involved a deliberate bypassing of written reasons in favour of a bureaucratic "third-person" observer's summary. Although we began our project with the assumption that *By the Court* was the product of a conscious and deliberate choice by the panel of judges, this seems not to have been the case at all – clearly not in either the first stage or the second.

This last period, after 1923, marked an important shift, in that the "third-person perspective" of the second stage was replaced by judicially written text. The records support the idea that the "By the Court" designation was judicially chosen (sometimes by the panel itself, sometimes by the chief justice), such that it can now be thought of as a judicial rather than an administrative phenomenon. At the same time, the reasons became modestly more substantive, with word counts no longer in the dozens but rather in the high hundreds or low thousands. However, it was almost never (we found only a single exception) used for the constitutional cases that were at that time a much smaller part of the Supreme Court caseload. It would be too much to turn this into a full-fledged "intermediate tradition" because the numbers were neither large nor increasing, but we think that the change is significant and consistent enough to merit our dramatic title "The Judges Take Control," below.

By the Court **as an Administrative Salvage Effort: 1886 and After**

In its early stages, *By the Court* was not a strategic judicial manoeuvre for dealing with some of the Supreme Court's most important cases. Indeed, to our surprise, it does not even appear that the judges themselves were directly involved initially. Rather, the device was developed by the registrar's office to accommodate publication of the court's decisions. During its early decades, the court took some time to develop a fully functional routine for the delivery and publication of its decisions, and in the process it experienced difficulties that required temporary work-around measures. *By the Court* was one such measure.

Snell and Vaughan identify the publication of judicial decisions as an issue that plagued the court for many years.[3] Both the Supreme Court and the Exchequer Court were responsible for publishing their own judgments, something that was very unusual at this time because private publishing firms were the typical vehicle for the publication of judicial decisions.[4] Formal responsibility for this was assigned to the registrar, who over time developed the appropriate support staff for timely publication in the Supreme Court's official reporting service, the *Supreme Court Reports.*

But this confronted the registrar's office with a new problem. The private publishers did not publish every decision, but only their selection of the more significant decisions of the Supreme Court and other courts. The logical implication was that the judges would focus their writing efforts on their reasons in the more significant cases, and the private publishers would not be concerned that reasons were not being completed for the more routine decisions because they would not have published them in any event. The registrar, however, had no such luxury. The office's statutory responsibility – an innovative requirement that had been included in the earliest version of the legislation – was to report all decisions of the court, not just the more important ones and not just the ones that the judges filed promptly.[5]

The process involved several time-consuming stages. Secretaries wrote up the justices' notes once those notes had been submitted, and in the *seriatim* era this included all the judges who had spoken to the matter when the decision was handed down. The notes then needed to be edited and reviewed, and finally submitted to the registrar for final preparation for publication in the *Supreme Court Reports.* The legal profession complained repeatedly about the published product in the *Supreme Court Reports,* which was sometimes so shoddy that the reasons were all but incomprehensible, a problem that only gradually yielded to improvements.

Even more problematic was the slowness of the process. There were extended delays between oral argument and the decision itself, and again in the publication of the judgment. Snell and Vaughan identify these delays as a serious impediment to the court's fulfillment of its responsibilities, one that persisted through many chief justiceships. Although the multi-stage publication process itself was part of the problem, even more so was the fact that during the court's earliest years, its operations were disrupted by the tardiness of the judges themselves. They often failed to submit their written notes to the registrar within a reasonable time, if at all, and the registrar lacked the power to do anything but request the missing submissions. Today, we would expect a chief justice to play some role in the prompting of colleagues, but on the early Supreme Court the chief justices were sometimes among the worst offenders. Thus, despite the expectation that all cases, including the most routine ones, should be reported, many were omitted from the *Supreme Court Reports* for the simple reason that only some, and sometimes none, of the judges had submitted their written notes.

Through repeated requests from the registrar and complaints from the legal profession, the government of the day became aware of the issues and took several steps to resolve the matter:

- In 1881, the reporter of the Supreme Court of Canada received authorization from the Minister of Justice to send written notes of the judicial hearing directly to the private law reporters. This provided an outline of the court's final decision as well as a brief indication of the pertinent legal principles. The full formal reasons would usually follow at a later date, but even if they did not, the legal profession had some general indication of what had happened and why.
- The government gradually allocated additional money to hire more support staff. For example, an assistant reporter was added to the staff in 1885, and in 1893 a stenographer was hired as a personal assistant to Chief Justice Samuel Strong – himself a major culprit and the cause of much of the backlog. This was only a partial solution, however, and no additional funds were provided for such resources.
- An agreement was reached with the Justice Department that judgments would be published in some form in the *Supreme Court Reports* even without complete sets of written reasons. This ensured that the legal community was made aware of the final result of many cases, although at the cost of accepting a lower quality of the *Supreme Court Reports.* Snell and Vaughan observe that "in four cases [in 1896] the result alone was given, with no reasons and no indications of the justices' votes."[6]

Being obliged to report decisions without full supporting reasons – the judicial equivalent of producing bricks without straw – the registrar had no alternative but to improvise. The general form of this improvisation was what we shall call the "third-person perspective" type of reported decision. Many of these identify the specific judge whose comments were being described, but the dozens of cases that included no such detail account for the earliest *By the Court* decisions.

Early examples will clarify this context. For example, *Shaw v The Canadian Pacific Railway Company* was decided on December 9, 1889, but it was not included in the *Supreme Court Reports* until three years later, splendidly making the point about the delays.[7] Although this was by no means a major case with precedential consequences, it is part of a broader set of decisions by the court that begin to clarify questions about its jurisdiction and procedure, for example, about the kinds of interlocutory rulings (in this case, a demurrer) for which an appeal lies to the Supreme Court. Yet after a delay of several years, all that we read after a short description of the factual background is: "By the court. The appeal must be quashed."

A second example more clearly demonstrates the third-person aspect. The reported decision in *Great North Western Telegraph Co. v The Montreal Telegraph Co.*, delivered six months after oral argument, consists in its entirety of the following paragraphs:

> The Supreme Court dismissed the appeal, agreeing with and adopting the reasons for judgment of Mr. Justice Wurtele of the Superior Court, which are reported in M.L.R. 6 S.C. 94.
>
> Justices Strong, Fournier, Taschereau and Patterson were also of opinion that as by the agreement of the 17th of August, 1881, the appellants had assumed all risk of diminished income in the working of the telegraph lines transferred by respondent and had entered into this agreement after the Canadian Pacific Railway Company had obtained authority from Parliament to establish telegraph lines for the transmission of messages for the public, the action should be dismissed on the merits, adopting the view of the case taken by Sir A.A. Dorion in the Court of Queen's Bench for Lower Canada (appeal side) whose judgment is reported at length in M.L.R. 6 Q.B. p. 258.[8]

This is clearly a brief summary of proceedings written from the point of view of an observer, and at most a short paraphrase of a longer set of reasons. Moreover, it is one that hints at there being more than one set of reasons involved, because after reporting a decision that involves a five-judge panel dismissing the appeal, we are then told that four of those five "also" had a further observation to make. We would now expect to find something of this sort in the headnotes as a summary of more extensive written reasons, but in the early decades those headnotes often presented the legal arguments made by the two parties, and even the questions posed to counsel by the judges during oral argument. At the same time, for all its brevity, there is enough information here to be helpful for lawyers or lower court judges concerned about the issue (which had to do with "damages under the lessors and lessees articles of the Quebec Code of Civil Procedure"), especially because we are specifically told that the Supreme Court "agreed with and adopted the reasons for judgment" of the lower court.

As a third example, consider *Bickford v Hawkins*.[9] The judgment was delivered four months after oral argument, there is a short statement of the issue, and the concluding paragraph reads: "The court held that the appeal should be dismissed the questions raised being entirely matters of fact, as to which the decision of the trial judge who saw and heard the witnesses, confirmed as it was by the Court of Appeal, should not be interfered with."

There is a clear sense in the *Reports* that these were treated as a "catch-up" exercise by the registrar. For example, in both Volume 20 (mostly 1891 decisions) and Volume 21 (mostly 1892 decisions), there are five brief third-person perspective "THE COURT" decisions on successive pages. To be sure, the third-person perspective does not always mean an unattributed set of reasons – sometimes dissents are acknowledged in the same third-person way, and sometimes the impassiveness of "the court decided" is supplemented by an equally brief "Justice X explained" (Justice X usually being the chief justice) – but usually these judgments were reported in such a way as not to attribute any specific reasons or legal arguments to any members of the panel. It is in this sense that we regard it a clear precursor of the modern *By the Court*.

We have provided a plausible explanation of why the innovation of anonymous unattributed reasons was necessary. As might be expected, these decisions were short; the seventy-one examples that we identified between 1886 and 1905 averaged only thirty-nine words each. And, to repeat our basic point, there is no suggestion here that the court itself had made any decision about these being the kinds of cases that deserved this kind of presentation.[10] They exist in the *Reports* as an administrative response on the part of the registrar to a clash between the requirements of the registrar's office and the actual performance of the judges.

Inevitably this raises the question of why the judges were unable to follow through with their written reasons (especially given that the early decisions of the Supreme Court tend to be considerably shorter than the massive legal essays that we often expect today). Why was the court so backlogged?

One factor was the government's reluctance to provide sufficient funding for adequate support staff. This was in part an endemic feature of the time – governments in the nineteenth century functioned with levels of support staff that were much lower than what we take for granted today.[11] This was aggravated by the fact that courts in general, and the Supreme Court in particular, did not enjoy the same obvious public importance that we see today, in the age of the *Canadian Charter of Rights and Freedoms;* furthermore, the Supreme Court itself enjoyed neither a high profile nor a particularly solid reputation. (There is, of course, something of a vicious circle here: low staffing contributes to poor performance, which contributes to a poor reputation, which undermines the claim for more staff.)

Snell and Vaughan also suggest that other considerations distracted the judges from their duties.[12] One was ill health, which caused problems in the formation of panels (always something of a problem for a court of six judges with five as the legal minimum size for a panel) and the delivery of reserved judgments within a reasonable time, as well as following up with written reasons. Another was that many of the judges were simply not as diligent about their court responsibilities as one would expect of an appellate high court today. For example, Snell and Vaughan describe problems arising from the way some judges sought frequent leaves of absence in order to pursue other professional and business opportunities. Finally, there were a number of strong personal disagreements within the court, with some judges refusing to conference with or even discuss legal issues with their colleagues, while certain judges were well known within and beyond the court for their rudeness and lack of cooperation.

In the end, it fell to the registrar to find a way of reporting decisions even when the judges failed to produce the notes for written reasons. The result was third-person perspective reports of judgments that were not attributed to any specific judge but simply to "the Supreme Court," "the court," "The Court," or even "*per curiam*" (there was no consistent format). This was a rather unpromising starting point for a device that reached its apogee in the *Quebec Secession Reference,* but we think it is a starting point nonetheless.[13]

By the Court as a Reporting Device: 1905 and After

Before describing the second stage in the evolution of the precursor of the modern *By the Court* practice, we need to first describe our method (based on searching the Supreme Court archives rather than working from the published reports), and second, to explain the nature of the archives and how it constrained the data collection process.

From the *Supreme Court Reports,* we generated a list of unattributed decisions, but a simple flat list does not in itself explain very much. Zanoni decided to revise his master's thesis to deal with this previously unsuspected precursor to the high-profile modern practice, and he turned to the Supreme Court archives to gain a better understanding of the context and process. This was made possible by a remarkable degree of accommodation and cooperation from the Supreme Court staff responsible for those archives, and both authors express their sincere appreciation for this assistance. Zanoni's necessarily vague initial request (vague because neither author had any real idea of what those archives would look like, or whether they were organized so as to easily yield the additional information we wanted) expanded into four weeks of full days in the archives, completely changing our thinking about the nature of the phenomenon at this early stage.

The nature of the archives themselves calls for additional explanation. In the early 1980s, Professor DeLloyd Guth (then of the University of British Columbia, more recently of the University of Manitoba), who was conducting research on the Supreme Court, walked through the wrong door and wound up in a sub-basement looking at piles of boxes that represented the accumulated material from several decades of earlier cases.[14] Communication of his concern to a former colleague who was serving as the new chief justice's executive assistant resulted in Guth's being seconded for a year to oversee the process of transferring the archival material into the latest data storage technology. That technology was microfilm, as anyone who was doing research around that time will instantly guess. This makes the Supreme Court archives a wonderful demonstration of a technological trap. Microfilm was indeed a marvelous advance for the time, and one that greatly reduced the physical space needed for storing information while simultaneously making it more available to lawyers and researchers. However, it also means that great patience is required to scroll through a continuous film to find the precise page with the desired information (and this after making sure that you have the right film), which is then projected onto a flat surface in front of you – quite cumbersome particularly for researchers who are accustomed to the convenience of hyperlinks and the wonders of digitized search engines.

Zanoni had to identify specific cases so that an archival assistant could locate the correct strip of microfilm and advance it to the right page for Zanoni's consideration, and Zanoni then had to scroll through all the case material to find the specific pages with the desired information. It was not quite a needle in a haystack, but it was often a few pages in a not always systematic collection that often ran to hundreds of pages, including lower court decisions, the factums of all the parties, and the court's own forms and procedural reports, including written exchanges between the registrar and judges on the panel. It was impossible under these circumstances to consider every single case on our list, so we were reduced to noting that "we found examples" rather than recording firm counts.

Zanoni's critical discovery was that starting in 1910, some of the third-person perspective *By the Court* decisions in the *Supreme Court Reports* matched up with archival collections that included attributed discursive reasons from the judges on the panel. For these cases, it was not judicial tardiness or delinquency that necessitated an administrative salvage effort; something else was needed to explain this.

The answer, we are confident, lies in the reporting process as it operated for much of the twentieth century. As previously indicated, both official and private reporting services (such as the *Dominion Law Reports*) were involved in the reporting of Supreme Court decisions to the legal community to keep them informed of recent developments in the law.[15] Official reporting services are those administered and controlled by the government. Canada has two: the *Supreme Court Reports*, which is exclusively dedicated to the documentation and dissemination of the

Supreme Court's decisions, and the *Federal Reports,* which plays a similar role for the federal courts of trial and appeal.

Anne Roland, a previous registrar, has described the Supreme Court's reporting procedures for much of the twentieth century as involving a practice of "selective reporting," which was particularly pronounced during the court's earlier decades. Not every decision of the court was published for the legal community, even when the judges had written and filed those full reasons with the registrar. Complete publication was precluded by the fact that only limited resources were available, and the demands of the process of preparing these decisions meant that those resources had to be appropriately rationed and allocated. (The *seriatim* nature of most of the court's decisions for several decades, with every judge on the panel often writing his own complete reasons rather than combining with colleagues behind a focused majority, aggravated the problem, in terms of both the volume of material to be processed and the number of judges who needed to provide their material.)

For the *Supreme Court Reports,* it was the registrar who made the final discretionary call for inclusion, although there was a measure of consultation with the chief justice and the other members of the court, with the registrar normally acceding to the judges' requests.[16] The basic criterion was the obvious one: the potential impact of the immediate case on future decisions. Those cases seen to provide useful guidance and clarification for the lower courts were published in full, while a second set of cases were reported only in terms of a clerical summary that picked up on the major points.[17] An even more routine set of cases were not reported at all.[18] This helped make the editing and publishing of extended judicial reasons more manageable, but when the summarized reasons were a clerical amalgamation of a number of different sets of reasons embodying overlapping rationales, it would have been inaccurate and misleading to attribute them to any single individual.[19] Such reasons were therefore attributed to a generic, institutional label – usually but not always "THE COURT."[20]

The appearance of *By the Court* remained much the same: there were still short summaries of the most important elements of a decision, using a third-person perspective that made it clear that the specific words and phrases were those of a clerical summarizer, not of any judge individually or of the court collectively. For the reasons indicated above about the nature of the archives and our access to them, we could not do a complete case-by-case breakdown that would have enabled us to plot the shift from "accommodating the absence of reasons" to "amalgamating written reasons to accommodate the imperatives of publication," but our sampling suggests that there was a steady swing from the former to the latter. For the period after 1905, Zanoni was able to follow 122 *By the Court* decisions in the archives. For 96 of them, one or more sets of reasons attributed to a particular justice had been submitted to the registrar. We believe this supports our description of a new practice emerging and then displacing the older practice.

We have read a "more routine, less legally significant" element into these third-person summaries, but this does not mean that such summaries were unimportant to the extent that simple non-publication would have been a workable strategy. Many of these decisions dealt with basic issues of jurisdiction, procedure, and standing, an essential element of fitting a new court into an existing judicial structure. Since the 1970s, almost all cases have arrived before the court by a leave process that screens out most (as much as 90 percent) applications for leave to appeal, but during earlier decades the court did not possess the same discretionary control over its agenda and was increasingly inundated with "appeal-by-right" cases. Justice Strong, for example, often complained about the "paltry amounts" at issue in some of the cases that came before the court, regarding them as a distraction from the important work of the court, and he called on the provinces to establish more meaningful limits and thresholds on appeals.[21] Other jurisdictional and procedural issues (such as interlocutory appeals) needed to be worked out over time, and for these, short summary reasons appended to an outcome were enough to make the point. This second type of *By the Court* decision fit the bill in a double sense: the more routine decisions were handled in a way that put minimal strain on the resources for publication of decisions while still transmitting the relevant information.

The Judges Take Control: The Emergence of the Regular Form, 1920 and After

We have described an early *By the Court* practice that was essentially an administrative and clerical convenience for the registrar – first as a way of dealing with the failure of some judges to submit written reasons within a reasonable period of time, and then as a way of reporting an outcome and summary reasons for the more routine cases in order to better cope with the limitations of the publication process. Especially in the second period, this presumably involved some degree of collaboration with the chief justice and the other members of the court, but the fact remains that it was largely a simplifying process of a clerical nature rather than a direct product of judicial choice. An important transition occurred after 1920 that transformed the appearance on the page of *By the Court,* and that involved abandonment of the third-person perspective and its replacement with judicially written reasons.

The unprepossessing case that marks this transformation is *Hamilton v Evans.*[22] At first glance, it looks like another example of the procedural/jurisdictional emphasis described earlier, briefly dismissing a motion involving how the statutory limit for appeals should be calculated. In the *Supreme Court Reports,* the full text of the decision reads: "By The Court: We agree with the position taken by counsel for the respondent. The motion will be dismissed with costs." Note the appearance of the pronoun "we": what we see here is not a third-person summary by the registrar of the spoken or written words of the justices but rather a direct reporting of the very simple and brief words of the judges themselves.[23] We refer to this as a "*By the Court* judgment in regular form" to distinguish it from a "*By the Court* judgment in third-person summary form," and despite this modest beginning, it was a change with powerful potential. Although the shift from the first to the second phase of the process described above involved no explicit change to the format and appearance within the reports themselves and could be identified only from the archival record, this new shift is visible on the face of the reported decision. After 1923, and before a date in the late 1960s that will be discussed in the next chapter, there were fifty examples of this new style, reproducing judicially created text that differed from other reported decisions only by the fact that it was not attributed to a specific author.

Equally noteworthy, the archives make clear that the new format was chosen by the judges themselves before the decision was filed with the registrar; it was not an administrative convenience or necessity but a deliberate judicial tactic. In the archives, the standard form includes an "author tracker" that identifies a specific writer, with the other judges indicating their agreement by signing their names. Many of these regular-form *By the Court* judgments were submitted to the registrar in such a way that the author was already identified as "THE COURT." Given that the long-standing *seriatim* practices of the court were still in place for many of its decisions, this development was all the more remarkable.

On a number of other occasions (we were able to find ten of them), the written judgment submitted to the registrar was not headed "THE COURT" but was accompanied by an author sheet identifying a specific judge; this name had at some point been scratched out and replaced by a "THE COURT" designation. One possibility is that this switch took place just before the written reasons were submitted; another is that the choice was made after submission, presumably by the chief justice or by the registrar after consultation with the chief justice. In three of the ten cases, the name that had been scratched out was that of the chief justice himself.

Figure 6.2 shows that the third-person perspective was in sharp decline after 1930 and that the new regular form had largely replaced it. This points to Chief Justices Francis Anglin (1924–33) and Lyman Duff (1933–44) as the architects of the change.

Table 6.1 compares the new regular-form *By the Court* decisions with the largely earlier set of third-person perspective decisions. Three differences are striking:

- The regular-form decisions are about five times as long, averaging a page and a half of explanatory text, compared with the earlier single paragraph or even single sentence. These decisions are still moderate in length, well below average for reasons for judgment

Figure 6.2 *By the Court* cases by type, 1885–1970

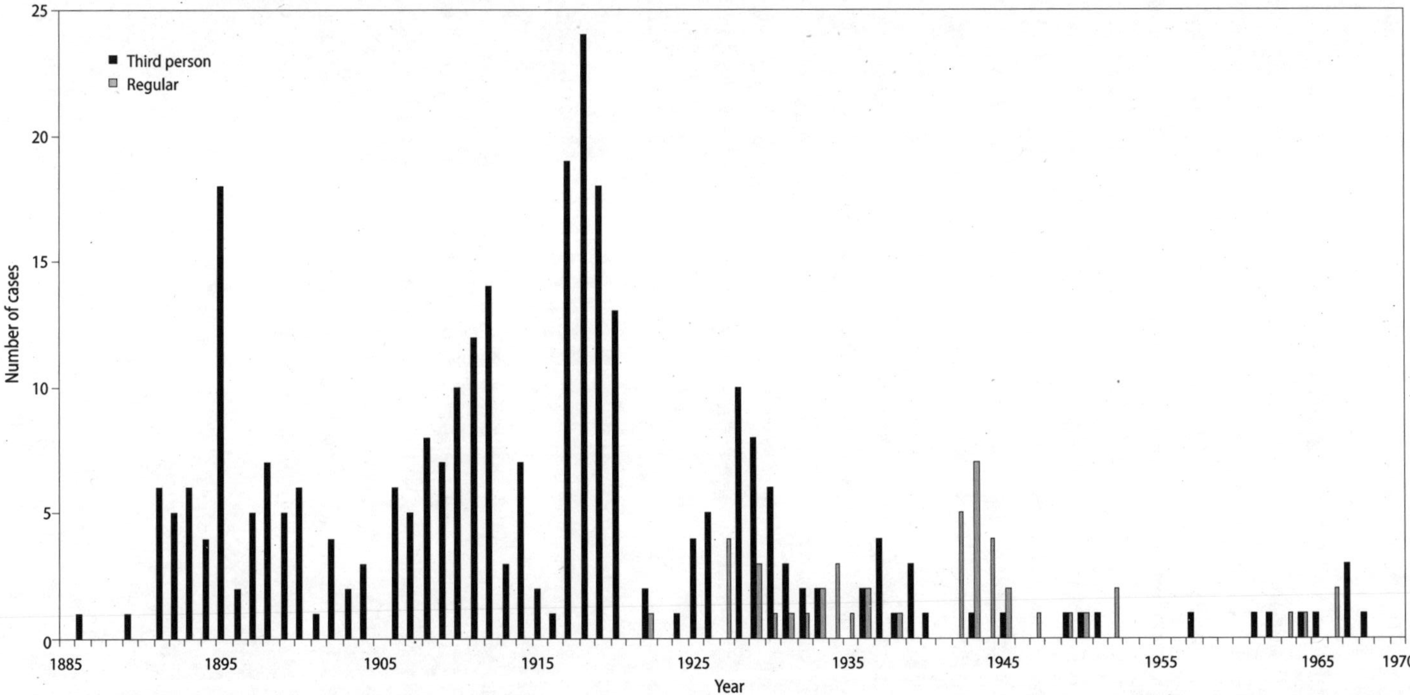

Table 6.1 Basic features of *By the Court* decisions in third-person summary form and regular form, 1885–1970

	Third-person summary	*Regular*
Average word count	108	525
Appeal success rate (%)	14.4	38.0
Average panel size	5.11	5.12
Origin (%)	Ontario 26.8	Quebec 30.0
	Quebec 23.2	British Columbia 18.0
	British Columbia 13.4	Ontario 16.0
Procedural and jurisdictional matters (%)	15.0	42.0
Private law (%)	72.0	22.0
Public law (%)	12.2	22.0
Criminal law (%)	0.7	14.0
Constitutional law (%)	0.7	0

even at a time when decisions tended to be much shorter, but they are long enough to convey some real substance.

- Many more of them deal with successful appeals, 14.4 percent for the third-person perspective compared with 38 percent for the regular form. If the older format invites a characterization of "routine dismissals," the newer one does not.
- The regular-form cases are even more clearly directed toward procedural and jurisdictional matters. This seems consistent with the fact that they were deliberately chosen rather than being the almost accidental product of judicial tardiness or a publication "squeeze."

Two similarities are equally obvious. The first is that such decisions clearly involved the less substantial elements of the Supreme Court caseload – the word count may be higher for the regular-form decisions but it is still modest even by the standards of the time. The second is that although the type of law dealt with in this style of judgment had evolved, the constitutional cases that have dominated the "grand tradition" were almost completely missing.

A handful of cases stand out from these generalizations, however, involving judge-written discursive reasons that exceed an arbitrary but not unreasonable cut-off of 1,000 words (two or three pages of text). These decisions show that at the same time that the judges were taking control of the device by using it to convey specific judge-written text, they were also beginning to do so for reasons that were becoming more substantive. Word count is not a perfect surrogate for importance, but clearly very short reasons (on the order of the third-person perspective average of 100 words) are generally less likely to represent substantive contributions to the law than, for example, the 6,500 words of *Prince* (described below).[24] There were four such cases:

- *Brooks v The King* in 1927 was a criminal law case with reasons that ran to 1,330 words.[25] The accused had been charged with "procuring an abortion" and was convicted at the trial level. His appeal to the Appellate Division of the Supreme Court of Ontario was unsuccessful, but a further appeal to the Supreme Court of Canada succeeded on the ground that the judge had misdirected the jury in a "material matter" that contributed inappropriately to the jury's decision, and a new trial was ordered. The court used a *By the Court* judgment to explain why the instructions given to the jury were insufficient.
- *R v McLean* in 1933 was a criminal case that similarly arose out of the trial judge's charge to the jury on a conviction for murder that drew a death penalty.[26] The conviction was upheld on appeal to the Appellate Division of the Supreme Court of Alberta, but a dissent by one of the judges on that panel brought the case before the Supreme Court to deal with the issues raised in the dissent. In a *By the Court* judgment of 1,933 words, the Supreme Court rejected the concerns of the dissenting judge and upheld the original trial decision.
- The longest of the decisions was *City of Toronto v Prince* in 1934, at almost 6,500 words.[27] The dispute involved the expropriation of

land by the City of Toronto, and specifically whether an exchange of letters about possible compensation was enough to constitute a binding contract after the project was dropped and the expropriating bylaw repealed. Mrs. Prince succeeded at trial and again before the Court of Appeal of Ontario, but a dissent by two of the judges on the Court of Appeal led the City of Toronto to appeal, successfully, to the Supreme Court.

- *Fiset v Morin* in 1945 was a *By the Court* judgment of 1,899 words dealing with a motion to quash an appeal from a decision of Quebec's Court of King's Bench, Appeal Side.[28] This court had dismissed an appeal from the trial decision, on the grounds that "there is no jurisdiction in this Court" to entertain such an appeal. Most unusually, the decision was delivered in French at a time before it was the practice for the *Supreme Court Reports* to provide a parallel English version.

Tempting though it may be to distinguish a fourth stage in this process with a label such as "the intermediate tradition," there are simply too few cases, spread out across two decades, to justify it, nor are the decisions (*Prince* aside) particularly long, even by the standards of the time. It is worth noting, however, that three of them were sufficiently noteworthy to be cited by the Supreme Court in subsequent decisions – *McLean* was cited once, *Fiset v Morin* was cited three times (most recently in 1970), and *Brooks* was cited a remarkable twenty-one times, most recently in 1989. Although these numbers (*Brooks* aside) may not seem particularly impressive, McCormick's research has shown that most Supreme Court judgments for reserved decisions are never cited at all, even in more recent decades, when the number of such citations by the Supreme Court has increased sharply; few cases are cited more than twenty times, and even fewer are still being cited several decades later.[29] If citability is one dimension of the legal importance of a case, then the judicial choice of the *By the Court* label for judge-written text of some length is a development worth noting, despite the small number of such cases.

Our goal in this chapter has been to show that there was a longstanding practice of the Supreme Court that preceded the emergence of the modern *By the Court,* and that this practice was showing modest signs of developing into something more substantial than merely an administrative convenience for routine cases. But this is only half of our hurdle; the other half, which we will tackle in the next chapter, is to explain how this modest beginning was reshaped into a device focused on constitutional decisions.

Emergence: The Birth of the "Grand Tradition"

7

We have suggested an answer to the question of where the *By the Court* judgment presentation format came from by showing that the Supreme Court of Canada itself had for many years followed an evolving practice of short, routine decisions attributed (for changing reasons) to "THE COURT," but we are only half-way to explaining the emergence of *By the Court.* There is still a large gap between the "short reasons for routine cases and not for constitutional cases" of the early period, and the "extended reasons for constitutional cases, very important ones" of the modern period – between Zanoni's "minor tradition" and the "grand tradition" of recent decades. If courts are institutions not usually open to innovation, how was this gap overcome? Why did it occur when it did rather than at some other time? In general terms, both questions have to be answered at the same time. The new format had to be a response to some unusual and pressing challenge that could not be adequately addressed by the standard format, such that the question of why at that time is answered by identifying the challenge.

There is a conventional explanation of the origins of *By the Court* that was widely accepted by the academic community, one to which McCormick was long exposed and to which (to his current embarrassment) his own publications occasionally contributed; we will call this "the Laskin thesis." On the basis of our own research, we are not satisfied with this origin story, and will devote the next section to an explanation of why it does not work and why a different sequence of events actually presents the transformative challenge to which *By the Court* is the response.[1]

The Laskin Thesis

The conventional explanation of the invention of *By the Court* goes like this: it first appeared in 1979 as a way of dealing with a pair of language decisions – one from Quebec (*Blaikie*) and the other from Manitoba (*Forest*) – that dealt with the status of official languages and the constitutional powers of provincial legislatures to modify that status.[2] For Manitoba, the issue was the province's shift from bilingualism to English-only for legislative purposes in 1899; for Quebec, it was the province's legislation ("Bill 1," subsequently revised to become "Bill 101," with the politically potent official title "The Charter of the French Language") that sought to constrain the role of English and make French the dominant language in the province. The explosive potential of these cases was obvious.[3] Small wonder, then, that the Supreme Court would be willing to consider something unusual in the way of judgment delivery, the more so because this was a court led by a most unusual chief justice who embodied reformist ideas. *By the Court* was, in this account, the response of this reformist court under its reformist leader to the politically explosive challenge in the early days of the court's assumption of a more robust role as a "constitutional court." It was all the more important because the device was something that the Supreme Court under Bora Laskin and his successors continued to use in comparable cases.

In this account, then, *By the Court* was invented by the Laskin court in response to the profound constitutional challenges occasioned by the election of a sovereigntist government in Quebec that proceeded with aggressive legislative initiatives. Canada has survived the Patriation controversy, the sovereignty referenda of 1980 and 1995, and two unsuccessful attempts at further constitutional change on the part of the federal government (Meech Lake and Charlottetown) to deal with the after-effects.[4] The language cases came at the front end of these challenges, when there was a real prospect of a more dramatic outcome, and they very much put the Supreme Court on the hot seat. It is not an exaggeration to say that this had the potential to be the Canadian equivalent of the US Supreme Court's *Dred Scott* decision, which has been called one of that court's three worst decisions and sometimes (a little simplistically) accused of triggering the American Civil War.[5] The language cases were an invitation to our Supreme Court to become involved in a *cause célèbre* with the potential for a major political showdown of comparable consequence. On the face of it, this makes it credible that even a traditionally inclined institution would be willing to act in an unusual way, especially under a reform-minded chief justice like Laskin. The fact that within the next few years the court used the device again for a number of comparably weighty cases – the *Upper House Reference* of 1980, the follow-up case to *Blaikie* in 1981, the *Quebec Veto Reference* of 1982, and the *Superior Court Reference* of 1983 – helps to anchor the reputation of this pair of decisions as the innovative turning point, and identifies *By the Court* as something that "had legs" in the context of constitutional cases.[6]

The plausibility of such a timing for an innovation is enhanced by the unusual circumstances of the Laskin court. Laskin became chief justice in a highly controversial way, given his lack of seniority on the court. No fewer than six justices had enjoyed longer service, with an obvious candidate for chief justice in Alberta's Ronald Martland, who was by some accounts profoundly annoyed at having been passed over.[7] This was particularly so given the firmly established convention (previously violated only twice, with Charles Fitzpatrick and Francis Anglin) that seniority was the pre-emptively important principle for succession to the chief justiceship.[8] The selection of Laskin was so unexpected and so controversial as to attract critical commentary from within the legal profession; it was considered unsettling for a prime minister to use discretionary choice to make an appointment with such significant institutional implications.[9]

Initially, this novel appointment had precisely the institutional effect that might have been anticipated – the more senior judges closed ranks under Martland's leadership and Laskin began earning his reputation as the Great Dissenter, authoring and joining dissents more frequently than any of his chief justice predecessors.[10] The senior cohort of the court suffered relentless attrition, however, and their replacements were appointed by the government that had appointed Laskin himself. Gradually, the balance shifted (most plausibly, the appointment of Antonio Lamer in 1980 marked the critical moment); Laskin stopped writing dissents and the court shifted to the style that became the Laskin court standard – an unusually high percentage of unanimous judgments, an unusually large proportion of which were delivered by the chief justice. The language cases of 1979 appeared to fit neatly into this story of shifting voting balances and emerging new practices.[11]

The two decisions also display a first-glance appearance that fits this story. They are brief, tight-lipped, and to the point, almost boilerplate rather than the expansive nuanced explanations we take for granted today. In short, they have the feeling of a somewhat tentative test drive. The literature often suggests that national high courts, besides giving final legal answers in a way that provides useful guidance to lower courts and future litigants, also have a public educative function.[12] Many of the later *By the Court* judgments fully deliver on this expectation, dealing at length with the background and logic and implications of the important matters they are deciding, striving for a completely persuasive resolution. Against that backdrop, these putative "first two" are curiously reticent and constrained. *Blaikie* is 4,000 words long, *Forest* is 2,000 – roughly ten and five pages of text, respectively, well below the average length of reasons for Supreme Court judgments. The 7,500 words of the *Upper House Reference* later that same year – more than the two language case decisions combined – is a better preview of what we have come to expect from this style of judgment in subsequent years.

But our major problem with the conventional explanation and the Laskin thesis is simply that they get the date wrong. The critical year is not 1979 but 1967, and the critical challenge is not Quebec separatism but one of the most embarrassing episodes in the court's history.

The True Origin of *By the Court:* The 1967 Trilogy

The calendar year 1967 saw an unusual trilogy of cases that mark the true birth of the *By the Court* format. None of the three used that precise label; all styled themselves as "joint opinions," the only three judgments in the history of the Supreme Court to have used that label. Indeed, the first of the three was not even unanimous but drew a solo dissent. The critical point, however, is that never before had an anonymous format been used in a major case. Together, the three cases mark the redeployment of that format from the routine and procedural that it had been used for over a period of almost a century to major high-profile cases, including (in two of the three examples) constitutional cases.

From the most recent to the earliest, the three cases were:

1 *The Queen v Board of Transport Commissioners*, a constitutional law case dealing with the federal-provincial division of legislative authority.[13] The question was whether the tolls charged for a commuter train service using provincial stock but operating on Canadian National Railway tracks were subject to the regulatory authority of the federal Board of Transport Commissioners.
2 *Reference re: Offshore Mineral Rights*, also a constitutional law case dealing with the federal-provincial division of legislative authority.[14] At stake were proprietary rights and legislative authority over certain lands adjacent to the British Columbia coast.
3 *Reference re: Steven Murray Truscott*, the first of the three cases and our candidate for the case that marked the critical transition to the modern *By the Court*.[15]

Steven Truscott and the *Truscott Reference*

The name of Steven Truscott has reverberated for decades throughout the Canadian justice system. He lived in the small town of Clinton, Ontario, and in 1959 he was convicted of the rape and murder of a twelve-year-old classmate, Lynne Harper. He was only fourteen years old when the judge announced the verdict and the sentence in the famous historic formula: "You will be kept in close confinement until Tuesday, the 8th day of December, 1959, and on that day and date, you be taken to the place of execution and that you there be hanged by the neck until you are dead. And may the Lord have mercy on your soul."

The verdict and sentence were immediately controversial for two reasons. One was the young age of the defendant, surprising in any event but even more so when the trial culminated in a death sentence; the other was the fact that there was only circumstantial evidence (some of it conflicting) to link him to the crime. An appeal to the Ontario Court of Appeal was unanimously dismissed on January 21, 1960, although the government of Canada commuted the death sentence to life imprisonment shortly afterward. An application for leave to appeal to the Supreme Court was refused by a unanimous panel of five Supreme Court justices on February 14, 1960.[16]

The unanimity of all these judges (one trial judge, three provincial appeal court judges, and five Supreme Court justices) is striking. It appears to signal a very straightforward legal case, and yet the controversy persisted, not only in this country but around the world. The picture of a fourteen-year-old boy being sentenced to death on the basis of circumstantial evidence was not the sort of thing that was expected from a country like Canada – it was a "Project Innocence" case before its time. The level of controversy was ratcheted upward considerably in 1966 when Isabel LeBourdais published her book *The Trial of Steven Truscott*, which provides an extensive analysis of the conduct of the police during the investigation and of the details of the trial proceedings themselves.[17] The public controversy reached such a point that the Canadian government felt obliged to make some formal response. It announced in April 1967 that there would be an official review of the case, and this ultimately took the form of a reference question to the Supreme Court of Canada.[18] The basic question was this: Had the Supreme Court of Canada heard the appeal in 1960 (as it would have been obliged to do had subsequent *Criminal Code* amendments been in place), would it have allowed the appeal?

We must admit that we find this a rather surprising manoeuvre.[19] Strictly speaking, it is the kind of question the court often gets in a reference case, in the sense that it starts with a counter-factual hypothesis and invites the court to explore such a possibility for the guidance of official actors. In the immediate circumstances, however, it carried quite different overtones. For one thing, the entire Canadian judicial system, of which the Supreme Court is the apex and in some sense the spokesperson and champion, had been the subject of unusual and sustained public criticism within Canada and around the world for a full decade; if the court system as a whole was the target of the criticism, the highest court within that system was perhaps not the obvious choice to look into it. In addition, the Supreme Court itself had already been directly involved in the events that had contributed to the controversy: a panel of five Supreme Court justices had unanimously denied an application for leave to appeal. Worse yet in terms of appearances, four of those justices were still on the Supreme Court and (compounding the problem) one was the chief justice himself.[20] The apparently neutral "how should this ten-year-old case have been resolved had the statute been different?" could not be entirely stripped of its overtones of "now that you have had time to think about it, will you admit that you made a mistake?" This could only be seen as a direct challenge to the four judges and an implicit challenge to the institution itself. These considerations made this reference case a unique existential challenge to the credibility and prestige of the Supreme Court and its sitting members, a case unlike anything else in memory.[21]

If the case was unique, so was its procedure. The court sat as a full panel of nine, something that was more unusual in the 1960s than it has since become. Because it was admitting new evidence, it effectively turned itself into a trial courtroom with witnesses and expert testimony and cross-examination, with Truscott himself taking the stand – that is, it did not look remotely like a normal appeal court proceeding. The hearings stretched over four full days, and the court delivered its judgment three months later, on May 4, 1967. The reasons were unusually long for the time – more than 30,000 words – and unlike anything else that we have ever seen in the *Supreme Court Reports*. They read like a trial judgment rather than an appeal judgment, replete with a close and detailed examination of the witness testimony, a careful dissection of expert evidence with extended quotations, and direct evaluations of witness credibility. In the end, the court concluded that the trial court had reached an appropriate verdict, that the Ontario Court of Appeal had been right to dismiss the appeal, and that the Supreme Court panel had been right to deny the application for leave. The evidence, they said, was "not only consistent with the guilt of Truscott" but, even more categorically, it was "inconsistent with any rational conclusion other than that Steven Truscott was the guilty person." Of Truscott himself, the court found "many incredibilities [*sic*]" in his evidence, and it flatly concluded that "we do not believe his testimony."[22]

But the decision was not unanimous: only eight of the nine judges supported it. The ninth, Justice Emmett Hall, wrote an extended dissent, finding grave errors in the conduct of the trial to such an extent that the verdict should be set aside. According to his biographer, Hall was the subject of considerable resentment within the court for his stand on this case, feelings that lingered for the rest of his service on the bench.[23] This again shows how unusually highly charged the case had been – dissents are a routine feature of the court's decisions, coming and going without generating lasting resentments, as must be the case if the institution is to continue functioning effectively. That these resentments lingered and remained strong is further indication of the unique significance of the *Truscott Reference* to the institution.

The most obvious way for the eight-judge majority to have presented its decision in such a high-profile case was a single set of reasons attributed to the chief justice with the concurrence of the other seven.[24] But they did not do this, perhaps because the chief justice was one of the four who had served on the implicitly impugned panel in 1960, which would have given such a presentation format an unavoidably defensive appearance, or perhaps because the direct challenge to the credibility of the court was so obvious as to demand a special response.[25] Instead, what was issued was a "joint opinion" of the eight judges listed in order of seniority, the first time the court had ever used such a label. They did not use the "THE COURT" designation, presumably because of Hall's solo dissent, and perhaps also because the case was not of the sort (minor, routine, short) that the court had for decades been deciding under this rubric. Instead, they presented a completely new phenomenon that justifies our treatment of it as the transition to *By the Court:* an anonymously authored set of extended reasons in a major case.[26]

This could of course have wound up being a one-off judgment, as the circumstances of the *Truscott Reference* were truly exceptional, like those once-in-a-century perfect storms we hear about in the news. But in fact it did not. Seven months later, on November 7 and November 20, the court handed down its decisions in two constitutional cases and, as in *Truscott,* each was presented as a joint opinion. *Truscott* constitutes a critically important first step toward the modern *By the Court,* employing as it did an anonymizing device for the resolution of a major case of broad significance, the first such example for the court. But the other two cases in the trilogy represent an equally important second step: they moved the anonymizing practice away from the unique circumstances of *Truscott* and applied it to significant constitutional cases. It is also worth noting that one of them was a constitutional reference from the federal government, the kind of case that has provided *By the Court* with its centre of gravity ever since.

There may have been only one *Truscott* case but questions about constitutional law were becoming a regular part of the court's caseload at the time. Because both decisions were unanimous (unlike *Truscott*), they were not joint opinions of listed judges but rather "Joint Opinion(s) of the court," making them an interesting terminological halfway house between the "joint opinion of listed judges" in *Truscott* and the "THE COURT" designation of 1979 and after.[27] Together, these three cases constitute a unique trilogy in which the Supreme Court of Canada first began to use an anonymous judgment format to deliver its decisions on major issues, departing from its long-standing tradition of specifically authored judgments for all but the most routine cases. This, we suggest, is where the panels of the Laskin court found their inspiration in 1979.

We might want to think of the *Offshore Mineral Rights Reference* as the first "pure" example of the modern *By the Court* because it did, and *Truscott* did not, deal with a question of constitutional law, but *Truscott* clearly provided the trigger for the emergence of anonymous judgments in major cases.[28] Before *Truscott* and the other cases of the 1967 trilogy, the anonymous and impersonal style of *By the Court* promised a short set of reasons dealing with routine or procedural matters; since then, it is frequently a marker of a major constitutional decision and often anticipated as such. And the origin of that new practice and style can, we suggest, be directly linked to a controversial murder trial involving a fourteen-year-old boy in 1959, and to a remarkable storm of public protest that shook even the federal cabinet and finally the Supreme Court itself.

Innovation and Path Dependency

Our comments assume a notion of judicial innovation that we will now make more explicit. Only reluctantly, only with powerful reasons, and only under unusual circumstances will an institution – and particularly an institution like a national high court, which relies heavily on continuity and consistency to optimize its influence – undertake significant change in some highly visible aspect of its operations. For the Supreme Court of Canada, the *Truscott Reference* created just such a situation. The Canadian justice system had been under sustained attack, drawing intense public criticism over the Truscott case for over a decade. Worse, the Supreme Court had, by denying Truscott's application for leave to appeal, linked itself to the trial result that had generated the waves of criticism. The court was forced into a defensive posture. The federal government eventually yielded to public pressure but did so in a way that put the Supreme Court firmly back in the spotlight. In the modern Charter era, the court is presumably no longer surprised when from time to time it finds itself out in the open and under fire in this way, but in an age when the court could without irony be described as a "quiet court" that eschewed political controversy, this was far from business as usual – it was the stuff of nightmares.[29]

It is not surprising, then, that the court essentially decided to double down – rather than saying "oops," rather than saying "different rules would have generated different results, how unfortunate that we weren't given those better rules in time," rather than retreating or equivocating or temporizing in any way, it stood firmly by its previous position. It did so by ramping up the rhetoric ("not consistent with any other conclusion"), by challenging the credibility of the person at the centre of the storm ("we do not believe his testimony"), and by embracing the original outcome even more vigorously and emphatically. Criticized by the media, excoriated by public opinion, condemned in other countries as well as their own, abandoned by the federal government that passed the buck with a problematic reference question, abandoned again by one of their own (Vaughan's biography of Justice Hall fully justifies this description of how Hall's colleagues felt about his solo dissent), the justices must have felt beleaguered as no previous members of that court had ever been.[30] Denied the solid front of a unanimous judgment, denied the chief justice as a fully credible institutional spokesperson by his own direct involvement with the earlier leave decision, but still anxious to make their point with a unified emphasis that was not normally necessary, the judges came up with a new-but-not-new idea. It was not new in that they had been using the anonymity of "THE COURT" to present a unified institutional position on routine and procedural matters for many decades, but it was distinctly new in that they had never used such institutional anonymity in the context of a major, controversial, high-profile case. Unique circumstances call for unique responses; exceptional pressure can produce innovation even in innovation-resistant institutions – necessity, as the old saying goes, is the mother of invention. The result was the novelty of the "joint opinion," of anonymity in the context of a not-quite-unanimous decision, which easily evolved into the modern *By the Court.*

If reluctant innovation under unique pressure explains the first emergence of *By the Court,* the concept of path dependence explains its subsequent use. There can be only one "first," after which it is less a question of *whether* than of *when* to consider doing it again. It may well be that the justices thought that their device had "worked," had deflected the challenge and brought the institution through in relatively good order. With the benefit of hindsight, including Truscott's vindication by the Ontario Court of Appeal in 2007, we have our doubts about whether it actually worked that well, but certainly the sense of crisis dissipated and the immediate fallout was directed elsewhere – for example, into public pressure to do away with the death penalty itself.[31] If the device was seen by the judges of the court itself to have succeeded, it must have made eminent good sense for the person we are about to identify as its architect to consider using it again later that same year for a tangentially similar purpose, to present a unified institutional response to a major question, such as a constitutional reference case brought by the national government.

Path dependence implies that the sequence matters. Had there been no *Truscott* case, no utterly exceptional circumstances generating the highly unusual response, there would probably have been no "Joint Opinion of (listed judges)" that could morph into a "Joint Opinion of the Court" and then into *By the Court.* There would therefore have been no new judgment-delivery device available as part of the court's repertoire for a broader set of future cases that posed little threat to the institution of the court itself but addressed major legal issues such as constitutional matters.

A single episode does not in itself establish a new practice, but repeated episodes over a period of time can gradually do so, in ways that may not have been contemplated (let alone intended) at the time. The subsequent story of *By the Court* judgments will unfold in subsequent chapters, but we will settle now for the most obvious generalization about its use: since *Truscott,* but never before *Truscott,* the *By the Court* judgment has become the normal way in which the court has dealt with federal reference cases as long as unanimity or near-unanimity could be achieved (which it usually could).[32]

It is neither fanciful nor forced to suggest that absent the *Truscott Reference,* this practice might never have emerged; this is what path dependence means. It is not that later cases of this sort were exactly like *Truscott* because they clearly were not: not only was the direct challenge to the institution much weaker but, unlike *Truscott,* almost all the later cases had constitutional overtones. The point is that once unusual circumstances have elicited an unusual response, that response is available for more calculated use in other circumstances and patterns may emerge that were not implicit in the first example. *By the Court* judgments are like a highly respected family that discovers that the original source of the family fortune was an embezzler. We are therefore not surprised that the academy has generated more genteel origin theories (the 1979 cases) or that the institution itself has begun to develop its own folk history.[33]

Naming Names

We have explained when and why *By the Court* emerged; what remains is the question of "who?" Given our explanatory theory, this actually turns out to be two questions: Who was responsible in 1979? Who was responsible in 1967?

As to who was responsible in 1979, someone at the post-hearing conference had to make the suggestion, had to say, "Why not an anonymous judgment, jointly attributed to the panel as a whole?" We doubt that it was Laskin – because he had strongly opposed a similar idea several decades earlier, because he was on the panel for only one of the two cases, and because he was absent from Ottawa for much of the term during which the two panels were working toward the December judgments.[34] A Laskin role is not impossible – he was part of the *Blaikie* panel, he could have been interacting with colleagues by mail or phone for part of his convalescent period in Vancouver, and he was definitely back in Ottawa and much more active than his doctors wanted him to be for the crucial weeks just before the judgments were delivered – but we remain doubtful. As well, we find it significant that the revival of *By the Court* occurred during the only half-term when Laskin was not present in Ottawa, not part of the ongoing interactions within the court, not physically present to act as a leader in the most obvious sense.

The justices we think most likely to have made the suggestion were those who had been there for the *Board of Transport Commissioners* case, the *Offshore Mineral Rights Reference*, and especially the *Truscott Reference* itself. These were the ones who could say, here is how we handled a challenging situation a dozen years ago that presented some real problems for the court; perhaps we should consider using that solution again now. The two justices who qualify – the two who served on all three of the 1967 panels and on both the *Forest* and the *Blaikie* panels – are Ronald Martland and Roland Ritchie. It seems to us that one or both of these justices are the most credible candidates for making the suggestion, and it is more poetically just to consider Martland the stronger candidate because he was the judge passed over when Laskin became chief justice.

The more tantalizing question is, who was responsible in 1967, when the idea was truly new and had no prior example to draw on? At first glance, the most logical candidate would be the chief justice at the time, namely Robert Taschereau, but from Vaughan's account in his biography of Hall, Taschereau was (to put it politely and delicately) failing, and the *de facto* leadership of the court had devolved onto Robert Cartwright, soon to become chief justice himself in time for the decisions in the other two cases in the joint opinion trilogy.[35] A major role for Cartwright might also explain why the device subsequently vanished for a dozen years. By 1970, Cartwright had retired and had been replaced by Gérald Fauteux, and the "Joint Opinion of the Court" device for constitutional cases fell into disuse – perhaps because Fauteux was less taken with the idea, perhaps because of a paucity of constitutional cases in general and federal reference cases in particular. Cartwright seems to us the more credible candidate, especially as the first two clear examples of *By the Court* occurred during his chief justiceship.

Remarkably, recent circumstances have provided a replay of the most critical moment of our story – a reference case that placed the court as an institution in a difficult and embarrassing corner, with a single dissent that kept it from presenting a truly united front, to which the majority responded with the anonymizing device of a joint judgment attributed equally to an all-but-one string of named judges. In 1967, this was the *Truscott Reference;* in 2014, it was the *Nadon Reference.*[36] History may not always repeat itself, but sometimes it echoes.

Our conclusion is that the *Truscott* case marks the transition of *By the Court* from the "minor tradition" of the court's first nine decades to the "grand tradition" that has given us a string of major constitutional judgments in the last five decades, and therefore the emergence of an important and unusual judgment presentation device. We will now provide a complete inventory of the practice, presenting it initially in the form a chronology and then proceeding to generate a typology that explains the multiple foci that it has displayed.

PART 3
The Modern *By the Court* Decisions

8 Inventory and Chronology of Decisions

We have defined the *By the Court* phenomenon, described its early history and emergence, and narrowed the focus to the "grand tradition" of major cases, somewhat generously defined as reserved judgments with reasons running over 2,000 words. There have been just under five dozen of these since 1967, slightly fewer if we treat companion cases (of which there have been four pairs and one triplet) as single examples. We have already spoken about the early examples from the Cartwright court in 1967. In this chapter, we provide an overview of the "grand tradition" *By the Court* judgments during the tenures of the various chief justices.

The Cartwright Court

The three cases listed in Table 8.1 stretch the point in two ways, as discussed in Chapter 7. First, we have been treating *Truscott* not as the first true *By the Court* but rather as the transitional case from which the modern *By the Court* followed. Second, the *Truscott* decision was handed down shortly before Robert Cartwright became chief justice, although we are following Vaughan's account and treating Cartwright as the *de facto* leader of the court for that case.[1]

Table 8.1 ***By the Court*** **judgments of the Cartwright court, 1967–70**

Case	*Citation*	*Words*	*Subject*
Reference re: Steven Murray Truscott	[1967] SCR 309	31,257	Other
Reference re: Offshore Mineral Rights	[1967] SCR 792	11,365	Federalism
The Queen v Board of Transport Commissioners	[1968] SCR 118	3,275	Federalism

At first glance, especially to readers who have come to take for granted the modern Supreme Court's constitutional caseload, the fact that our alleged innovator delivered only two *By the Court* judgments during his entire chief justiceship might seem to undermine our argument, but such a conclusion overlooks the impact of two facts: 1) constitutional cases were considerably less common in the 1960s; and 2) Cartwright was chief justice for only two and a half years. As a result, the Cartwright court decided only six constitutional cases, all dealing with the federal-provincial division of legislative authority:

- *Attorney-General of British Columbia v Smith*, [1967] SCR 702, concerning the interaction between the federal *Juvenile Delinquents Act* and the provincial *Motor Vehicle Act* and *Summary Convictions Act*[2]
- *Reference re: Offshore Mineral Rights*, [1967] SCR 792 (discussed in Chapter 7), on the question of the respective proprietary rights and legislative jurisdiction of Canada and the province of British Columbia with respect to lands adjacent to the BC coastline
- *The Queen v Board of Transport Commissioners*, [1968] SCR 118 (discussed in Chapter 7), concerning the jurisdiction of the provincial Board of Transport Commissioners with respect to the tolls to be charged by a provincial government–owned and operated commuter train service using Canadian National Railway tracks
- *Carnation Co. Ltd. v Quebec Agricultural Marketing Board*, [1968] SCR 238, dealing with the validity of a provincial joint marketing plan for a product that was in large part exported from the province

- *Coughlin v The Ontario Highway Transport Board*, [1968] SCR 569, concerning a federal legislative delegation authorizing a provincial board to issue a licence permitting the interprovincial transport of goods
- *Walter v Attorney-General of Alberta*, [1969] SCR 383, an unsuccessful challenge by a Hutterian religious community against provincial legislation on property rights, on the grounds that it was *ultra vires* the provincial legislature by virtue of being legislation with respect to religion rather than legislation with respect to property rights within the province.

As already indicated, *Board of Transport Commissioners* and the *Offshore Mineral Rights Reference* were the earliest examples of a constitutional use of *By the Court*. Although the decision in *Attorney-General of British Columbia v Smith* was handed down at about the same time, it had been argued months earlier than the other two, when Robert Taschereau was still chief justice and on the panel. It is therefore not in a complete sense a decision of the Cartwright court, the dates notwithstanding. *Coughlin* was not a unanimous decision, with Cartwright delivering the majority judgment over the dissents of Ronald Martland and Roland Ritchie; Cartwright was not a member of the panel in the unanimous decision delivered by Martland in *Carnation*. This leaves *Walter* as the odd one out – a unanimous decision on a constitutional matter (division of powers) presided over by Chief Justice Cartwright, but with the judgment delivered by Martland.

In some accounts, *The Queen v Drybones*, [1970] SCR 282, is also treated as a constitutional case, and it is considered as such on the Lexum website. *Drybones* is still celebrated as the clearest judicial invocation of the 1960 Diefenbaker *Canadian Bill of Rights*,[3] using that statute as the basis for striking down part of a federal statute, although we find the constitutional labelling dubious because the *Bill of Rights*, unlike the *Canadian Charter of Rights and Freedoms*, was not constitutionally entrenched. In any event, it was also not a unanimous decision, with Chief Justice Cartwright among the dissenters.

But Cartwright was chief justice for only thirty-one months, and the practice clearly did not extend to his successor. Gérald Fauteux was chief justice for forty-five months, during which time the Supreme Court dealt with ten constitutional cases.[4] Five of these resulted in unanimous decisions, but not a single one emulated the Cartwright court's *By the Court* style. The most telling omission occurred almost immediately after Fauteux became chief justice, with the federal *Criminal Law Amendment Act, Reference,* [1970] SCR 777. At issue was whether it was valid for the governor in council to proclaim certain sections of the *Act* but not others. The court delivered five different sets of reasons (all of which are identically labelled "opinions" in the *Supreme Court Reports*), further complicated by the fact that four of the justices signed more than one of those sets of reasons. There are a number of cross-references within the reasons, so it is not an example of the "pure *seriatim*" practice; we might think of the combination of multiple judgments and cross-referencing as what decisions look like when the *seriatim* practice meets the post-hearing judicial conference. Nor did the Laskin court promptly return to *By the Court;* it was only at the end of the fifth year of Laskin's tenure as chief justice that it was revived. Cartwright's was an innovation that languished for a dozen years, hardly a promising start and one that demonstrates the real threshold that must be overcome for major changes to the way the court operates.

The Laskin Court

The Laskin court handed down nine major *By the Court* judgments over a period of five years (stretching over six calendar years) (see Table 8.2). The focus is striking: six of the nine cases are reference cases posed by governments (federal or provincial), and the other three are direct constitutional challenges to the actions of provincial governments. The loose generalization that one can often find in the literature is that *By the Court* judgments are all about constitutional law, and this string of decisions by the Laskin court completely supports this notion. Indeed, for the Laskin court, we can be even more specific: *By the Court* judgments are all about federalism, and mostly about reference cases.

But if we say "the Laskin court," are we necessarily saying Laskin? This may seem a strange question, since there is some indication in the literature that Laskin was a forceful leader. Nonetheless, there is reason

Table 8.2 ***By the Court*** **judgments of the Laskin court, 1973–84**

Case	*Citation*	*Words*	*Subject*
*Att. Gen. of Quebec v Blaikie et al. [Blaikie 1]**	[1979] 2 SCR 1016	4,032	Federalism/ language
*Attorney General of Manitoba v Forest**	[1979] 2 SCR 1032	1,816	Federalism/ language
Re: Authority of Parliament in Relation to the Upper House	[1980] 1 SCR 54	7,245	Federalism
Attorney General of Quebec v Blaikie et al. [Blaikie 2]	[1981] 1 SCR 312	6,424	Federalism/ language
Re: Resolution to Amend the Constitution [Patriation Reference]	[1981] 1 SCR 753	28,743	Federalism
Re: Exported Natural Gas Tax	[1982] 1 SCR 1004	12,811	Federalism
Re: Objection by Quebec to a Resolution to Amend the Constitution [Quebec Veto Reference]	[1982] 2 SCR 793	7,768	Federalism
McEvoy v Attorney General of New Brunswick et al.	[1983] 1 SCR 704	5,569	Federalism
Reference re Newfoundland Continental Shelf	[1984] 1 SCR 86	12,758	Federalism

Notes: * = companion cases. We note that *Blaikie 1* and *Forest* are not "pure" companion cases because they were not argued before the court on the same day, nor were they considered by the same panel of judges, although judgment was delivered on the same day and they are directly sequential in the *Supreme Court Reports*. We think that under the circumstances it is more useful than misleading to consider them as companion cases.

to doubt that Laskin himself played a strong part in the re-emergence of *By the Court* in 1979 and some reason to doubt that he was a major player in the *By the Court* decisions after that year. When the device was redeployed in the fall of 1979, Laskin was absent for almost the entire term, seriously ill and hospitalized in Vancouver for several months and returning to Ottawa, but not to full service on the court, shortly before the decisions were handed down. He is therefore more likely to have been a follower than the leader in these important examples. It is also striking that the use of *By the Court* dates not from the early stages of Laskin's tenure but rather from the midpoint, particularly from the half-term when he was away. This does not rule out Laskin's having played some role in the innovation, but it makes it less likely.

The Dickson Court

By the Court judgments are more numerous for the Dickson court, but their use is considerably more diffuse (Table 8.3). Only two involved federalism issues, and one of these was the extended follow-up to *Forest* in the same way that *Blaikie 2* expanded and fulfilled *Blaikie 1*. Three others grew out of the Supreme Court's new challenge of an entrenched *Charter of Rights*. A pair of cases involved First Nations issues, but these are not decisions that loom large in the court's development of First Nations jurisprudence. Finally, there was a curious quartet of relatively short decisions – *Dorval, Carrières Ste-Thérèse, Lamb,* and *Wigman* – that are noteworthy for the fact that none raises any constitutional issue at all. Their inclusion in the "grand tradition" is therefore somewhat suspect. These aside, the generalization that *By the Court* is about constitutional law is generally sustained, although the scope of constitutional concerns addressed is considerably broader. Only one of the cases (*Manitoba Language Rights*) is a reference question, federal or provincial; all the others involved a more discretionary proactive choice by the panel to treat a particular case anonymously, although the reasons for this choice (*Healy* aside) were never made explicit.

Fourteen examples in six years certainly suggests a vigorous and deliberate *By the Court* strategy on the part of Chief Justice Brian Dickson, but the impression needs to be adjusted in light of the fact that some of the examples are clearly less a matter of strategic choice than of administrative convenience, a way of dealing with "problem" cases where a judgment simply could not be attributed in the "normal" way. We will suggest in the next chapter that this count is actually somewhat inflated, as a pair of the most significant cases, and possibly some of the curious shorter ones, can be explained in these terms.

Table 8.3 ***By the Court*** **judgments of the Dickson court, 1984–90**

Case	*Citation*	*Words*	*Subject*
Attorney General of Quebec v Quebec Association of Protestant School Boards et al.	[1984] 2 SCR 66	8,418	Language/ Charter
Air Canada v City of Dorval	[1985] 1 SCR 861	4,217	Municipal law
Re Manitoba Language Rights	[1985] 1 SCR 721	18,068	Federalism/ language
A.G. (Que.) v Carrières Ste-Thérèse Ltée	[1985] 1 SCR 831	2,604	Administrative law
Lamb v Lamb	[1985] 1 SCR 851	2,446	Family law
Québec (A.G.) v Healy	[1987] 1 SCR 158	6,972	First Nations
R v Wigman	[1987] 1 SCR 246	4,783	Criminal law
Canadian Pacific Ltd. v Paul	[1988] 2 SCR 654	8,529	First Nations
Clark v Canadian National Railway Co.	[1988] 2 SCR 680	9,190	Federalism
*Ford v Quebec (Attorney General)**	[1988] 2 SCR 712	24,634	Language/ Charter
*Devine v Quebec (Attorney General)**	[1988] 2 SCR 790	9,277	Language/ Charter
R v Chaulk (Application)	[1989] 1 SCR 369	2,230	Supreme Court procedures
Irwin Toy Ltd. v Quebec (Attorney General)	[1989] 1 SCR 927	22,707	Charter
Tremblay v Daigle	[1989] 2 SCR 530	13,593	Charter

Note: * = companion cases

The Lamer Court

The Lamer court delivered seven *By the Court* judgments (Table 8.4). One was yet another installment of the Manitoba language litigation (*Forest* being "Manitoba 1," "Manitoba 2" showing up under Dickson, and now "Manitoba 3" under Lamer), and a second was a relatively short and minor case on a municipal vote in Quebec (*Sinclair*). The others, however, bracket the major constitutional issues of recent decades, with two significant Charter cases (*Tobiass* on judicial independence, *Libman* on limiting election expenses), arguably the most important case to date on federalism (*Quebec Secession Reference*), and one of the most important (certainly the most explosive and controversial) of recent cases dealing with First Nations issues (*Marshall* 2). Compared with the Dickson court, the frequency of *By the Court* decisions is much lower, but the subject matter is wider and the importance of some of the cases is unquestionable.

The McLachlin Court

The *By the Court* list for the McLachlin court is by far the longest and most impressive. This is not just a reflection of the fact that Beverley

Table 8.4 ***By the Court*** **judgments of the Lamer court, 1990–99**

Case	*Citation*	*Words*	*Subject*
Reference re Manitoba Language Rights	[1992] 1 SCR 212	5,985	Federalism/ language
Sinclair v Quebec (Attorney General)	[1992] 1 SCR 579	4,046	Federalism/ language
Reza v Canada	[1994] 2 SCR 394	2,530	Charter
Canada (Minister of Citizenship and Immigration) v Tobiass	[1997] 3 SCR 391	13,765	Charter
Libman v Quebec (Attorney General)	[1997] 3 SCR 569	15,477	Charter
Reference re Secession of Quebec	[1998] 2 SCR 217	21,587	Federalism
R v Marshall [Marshall 2]	[1999] 3 SCR 533	9,108	First Nations

McLachlin was the longest-serving chief justice in the history of the institution; the per-year count is comparable to that of the Dickson court. More to the point, a high proportion of the cases on the McLachlin list are robust cases of considerable weight, well above the 9,000-word average length of the reasons for judgment in a reserved decision. This suggests that the use of *By the Court* was becoming not just more frequent but also more targeted and deliberate.

Two cases in particular make the point about this targeting. The first is the *Provincial Court Judges' Assn. of New Brunswick v New Brunswick (Minister of Justice)* case, which is directed toward clarifying certain aspects of the process for determining judicial salaries that remained problematic after the blockbuster judicial independence decision in

Table 8.5 ***By the Court*** **judgments of the McLachlin court, 2000–17**

Case	*Citation*	*Words*	*Subject*
Reference re Firearms Act (Can.)	2000 SCC 31	13,655	Federalism
R v Latimer	2001 SCC 1	10,672	Charter
United States v Burns	2001 SCC 7	20,051	Charter
Suresh v Canada (Minister of Citizenship and Immigration)	2002 SCC 1	18,008	Charter
Ahani v Canada (Minister of Citizenship and Immigration)	2002 SCC 2	2,460	Charter
*R v Powley**	2003 SCC 43	6,422	First Nations
*R v Blais**	2003 SCC 44	5,460	First Nations
Wewaykum Indian Band v Canada	2003 SCC 45	11,497	Supreme Court
Reference re Same-Sex Marriage	2004 SCC 79	7,140	Federalism/ Charter
*Solski (Tutor of) v Quebec (Attorney General)**	2005 SCC 14	10,669	Language/ Charter
*Gosselin (Tutor of) v Quebec (Attorney General)**	2005 SCC 15	4,034	Language/ Charter

►

Case	*Citation*	*Words*	*Subject*
*Okwuobi v Lester B. Pearson School Board; Casimir v Quebec (Attorney General); Zorrilla v Quebec (Attorney General)**	2005 SCC 16	9,355	Language/ Charter
Mugesera v Canada (Minister of Citizenship and Immigration)	2005 SCC 40	19,749	Charter
Provincial Court Judges' Assn. of New Brunswick v New Brunswick (Minister of Justice); Ontario Judges' Assn. v Ontario (Management Board); Bodner v Alberta; Conférence des juges du Québec v Quebec (Attorney General); Minc v Quebec (Attorney General) [Provincial Judges]	2005 SCC 44	19,523	Judicial independence
British Columbia (Attorney General) v Christie	2007 SCC 21	2,979	Courts/access to justice
Canada (Attorney General) v Lameman	2008 SCC 14	2,356	Courts/ discretion
Canada (Justice) v Khadr	2008 SCC 28	4,448	Charter
BCE Inc. v 1976 Debentureholders	2008 SCC 69	15,709	Commercial law
Canada (Prime Minister) v Khadr	2010 SCC 3	5,446	Charter
R v Ahmad	2011 SCC 6	9,576	Charter
Reference re Securities Act	2011 SCC 66	14,042	Federalism
Reference re Supreme Court Act, ss. 5 and 6 [Nadon]	2014 SCC 21	18,513	Federalism
Reference re Senate Reform	2014 SCC 32	12,575	Federalism
Carter v Canada (Attorney General)	2015 SCC 5	16,309	Charter
R v Smith	2015 SCC 34	3,778	Charter
R v Cody	2017 SCC 31	6,056	Charter

Note: * = companion cases

1997.[5] The point here is not simply that this decision is *By the Court* or that it is one of the longest and therefore presumably most comprehensive of the McLachlin court's *By the Court* judgments, although this is no small thing. More importantly, this is the first *By the Court* judgment in a remarkably extended string of Supreme Court decisions touching on the matter of judicial independence, those earlier decisions having been delivered by a surprising diversity of judges.[6] It has something of the feeling of a very deliberate period at the end of a long sentence, and therefore a marked and significant use of *By the Court.*

The second is in some ways the most curious: the decision in *BCE,* which has been welcomed (and also criticized) as an important landmark decision in company law, dealing with the obligations of corporate boards.[7] This is only the third *By the Court* judgment not to raise any constitutional issues whatsoever, the other two being the Dickson court's short and clearly less portentous decisions in *Dorval* and *Wigman.* With the obvious caveat that it takes more than one swallow to signal a summer, this may be a first step toward the conscious use of *By the Court* judgments for decisions intended as major and hopefully landmark contributions to unsettled corners of the law, done with a somewhat wider sweep than the constitutional law issues that have provided the focus of the practice to date. However, this is not to deny for a moment that the centre of gravity of the device remains in the area of constitutional law, especially decisions dealing with federalism issues and Charter questions.

But this inventory is only a beginning. In the next chapter, we will develop a typology of four different subsets from this larger list, each driven by a somewhat different logic and with a different type-of-law focus.

A Typology of Decisions 9

In Chapter 8, we presented a brief chronology of *By the Court* decisions, from the 1967 trilogy to the McLachlin court's three dramatic rebuffs of some of the Harper government's major initiatives (the *Securities Act Reference*, the *Nadon* case, and the *Senate Reform Reference*). The number of cases approaches five dozen cases in fifty years extending over five chief justiceships, including some of the Supreme Court of Canada's most dramatic and high-profile constitutional cases. At the same time, there has been a considerable degree of both variety and selectivity, which makes it useful to identify more precisely the types of cases for which *By the Court* has been used. The purpose of this chapter is to provide a typology of the practice.[1] To this end we will identify and consider four basic categories of *By the Court* decisions:

- federal constitutional references
- institutional defensive cases
- *faut de mieux* ("accidental") cases
- proactive uses of *By the Court*.

Federal References: The Institutional Conversation Cases

Canada has developed an unusual instrument of governance – the constitutional reference.[2] This is a device whereby a national or provincial government can ask its highest court of appeal (the Supreme Court, or very occasionally the Federal Court of Appeal, for the federal government, the provincial court of appeal for a provincial government) an abstract or hypothetical question, for the purpose of receiving advice as to the relevant legal and constitutional considerations before proceeding with any policy or legislative action.[3]

When we refer to the Canadian practice as "unusual," we mean that few national high courts of comparable countries have any similar procedure. In the United States, the possibility was clearly precluded in the US Supreme Court's earliest days, when President George Washington sought the advice of the court only to be rebuffed on the grounds that the procedure failed to satisfy the "causes and controversies" clause in Article III of the US Constitution, which defines the Supreme Court's jurisdiction. The same exclusionary argument applies to Australia, where a similar phrase in the constitution has been taken as providing the same prohibition (although not without persistent advocates of the establishment of such a power).[4] In a handful of countries (such as Pakistan or India) where the relevant legislation contemplates a similar advisory jurisdiction, it is seldom exercised, and even then the court in question sometimes refuses to answer on the grounds that the question is too hypothetical.[5]

Why is Canada such a striking exception? This is apparently a legacy of our colonial history, and specifically of the existence of the Judicial Committee of the Privy Council. The Judicial Committee is often described as the judicial body that functioned as a final court of appeal for Canada until 1949, but it did so not as part of the English judicial hierarchy but rather as an advisory body to the government (hence "Privy Council") on whether colonial statutes were in accord with imperial authorizing statutes. When it was subsequently asked (in a reference case delightfully called *Reference re References*), the Judicial Committee concluded that the giving of advice to the Crown was an entirely appropriate practice that could indeed be extended to the Supreme Court.[6] The real issue in Canada was therefore more the question of how provincial governments fit into the practice, and it took several decades to work out the current set of practices and expectations.

What Is at Stake and Why Does It Matter?

Normally, a judicial proceeding involves two, possibly more, direct parties to a dispute that hinges on what one of the parties did or did not do at some specific time in the past, such that a legally recognized duty or prohibition was violated. The two parties take their dispute to a court, presided over by a neutral judge (sometimes, although increasingly rarely, with a jury), where they present both evidence relating to that action or inaction and arguments about the precise nature and scope of the legal duty or prohibition involved, after which the judge or the jury renders a decision as to which party has the better case. If the decision is made by a judge, the decision includes extensive reasons explaining why this was the appropriate resolution of the case.

These are the basic elements of a normal case: a focus on specific concrete events and circumstances, directly contending parties, and adversarial proceedings to test the evidence and argument presented by those parties. Broader legal principles, including constitutional issues, are referenced, and the judgment may, particularly if it is by a higher court, itself have precedential effect that alters the application of those rules and principles going forward, but only in a way that grows directly out of the parties/adversary argument/concrete circumstances nexus. Normal litigation is essentially concrete, backward-looking, and grounded in a single case.

A reference floats free of such grounding. The question can be abstract or hypothetical – for example, it can ask about the status or meaning of statutes that do not yet exist, or phrases that have not yet been inserted into existing statutes, or actions that have not yet been taken. It can ask a series of more or less related questions, or it can lay out a string of possible responses to a situation and ask the court to comment on the status of each one. Unlike normal litigation, the judicial deliberation called for in references is essentially abstract, forward-looking, and general.

For a government, this suggests a number of advantages:

- It controls the timing of the question. Rather than await the normal movement of a case – time consuming, unpredictable, and uncontrollable – from a trial court up through one or more levels of intermediate appeal courts and finally to the Supreme Court, a government can place the matter directly before the Supreme Court. Although it cannot set a time frame on the court's response, it does bypass most of the elements that add up to lengthy delays.[7] And, of course, for the entire period between the filing of the inquiry and the handing down of an opinion, the government can deflect any questions on the grounds that it would be improper to comment on a matter that is before the courts.

- It can frame the question or questions carefully and deliberately, and in such a way as to attempt to steer the court away from awkward aspects or issues and focus on those aspects or issues that are most advantageous. The tactic may not always work – the court can sometimes decide to answer some but not all the elements of a multiple-question set, or it may take the bit between its teeth and answer questions it was not specifically asked – but it often does.
- There is no direct adversarial confrontation built into the reference process, no theoretically equal opposing side with the perfectly equal opportunity to challenge arguments or to present counter-arguments. Cognizant of this imbalance, the Supreme Court is willing to consider additional measures (such as intervener status, or the *amicus curiae* participation in the *Quebec Secession Reference*), but this does not fully level the playing field.[8]
- There is no fact situation around which evidence accumulates, but rather the kind of purely abstract reasoning process that is more typical of policy formulation than of judicial deliberation. Instead of responding after the fact to a specific event as courts normally do, the court is obliged to speculate before the fact. This process is less like normal adjudication and more like legislating, which takes the courts away from their real expertise and obliges them to work with the kinds of facts that governments routinely collect and organize.
- Tushnet has identified the problem of policy distortion – the fact that when legislatures act in the shadow of anticipated judicial review, they can get caught up in the problem of trying to guess what the courts will decide when the matter comes before them, and the legislature may settle for something less than, or at least

rather different from, what it would have preferred.[9] The reference procedure allows the legislative process to proceed without such potentially distorting guesswork.
- Whatever embarrassment might attach to an unexpected answer, it avoids the wasteful and disruptive inconvenience of establishing a policy structure only to have it retroactively delegitimized some years later.

The major point of the practice for governments is, of course, to reduce uncertainty by clarifying legal and especially constitutional questions before erecting statutory and regulatory structures on what might turn out to be thin jurisdictional ice. Depending on the circumstances, however, this quest for clarity can be used to serve other purposes as well. It can be used to blunt opposition to a policy by gaining an implicit judicial endorsement, or even a "the judges made me do it" defence if an unpopular measure can be framed as being constitutionally required.[10] It can be used to establish negotiating high ground for setting the details of federal-provincial cooperation.[11] It can even be used by a provincial government to challenge a neighbouring province's disadvantageous public policy.[12] In short, whatever its core principled purpose, the device of the reference case can be used tactically by governments to recruit the prestige of the courts to serve political or even partisan purposes.

What does the arrangement imply for the courts? Clearly, they get the opportunity to influence public policy and constitutional evolution. They cannot control the timing of the opportunity or the subject matter, and sometimes they might prefer to have been left out of it. They might hedge their bets by insisting that such a decision is advisory only, and that they would not necessarily be bound by it in the future should litigation arise in more normal circumstances, but the hedging does not really convince. For the governments that asked the question, the court's opinion is very much a binding statement about the rules of the game that cannot be directly challenged but only "nibbled" with great caution; the same is true of other governments similarly positioned. These opinions are not "advisory" in the way we normally think of "advice" – that is, as something the recipient can heed or ignore at pleasure (such as advice from parents that a university student should study more and party less). An advisory opinion in a reference case is advice that cannot be ignored, recommendations that compulsorily reshape the parameters of policy formulation.

In short, the reference process makes the courts full partners in the process of governance, able to give strong "advice" that cannot be ignored, and to do so in light of the considerable publicity generated by the very fact that they were asked for the advice in the first place, with the unavoidable implication of becoming a part of the resulting policy process.

Reference Cases: How Common?

Reference cases have been a regular if not necessarily large part of the Supreme Court's caseload. Huffman and Saathoff count a total of 115 Supreme Court decisions that involved reference cases.[13] This count ended in 1987, but based on our own count of such cases since 1987, we would add a further 11 references by the federal government and 19 from provincial governments, for a grand total of 145 Supreme Court advisory opinions.[14] Thus, since the Supreme Court was first established in 1875, it has dealt with roughly one advisory opinion case each year, or about 1 percent of the total caseload, although since reference cases are almost always constitutional cases, the mere number understates their significance. Huffman and Saathoff's conclusion is that these cases have frequently been contentious, that the decisions have often been significant in terms of the evolving balance between the federal and provincial levels of government, and that the Supreme Court's contribution to the functioning of Canadian federalism through the reference process has been important.

Huffman and Saathoff are content to work with an overall total count of reference cases, combining those initiated by the federal government with appeals from provincial court of appeal decisions on references from the provincial government. This aggregated view of the reference caseload is not unreasonable. Since the important thing is that the court is responding to a hypothetical or abstract question from a government, something that not all national high courts are able or willing to do, it is from that angle just a detail that some of these cases are initiated by the federal government and some by a provincial government. It was because of their understanding of this potential that the provincial governments tried at first to contain the federal reference power by judicial or political means; having failed, they established their own parallel power and then strove mightily for the right to appeal those provincial references to the Supreme Court itself.[15] The modern reference power is the product of both the initial federal initiatives and the series of provincial responses. For the purposes of this chapter, however, we will consider federal references and provincial references separately, for two reasons.

The first reason is conceptual and theoretical. The structure of the Canadian court system roughly maps that of the political order. Corresponding to the provincial/territorial governments, we have the provincial/territorial courts, capped by a provincial/territorial court of appeal; corresponding to the national government, we have the federal courts, capped by the Supreme Court of Canada. But although organization of the courts is hierarchical – the Supreme Court is "the highest court in the land" and makes binding decisions on appeals from provincial and territorial courts – there is no corresponding hierarchy of governments; the two orders of government are not "levels" but rather "orders," that is, coordinate sovereign partners. In such a context, the reference power, like the broader power of judicial review of which it is a part, imposes hierarchical judicial ideas into a non-hierarchical political system. Small wonder that the provinces challenged it early on, then sought a share of the same power at the cost of conceding its hierarchical overtones.

The second reason is practical. As we will demonstrate, the Supreme Court itself has systematically and consistently treated the two types of reference differently, and at the heart of that difference is the *By the Court* format.

Federal Government References

There have been twenty-nine federal constitutional references since 1945.[16] We have expanded the reference period beyond our 1967 starting point in order to justify it, with the fifth column in Table 9.1 performing this service. The year 1967 presents a remarkably clear dividing point, with a *seriatim* "before" and a joint judgment "after." The only problematic case on the list, as we discussed in Chapter 8, is the single federal reference decided by the Fauteux court in 1970, where a nine-judge court delivered five different sets of reasons, with several judges signing on to more than one set. We suggest that this can be thought of as the product of Fauteux's lack of enthusiasm for Cartwright's innovation, and the last gasp of the *seriatim* practice.

The cases are unevenly spaced over the seventy years, with a definite low point during the 1960s and 1970s but offsetting high points at the "bookends" of the 1940s and 1950s on one end, and the 2010s on the other. To make the impression even stronger, the table both starts and ends with a period of six reference cases in only five years.

But the most powerful message from Table 9.1 is the emergence and consistent use of the anonymous style of judgments. The critical date we have suggested is 1967 – all the nine federal references in the two decades leading up to this date are decided in the same way, through a *seriatim* judgment. Of the twenty federal references since 1967, two-thirds are unanimous decisions, all but one of which are *By the Court* judgments. In addition, two of the non-unanimous decisions are also resolved with joint judgments – that is, they were anonymous without being unanimous.

The practice of *seriatim* judgments was discussed in Chapter 3 as part of our argument that judgment presentation styles matter. The early practice of the court was for many or all of the judges to write extended and often largely duplicative reasons, and this persisted for constitutional cases even while the plurality of judgments for other cases declined.[17] The effect of *seriatim* is to create multiple judgments, none of which is assigned a higher status than any of the others; the modern distinction between the "judgment" of the majority and the "reasons" of the minority or minorities emerges in the 1960s and solidifies in the 1970s.

Seriatim and *By the Court* are polar opposites. Nothing says "individual" like a *seriatim* judgment; nothing says "institution" like "THE COURT." There is no longer a series of largely parallel judgments to wade through, possibly differing slightly with no clear signal as to which voice prevails should there be such differences; later courts (and

Table 9.1 References brought by the federal government since 1945

Chief justice	Reference	*Citation*	*Panel*	*Unanimous?*	*Joint?*
Rinfret	Reference to the Validity of Orders in Council in Relation to Persons of Japanese Race	[1946] SCR 248	7	Seriatim	No
	Reference as to the Validity of Section 6 of the Farm Security Act, 1944 of Saskatchewan	[1947] SCR 394	6	Seriatim	No
	Reference Re Minimum Wage Act of Saskatchewan	[1948] SCR 248	6	Seriatim	No
	Reference re Validity of Section 5 (a) Dairy Industry Act	[1949] SCR 1	7	Seriatim	No
	Reference re Wartime Leasehold Regulations	[1950] SCR 124	7	Seriatim	No
	Reference re Bowater's Pulp & Paper Mills Ltd.	[1950] SCR 608	7	Seriatim	No
Kerwin	Validity and Applicability of the Industrial Relations and Disputes Investigation Act	[1955] SCR 529	9	Seriatim	No
	Reference re Regina v Coffin	[1956] SCR 191	7	Seriatim	No
	Re The Farm Products Marketing Act	[1957] SCR 198	8	Seriatim	No
Cartwright	*Reference re: Steven Murray Truscott*	*[1967] SCR 309*	9	*Divided*	*Yes*
	Reference re: Offshore Mineral Rights	*[1967] SCR 792*	7	*Unanimous*	*Yes*
Fauteux	Criminal Law Amendment Act, Reference	[1970] SCR 777	9	Divided	No
Laskin	Re: Anti-Inflation Act	[1976] 2 SCR 373	9	Divided	No
	Re: Authority of Parliament in Relation to the Upper House	*[1980] 1 SCR 54*	8	*Unanimous*	*Yes*
	Reference re Newfoundland Continental Shelf	*[1984] 1 SCR 86*	7	*Unanimous*	*Yes*

Dickson	*Re Manitoba Language Rights*	*[1985] 1 SCR 721*	*7*	*Unanimous*	*Yes*
Lamer	*Reference re Milgaard (Can.)*	*[1992] 1 SCR 866*	*5*	*Unanimous*	*Yes*
	Reference re Milgaard (Can.)	*[1992] 1 SCR 875*	*5*	*Unanimous*	*Yes*
	Reference Re Ng Extradition (Can.)	[1991] 2 SCR 858	7	Divided	No
	Reference re Manitoba Language Rights	*[1992] 1 SCR 212*	*9*	*Unanimous*	*Yes*
	Reference re Quebec Sales Tax	**[1994] 2 SCR 715**	**7**	**Unanimous**	**No**
	Reference re Secession of Quebec	*[1998] 2 SCR 217*	*9*	*Unanimous*	*Yes*
McLachlin	*Reference re Same-Sex Marriage*	*2004 SCC 79*	*9*	*Unanimous*	*Yes*
	Reference re Assisted Human Reproduction Act	2010 SCC 61	9	Divided	No
	Reference re Securities Act	2011 SCC 66	9	Unanimous	Yes
	Reference re Broadcasting Act*	2012 SCC 4	9	Unanimous	Yes
	Reference re Broadcasting Regulatory Policy CRTC 2010–167 and Broadcasting Order CRTC 2010–168*	2012 SCC 68	9	Divided	No
	Reference re Supreme Court Act, ss. 5 and 6 [Nadon]	*2014 SCC 21*	*7*	*Divided*	*Yes*
	Reference re Senate Reform	*2014 SCC 32*	*8*	*Unanimous*	*Yes*

Notes: * = federal reference to Federal Court of Appeal, appealed to the Supreme Court of Canada; italics indicate anonymous decisions by the Supreme Court; and boldface indicates the lone example of a unanimous but authored judgment.

governments) can no longer construct their own precedent from a diversity of voices; and the impassivity of "THE COURT" precludes any appearance of a lead author whose subsequent departure from the court might imply some openness to reconsideration. *By the Court* is impossible to ignore and profoundly difficult to finesse, and for this reason it is the purest opportunity for a collegial, organized court to exercise significant strategic influence. A "judgment" of the Supreme Court is no small thing; a "judgment of the Court" presented by a single judge is something rather stronger; "A judgment by THE COURT" is simply in a different league altogether. The court's choice of labels may obscure these distinctions, but their implications are far from trivial.

The 1967 turning point is transparent: every federal reference case between 1949 and 1967 was decided *seriatim*, but no federal reference case since 1967 (with the exception of the 1970 *Criminal Law Amendment Act Reference*) has been dealt with in any comparable way. Conversely, two-thirds of all federal reference cases since 1967 have been unanimous and two-thirds have been decided *By the Court* (although, as we will discuss below, these are not quite the same two-thirds). Only one unanimous decision in a reference case (the *Quebec Sales Tax Reference*) was attributed to a single judge; two cases (the *Truscott Reference* and *Nadon* – virtual bookends for the period) were solid majority decisions over a solo dissent, presented as joint judgments whose anonymity makes them, for our purposes, the same thing as *By the Court.*

Provincial Government References

Over the same period, the Supreme Court has decided slightly more provincial reference cases on appeal: forty provincial versus twenty-nine federal. Considering that there have been, at least since 1949, ten provincial governments compared with only one federal government, this suggests that provincial governments make much less use of the device. (This may be slightly misleading because we do not have the count of provincial references that were not appealed beyond the provincial court of appeal.) The list of all provincial references considered by the Supreme Court of Canada since 1945 is provided in Table 9.2.

Federal references appear to have been more frequent during the decades at the beginning and end of the period, whereas the bulge for

Table 9.2 Provincial government reference cases heard on appeal since 1945

Chief justice	*Reference*	*Citation*	*Province*	*Panel*	*Unanimous?*	*Joint?*
Rinfret	Reference as to the Interpretation of the Jury Act of the Province of Alberta	[1947] SCR 213	AB	5	Unanimous	No
	Canadian Pacific Railway Co. v Attorney-General of British Columbia	[1948] SCR 373	BC	5	Seriatim	No
	Esquimalt and Nanaimo Railway Co. v Attorney-General of British Columbia	[1948] SCR 403	BC	5	Seriatim	No
	Attorney General of Nova Scotia v Attorney General of Canada	[1951] SCR 31	NS	7	Seriatim	No
Kerwin	The Queen v Snider	[1954] SCR 479	BC	9	Seriatim	No
	The Attorney General of Canada v The Canadian Pacific Railway Company and Canadian National Railways	[1958] SCR 285	MB	9	Majority	No
	Validity of Section 92 (4) of The Vehicles Act, 1957 (Sask.)	[1958] SCR 608	SK	9	Seriatim	No
	The Attorney-General for Manitoba v Canadian Pacific Railway Company et al.	[1958] SCR 744	MB	7	Majority	No
	Validity of Orderly Payment of Debts Act, 1959 (Alta.)	[1960] SCR 571	AB	9	Majority	CJ

►

Chief justice	*Reference*	*Citation*	*Province*	*Panel*	*Unanimous?*	*Joint?*
Taschereau	Reference re Magistrate's Court of Quebec	[1965] SCR 772	QC	9	Unanimous	CJ
Fauteux	Attorney-General for Manitoba v Manitoba Egg and Poultry Association et al.	[1971] SCR 689	MB	9	Majority	No
Laskin	Jones v A.G. of New Brunswick	[1975] 2 SCR 182	NB	9	Unanimous	CJ
	Reference re Agricultural Products Marketing	[1978] 2 SCR 1198	ON	9	Majority	No
	Re Residential Tenancies Act	[1981] 1 SCR 714	ON	7	Unanimous	No
	Re: Resolution to Amend the Constitution	*[1981] 1 SCR 753*	*MB, NL, QC*	9	*Majority*	*Yes*
	Re: B.C. Family Relations Act	[1982] 1 SCR 62	BC	7	Majority	No
	Re: Exported Natural Gas Tax	*[1982] 1 SCR 1004*	*AB*	9	*Majority*	*Yes*
	Re: Objection by Quebec to a Resolution to Amend the Constitution	*[1982] 2 SCR 793*	*QC*	9	*Unanimous*	*Yes*
	McEvoy v Attorney General for New Brunswick et al.	*[1983] 1 SCR 704*	*NB*	7	*Unanimous*	*Yes*
	Reference re: Ownership of the Bed of the Strait of Georgia and Related Areas	[1984] 1 SCR 388	BC	7	Majority	No
	Reference re Upper Churchill Water Rights Reversion Act	[1984] 1 SCR 297	NL	9	Unanimous	No

Dickson	Wiretap Reference	[1984] 2 SCR 697	AB	7	Majority	No
	Reference re Bill 30, An Act to Amend the Education Act (Ont.)	[1987] 1 SCR 1148	ON	7	Majority	No
	Reference re Public Service Employee Relations Act (Alta.)	[1987] 1 SCR 313	AB	7	Plurality	No
	Reference re Workers' Compensation Act, 1983 (Nfld.)	[1989] 1 SCR 922	NL	7	Unanimous	No
	Reference re ss. 193 and 195.1(1)(C) of the Criminal Code (Man.)	[1990] 1 SCR 1123	MB	7	Plurality	No
Lamer	Reference re Young Offenders Act (P.E.I.)	[1991] 1 SCR 252	PEI	7	Plurality	CJ
	Reference re Prov. Electoral Boundaries (Sask.)	[1991] 2 SCR 158	SK	9	Majority	No
	Reference re Canada Assistance Plan (B.C.)	[1991] 2 SCR 525	BC	7	Unanimous	No
	Reference re Goods and Services Tax	[1992] 2 SCR 445	AB	9	Majority	CJ
	Reference re Public Schools Act (Man.), s. 79(3), (4) and (7)	[1993] 1 SCR 839	MB	7	Unanimous	CJ
	Reference re Education Act (Que.)	[1993] 2 SCR 511	QC	7	Unanimous	No
	Reference re Amendments to the Residential Tenancies Act (N.S.)	[1996] 1 SCR 186	NS	9	Majority	No

▶

Chief justice	*Reference*	*Citation*	*Province*	*Panel*	*Unanimous?*	*Joint?*
Lamer	Reference re Remuneration of Judges of the Provincial Court of Prince Edward Island; Reference re Independence and Impartiality of Judges of the Provincial Court of Prince Edward Island	[1998] 3 SCR 3	PEI	9	Majority	CJ
McLachlin	Reference re Gruenke	2000 SCC 32	MB	9	Unanimous	CJ
	Reference re Firearms Act (Can.)	*2000 SCC 31*	*AB*	9	*Unanimous*	*Yes*
	R v Kelly	2001 SCC 25	ON	5	Majority	No
	Reference re Earth Future Lottery	2003 SCC 10	PEI	9	Unanimous	CJ
	Reference re Employment Insurance Act (Can.), ss. 22 and 23	2005 SCC 56	QC	7	Unanimous	No
	Reference re Broome v Prince Edward Island	2010 SCC 11	PEI	9	Unanimous	No

Note: Italics indicate anonymous decisions by the Supreme Court.

provincial references comes in the middle, during the 1980s and the 1990s, with those two decades accounting for fully one-half of the total. This suggests that the political or policy dynamics that lead governments to resort to an advisory opinion are working on different cycles for federal and provincial governments, rather than both of them responding through this important legal device to a common set of triggers. The provinces whose advisory opinions were before the Supreme Court most often were Alberta (seven cases) and British Columbia and Manitoba (six cases each), but there is at least one reference from each province.

For our purposes, what is important is again the shift in Supreme Court practices during and after the 1960s. For the earlier decades, the *seriatim* style that prevailed for federal references was used less consistently for provincial references, with an equal number of majority (three) or unanimous (two) decisions. What seems to have been a strict protocol whereby federal references called for a *seriatim* response was much less strictly applied to provincial references, although for both it was more common than for the rest of the caseload. For both federal and provincial references, *seriatim* judgments disappeared after the 1960s, but except for a brief four-year interval during the Laskin court, the *By the Court* judgments that are so common for federal references were not used for provincial references.

The Intersection of Reference Cases and *By the Court*

The roster and focus of *By the Court* decisions have been obscured by the way they were folded into the two longer lists of reference cases in Tables 9.1 and 9.2. We will now isolate the reference cases from this larger set of cases, and the central message of that isolation is clear: *By the Court* and reference cases are about federalism, to the virtual exclusion of any other aspects of constitutional law, such as the *Canadian Charter of Rights and Freedoms* and First Nations issues.

The *Quebec Secession Reference* is arguably the "poster child" of the list. It was a highly significant case, dealing with a major issue not directly addressed by the constitutional amendment formulas (the possible secession of a province), and fraught with potential political fallout as it came shortly after a provincial referendum had fallen just short of supporting

Table 9.3 ***By the Court*** **decisions on reference cases**

Reference	*Citation*	*Subject matter*
Reference re: Steven Murray Truscott	[1967] SCR 309	Courts
Reference re: Offshore Mineral Rights	[1967] SCR 792	Federalism
Re: Authority of Parliament in Relation to the Upper House	[1980] 1 SCR 54	Federalism/amendment
Re: Resolution to Amend the Constitution [Patriation Reference]	*[1981] 1 SCR 753*	*Federalism/amendment*
Re: Exported Natural Gas Tax	*[1982] 1 SCR 1004*	*Federalism*
Re: Objection by Quebec to a Resolution to Amend the Constitution [Quebec Veto Reference]	*[1982] 2 SCR 793*	*Federalism/amendment*
McEvoy v Attorney General of New Brunswick et al.	*[1983] 1 SCR 704*	*Federalism*
Reference re Newfoundland Continental Shelf	[1984] 1 SCR 86	Federalism
Re Manitoba Language Rights	[1985] 1 SCR 721	Federalism
Reference re Milgaard (Can.)	[1992] 1 SCR 866	Courts
Reference re Milgaard (Can.)	[1992] 1 SCR 875	Courts/contempt
Reference re Manitoba Language Rights	[1992] 1 SCR 212	Federalism
Reference re Secession of Quebec	[1998] 2 SCR 217	Federalism/amendment
Reference re Firearms Act (Can.)	*2000 SCC 31*	*Federalism*
Reference re Same-Sex Marriage	2004 SCC 79	Federalism/Charter
Reference re Securities Act	2011 SCC 66	Federalism
Reference re Broadcasting Act*	2012 SCC 4	Statutory interpretation
Reference re Supreme Court Act, ss. 5 and 6 [Nadon]	2014 SCC 21	Federalism/amendment
Reference re Senate Reform	2014 SCC 32	Federalism/amendment

Notes: Italics indicate references initiated by provincial governments. An asterisk indicates a reference directed to the Federal Court of Appeal.

such an act of secession – the obvious danger being that a Supreme Court decision could trigger a third referendum with a majority in the other direction. It is also striking as an example of over-reach, given that the court turned an apparently "easy" question (is there an explicit right to unilateral secession in the Constitution?) into a much trickier one (given that the Canadian people must be capable of achieving any constitutional outcome they wish, what is the appropriate procedure for dealing with the matter when the outcome is secession?).

The federalism focus is equally clear for the intersection of *By the Court* and provincial references, but we shall detour here to consider a possible objection to this provincial list, namely, its inclusion of *Re: Resolution to Amend the Constitution* (better known as the *Patriation Reference*), the problem being that the decision was not unanimous.

Briefly, appeals from provincial references in three different provinces (Quebec, Newfoundland, and Manitoba) were combined into a single case before the Supreme Court, but the slightly different questions directed to those three provincial courts were turned into two questions for the Supreme Court. The first was whether there was a legal requirement that the federal government's constitutional proposals should not be submitted to the British Parliament absent provincial concurrence. The court decided that there was no such requirement, splitting seven (Laskin, Dickson, Beetz, Estey, McIntyre, Chouinard, and Lamer) to two (Martland and Ritchie) on the matter. The second question was whether such provincial concurrence was required as a matter of constitutional convention. The court decided that there was such a requirement, splitting six (Martland, Ritchie, Dickson, Beetz, Chouinard, and Lamer) to three (Laskin, Estey, and McIntyre).

For present purposes, what is particularly interesting about this pair of judgment-and-dissent combinations is that none of the four sets of reasons had an attributed author in the normal way. The majority reasons on the "matter of law" issue were jointly attributed to all seven judges in the majority bloc, and the dissent was jointly attributed to the two dissenters. The majority reasons on the "matter of convention" issue were jointly attributed to all six judges in the majority bloc, and the dissent jointly attributed to the three dissenters. More interesting still, the same practice was echoed nine months later in the *Exported Natural Gas Tax Reference,* involving a levy on the export of natural gas owned and produced by the government of Alberta. A majority of six judges (Martland, Ritchie, Dickson, Beetz, Estey, and Chouinard) upheld the lower court finding that the tax was *ultra vires* the Parliament of Canada, and three judges (Laskin, McIntyre, and Lamer) dissented – but again the majority judgment was jointly attributed to all six judges in the majority, and the dissenting reasons were jointly attributed to all three dissenters.[18]

The lack of unanimity necessarily means that these are not *By the Court* decisions in a pure sense, but the anonymity of the majority bloc makes them more like *By the Court* than the normal "attribution to a specific author" style that is otherwise used by the court. It is the anonymity that contributes to the institutional character of the judgment, and this justifies the inclusion of the very small set of "anonymous but not unanimous" decisions as part of the phenomenon under consideration.

Since 1967, *By the Court* has emerged as the device of choice for federal references, replacing the fragmented judgment style of earlier decades with something more direct, more institutional, more organized, and more coherent. This appears to have been accompanied by a concerted attempt at unanimity, since two-thirds of federal references have been unanimous and all but one of these unanimous decisions have taken the form of a joint judgment. The same pattern does not hold for provincial references, with a lower unanimity level and only a single anonymous judgment since the Laskin court.

By the Court is an effective mechanism for making the most of the partnership with the federal government that is created by Canada's unique advisory opinion process. Whereas the earlier *seriatim* practice turned the court into a collection of solo advisers presenting a fragmented and sometimes less than fully coherent position, the current anonymous practice presents the court as a unified institution that returns a solid institutional position. As a result, the federal reference process now takes the form of a conversation of equals between two major national institutions, a conversation in which the Supreme Court ultimately enjoys the advantage. At the same time, it is clear that the court has shown no interest in using provincial references in the same way, and the hierarchical context of the provincial reference power, not to mention the fact that provincial governments do not appoint their own appeal court judges, makes it less likely that any provincial government could develop a comparable partnership with its own court of appeal.

Institutional Defensive Cases

The second use of *By the Court* is for cases that deal with major issues relating to the Supreme Court or to structural issues involving the judicial system more generally.[19] These can sometimes be reference cases (we have two specific cases in mind) but more often they are not. Indeed, they deal with so many disparate issues relating to the judiciary that at first glance they may seem not to form a "set" at all, so we will briefly describe each in turn to justify our characterization. The complete set of these cases is presented in Table 9.4.

We will deal first of all with the bookends of the set, namely, *Truscott* and *Nadon*, which are also the only two of the set that took the form of federal references. Our point in this double-counting is that both of them involved the Supreme Court in an intense and unprecedented controversy, constituting a challenge to the status and reputation of the institution itself. It is also worth noting that they are among the few non-unanimous decisions that nonetheless take an anonymizing form.

The Major Challenge Duo: *Truscott* and *Nadon*

Truscott, as discussed in Chapter 7, represented an unusually direct challenge to the court by implicitly requiring it to revisit an earlier decision (a denial of an application for leave to appeal) in the context of an unusually sustained public outcry against the judicial system.[20] The nine-judge panel was unusual for the time; a solid eight-to-one majority for a major decision was also unusual at a time when more divided panels were the norm, and when there was no institutional emphasis on a "judgment" distinguished from other sets of reasons. And of course the anonymity of a "joint opinion" was not just unusual but absolutely unprecedented.

Table 9.4 The institutional defensive set of *By the Court* decisions

Case	*Citation*	*Words*	*Subject*
Reference re: Steven Murray Truscott	[1967] SCR 309	30,000	Other
R v Chaulk (Application)	[1989] 1 SCR 369	2,230	SCC procedure
Canada (Minister of Citizenship and Immigration) v Tobiass	[1997] 3 SCR 391	13,765	Chief justice
R v Marshall [Marshall 2]	[1999] 3 SCR 533	9,108	First Nations
Wewaykum Indian Band v Canada	2003 SCC 45	11,497	Recusal
Mugesera v Canada (Minister of Citizenship and Immigration)	2005 SCC 40	19,749	Recusal
Provincial Court Judges' Assn. of New Brunswick v New Brunswick (Minister of Justice); Ontario Judges' Assn. v Ontario (Management Board); Bodner v Alberta; Conférence des juges du Québec v Quebec (Attorney General); Minc v Quebec (Attorney General)	2005 SCC 44	19,523	Judicial independence
British Columbia (Attorney General) v Christie	2007 SCC 21	2,979	Access to justice
Canada (Attorney General) v Lameman	2008 SCC 14	2,356	Judicial discretion
R v Ahmad	2011 SCC 6	9,576	S 96 jurisdiction
Reference re Supreme Court Act, ss. 5 and 6 [Nadon]	2014 SCC 21	18,513	Appointments to SCC

The *Nadon* case was a challenge of quite a different kind, its importance dramatically enhanced after the fact by a highly unusual public criticism of the chief justice by the prime minister of the day.[21] In 2013, Marc Nadon, a supernumerary judge of the Federal Court of Appeal, was appointed to the Supreme Court, replacing Justice Morris Fish as one of the three judges from Quebec. This appointment was immediately challenged in Federal Court by a Toronto lawyer, Rocco Galati, on the grounds that a judge of the Federal Court of Appeal did not meet the appointment eligibility rules in the *Supreme Court Act*, and the resulting public controversy led the government to put this question to the Supreme Court in a reference case. With one judge (Michael Moldaver) dissenting, the six majority judges issued an anonymous joint opinion finding that Nadon was not qualified and that his appointment was therefore of no effect.[22]

The case is also significant in that it resolved an important question relating to the amendment of the Canadian Constitution with respect to the Supreme Court itself.[23] The fact that there was even a question here is at first glance curious, because the amending formulas in Part IV of the *Constitution Act, 1982* seem to address this directly.[24] Among the types of amendments mentioned in section 41 as requiring resolutions of the Parliament of Canada and all the provincial legislatures are those that deal with the "composition" of the Supreme Court (which we assume means the nine-judge court with one-third appointed from Quebec); among the types of amendments mentioned in section 42 as requiring the General Amending Formula (resolutions of the Parliament of Canada and of the legislatures of at least two-thirds of the provinces, those provinces including at least 50 percent of the population of all the provinces) is any other change to the Supreme Court. But Peter Hogg, arguably Canada's most highly regarded constitutional scholar, has pointed out that the legal language speaks of "amendments to the Constitution of Canada with respect" to these items, and the Supreme Court itself is not actually "in" the constitution – the *Constitution Act. 1867* only gives permission for Parliament to create a "General Court of Appeal," and the *Supreme Court Act*, which accomplished that creation, is not included in the schedule to the *Constitution Act, 1982* that defines the Constitution of Canada under section 52. Therefore, Hogg suggested, these elements of the amending formula are embarrassingly empty: there is no part of the Constitution of Canada that deals with the Supreme Court in such a way that the indicated resolutions are necessary to change it, and when the Parliament of Canada wishes to make changes to the Supreme Court, it does so simply by the regular process of amending the *Supreme Court Act* as it would amend any of its statutes.[25]

The *Nadon* case has resolved this question, first by describing the institution as having evolved through Canadian practice to gain the status that made it appropriate for it to be addressed by the development of the new constitutional amending formulas, and then by simply eliding the apparent gap between "amendments to the constitution with respect to the Supreme Court of Canada" and "changes to the Supreme Court." Since (as Hogg himself has told us) decisions of the Supreme Court of Canada with respect to the Constitution are themselves part of the Constitution, the matter is now settled.

This made the *Nadon* question a double challenge for the court. First, it necessarily involved it in an unusually direct and high-profile confrontation with the prime minister, given that the outcome of the case was that the prime minister suffered a rebuff that is unique in the history of Canada. The aftermath of the decision – with the prime minister publicly accusing the chief justice of having acted improperly by "lobbying" regarding a judicial appointment, and the chief justice defending herself as simply carrying out her duties, and with national legal organizations (futilely) calling on the prime minister to apologize – clearly demonstrated the seriousness of the court/government rift. Second, it dealt with the question of how changes can be made to the Supreme Court of Canada, and therefore with the constitutional status of the court – that is, who can make what changes to the institution through what procedures. Either of these elements would have made the case important; the combination of the two ratcheted the stakes even higher.

The Recusal Duo: *Wewaykum* and *Mugesera*

The second pair of decisions involves the issue of recusals, or the withdrawal of judges from consideration of a particular case because of some involvement with an earlier stage of the proceedings. The question of recusal is a sensitive one, because it strikes at the heart of the court's claim to impartiality and neutrality regarding the issues that appear before it. Any direct connection between any of the judges and either of the parties has the appearance of a heavy and inappropriate thumb on the scales of justice.[26] The two cases are also linked by the fact that although they were unanimous decisions, they did not self-label themselves as being delivered by "THE COURT" but instead as a joint judgment of all the members of a panel that was one judge short of the full nine judges.[27]

Wewaykum was a challenge to the court's credibility in somewhat embarrassing circumstances.[28] In an earlier decision, the unanimous judgment had been delivered by Justice Ian Binnie, only for it to be subsequently discovered that Binnie had been involved in earlier stages of the case while serving as Associate Deputy Minister of Justice.[29] On the one hand, this clearly meant that he should have recused himself from participating on the panel, an oversight compounded by the fact that he delivered the judgment; on the other hand, nobody doubted either that his earlier involvement had been extremely limited, or that he had simply forgotten about it and had failed to make the connection when the case was heard. Nonetheless, a reasonably grounded motion to vacate a unanimous Supreme Court judgment is an unpleasant corner for the court to find itself in, and the unusual decision-delivery format reflects this discomfort. The joint reasons dismissed the motion while exploring the expectations surrounding recusal and (in an interesting aside) described the court's own decision-making procedures with unusual detail and candour.

Mugesera was superficially similar in that it also involved a recusal of a Supreme Court justice from a specific case.[30] On this occasion, it was Rosalie Abella, because of her husband's involvement with an organization that was intervening in a case coming before the court, although the litigant's application seemed redundant since she had already voluntarily recused herself for this reason. An appeal on the substantive issue was before the court when Mugesera made an application for a permanent stay of proceedings on the grounds that the proceedings revealed a pervasive Jewish conspiracy such that it was impossible for the court to serve as an impartial adjudicator. The application was dealt with by an eight-judge panel (all but Abella) and the decision was presented as a joint judgment. The court's annoyance with the tone and substance of the application is transparent in the short reasons given for dismissing the application (describing it as including "anti-Semitic sentiment and views that most might have thought had disappeared from Canadian society"). The same eight-judge joint judgment format was used for the substantive decision on the appeal itself, handed down on the same day.[31]

The use of an anonymous judgment format for two successive cases involving recusal issues makes the choice seem deliberate rather than haphazard, and justifies our treatment of this type of case as raising institutional issues that call for an unusual style of judgment. We note that recusal issues were also part of the *Tobiass* decision, discussed below.

The Judicial Independence Decisions: *Tobiass* and *Provincial Court Judges' Assn.*

These two cases are interesting because they are part of a long string of more than a dozen Supreme Court decisions reaching back twenty years, all dealing with the concept of judicial independence and its implications.[32] A dozen cases is quite a string, and it can be expanded to twenty if we redefine the central notion as "decision-maker autonomy," of which judicial independence is the strong centre but with implications that ripple wider. What provoked this flurry of judicial activity was, of course, the *Charter of Rights and Freedoms,* particularly section 11(d), which declares a right to trial before an "independent and impartial tribunal." This challenged the long historical understanding that only the provincial superior courts of trial and appeal were formally guaranteed judicial independence (in sections 96–100 of the *Constitution Act, 1867*). The new Charter guarantee therefore required a major rethinking with respect to the full range of Canadian courts.

By far the most important of these cases was the 1997 *Remuneration Reference.*[33] This case redefined judicial independence as an "unwritten constitutional principle" that was grounded not in sections 96–100 or in section 11(d), but rather in the preamble to the *Constitution Act, 1867,* which speaks of "a constitution similar in principle to that of the United

Kingdom." Since judicial independence is clearly part of the United Kingdom's (unwritten) constitution, dating back to the *Act of Settlement* of 1701, this makes judicial independence a key Canadian concept as well, with both sections 96–100 and section 11(d) now presented as examples of the principle rather than as the mechanisms of this constitutional entrenchment.[34] Based on our argument about *By the Court* decisions, this should have been an anonymous and unanimous decision. In fact, it was neither, with Chief Justice Lamer delivering the judgment over a solo dissent by Gérard La Forest.

The first case of the pair was *Canada (Minister of Citizenship and Immigration) v Tobiass.*[35] One of the important dimensions of judicial independence in the English tradition is that judges must not be supervised by or answerable to politicians or bureaucrats but only other judges. It was therefore an important step in the evolution of the Canadian judicial system when the provincial reforms of the 1970s (predating the Charter) created two major institutions within the judicial system that operationalized this dimension of judicial independence. The first was the office of Chief Judge of the Provincial Court, as a buffer between the bureaucracy and the politicians on one hand and individual judges on the other; the second was the creation of Judicial Councils for Provincial Court Judges in many provinces, with a role with respect to complaints lodged against provincial court judges as well as (in some provinces) the screening of candidates for judicial appointment. In an earlier article, McCormick celebrated these two institutions as the new pillars of judicial independence as it applied to provincial court judges.[36]

But although Judicial Councils remain very much in good form, praised highly in cases such as *Mackin* and *Ell,* chief judges have fared rather less well, and have instead become one of the forces from which judicial independence must be protected rather than one of the mechanisms by which independence is reinforced.[37] Lamer referred to Chief Judges in this manner in the landmark *Remuneration Reference; Tobiass* is the more expansive follow-up.

The case involved parties who had been informed that the government of Canada was moving to strip them of their Canadian citizenship on the grounds that they had failed to divulge relevant information. The matter was put before the Trial Division of the Federal Court, but there were a series of procedural disputes followed by a number of other delays at the hands of a Federal Court judge who had a reputation for not always dealing with cases expeditiously. An official of the Department of Justice met with the chief justice of the Federal Court, after which the two exchanged formal letters, and the chief justice instructed the trial judge to schedule prompt hearings to deal with matters more expeditiously. However, the men who were the subject of the proceedings objected to the fact that they and their lawyers had not been a party to these discussions and arrangements, and they moved for a stay of proceedings on the grounds that the judicial independence of the trial judge had been compromised. At this point, the judge in question recused himself.

The Supreme Court agreed with the complainants that there had been inappropriate behaviour, and that an objective observer would have reason to think that the chief justice and the trial judge had been improperly influenced by one of the parties. It declined to grant the stay, however, ordering instead that the case proceed under the supervision of a new trial judge, and that neither the chief justice nor the original trial judge have anything to do with the cases.

The second case of the pair was *Provincial Court Judges' Assn. of New Brunswick v New Brunswick* in 2005.[38] The reason the word "remuneration" figures prominently in the *Remuneration Reference* is the fact that the early 1990s saw provincial governments facing a major budget crunch, which they one after another attempted to deal with by rolling back the salaries of all provincial employees through a variety of mechanisms. Among those provincial employees were provincial judges, who promptly went to court to argue that such a rollback violated the principle of judicial independence. An eight-to-one majority of the Supreme Court of Canada agreed, and the court unfolded the concept of constitutionally entrenched judicial independence in such a way as to require a new mechanism to deal with provincial judicial salaries: the Judicial Compensation Committee. This solution has itself generated a considerable amount of controversy and conflict, including a string of cases involving appeals from the awards of these committees.

Provincial Court Judges' Assn. is (at the time of writing) the last of these to reach the Supreme Court, and it is also one of the very few cases in the extended judicial independence string (*Tobiass* is the other) to be resolved *By the Court.* The short label we are using for the case is an understatement: it is actually five separate appeals from four different provinces – New Brunswick, Ontario, Alberta, and Quebec – combined for this single decision. Put simply, the *Remuneration Reference* of 1997 had required the creation of Judicial Compensation Commissions for provincial court judges, had laid down expectations for the compensation of those committees, and had directed that they should receive submissions from both the relevant judges' associations and the government before making a recommendation on adjustments to judicial salaries. Although governments could appeal in provincial superior court awards that they thought too generous, they found themselves in an awkward corner: if they raised issues that had not been presented to the Judicial Compensation Commission, then the appeal was liable to be dismissed on the grounds that the government had not been acting in good faith; however, if they re-raised issues that had been presented to the commission, then they were liable to lose because their concerns had already been dealt with.

Had the Supreme Court been so inclined, it could have used the ten years of experience with this new financial compensation regime to modestly reshape a decision that had been widely regarded as both unexpected and audaciously creative.[39] *Provincial Judges' Assn.* resulted in a degree of clarification, but in the way of consolidation rather than retreat. Given that most of the earlier decisions in this judicial independence string had not been unanimous, and only one (*Tobiass*) had been *By the Court,* we are inclined to take the use of that format in this decision as a deliberately emphatic way of showing a conclusive unanimity in what had been an evolving doctrine, like putting a period at the end of a sentence.

The Judicial Jurisdiction Case: *R v Ahmad*

The immediate issue in *Ahmad* involved criminal proceedings against individuals charged with plotting terrorist attacks.[40] Fahim Ahmad was one of the "Toronto Eighteen," as the case was referred to in the media. Any such prosecution involves a delicate balance between the rights of accused to know the case against him and the concerns of the government that sensitive information not be disclosed; thus, the case raised *Charter* issues concerning the proper balance between individual rights and national security. Part of the legislative scheme for achieving this balance was a statute giving a judge of the Federal Court the power to order that specific sensitive information not be disclosed to the defendants or the trial judge; this is the procedure that the federal government had invoked and that the accused challenged. The trial judge held that the legislation in question was unconstitutional. His reasons for doing so involve "Section 96 doctrine," which requires some explanation.

Historically, the provincial superior courts that are referred to in sections 96–100 of the *Constitution Act, 1867* are (as the Judicial Committee of the Privy Council once called them) the pillars of the Canadian judicial system. For one thing, they are the only courts specifically mentioned in the Constitution – the Supreme Court appears only in the form of a constitutional permission for Parliament to establish a "General Court of Appeal," and the "purely provincial" courts at the bottom of the formal judicial pyramid similarly appear only in the form of a constitutional permission for provincial legislatures to establish courts of civil and criminal jurisdiction. In addition, the provincial superior courts were the only courts that were formally guaranteed a constitutionally protected judicial independence along the lines of the English tradition described above.[41] Finally, given the prevalence of lay magistrates rather than legally trained professionals in those "purely provincial" courts well into the 1960s, it was the provincial superior courts that provided fully professional adjudication.

But there is little point in establishing a court that provides fully professional, procedurally formal, and completely independent adjudication unless you have walled off a set of matters that must be considered by this court and only by this court, and on this the Constitution said nothing specific, simply assuming continuity with the superior courts of the colonies that were brought together in 1867. Over time, the courts (the Judicial Committee of the Privy Council when it was still the highest court of appeal for Canada, and the Supreme Court of Canada since) have developed the notion of a historically grounded "core jurisdiction" for these section 96 courts.[42] The consequence is that any statute, federal or provincial, is invalid to the extent that it unduly restricts the jurisdiction of a provincial superior court, and this is precisely what the provincial superior court trial judge ruled in the *Ahmad* case.[43]

On an unusual *per saltum* appeal (from the provincial superior trial court directly to the Supreme Court, bypassing the provincial court of appeal), this ruling was overturned. The Supreme Court found that the federal legislation "correctly interpreted" does not violate section 96 of the *Constitution Act, 1867,* insisting only that the trial judge must be directly notified of any such federal government application.

Retrieving an Embarrassment: *Marshall 2*

Donald Marshall, a Mi'kmaq from Nova Scotia, was the occasion for a pair of decisions in 1999. The first brought the Supreme Court considerable controversy and the second attempted to repair the damage, although at some cost to the court's reputation.

The first *Marshall* decision (which we shall call *Marshall 1*) involved a criminal proceeding against Marshall for fishing in a prohibited manner during a prohibited period and for selling fish without a licence.[44] His defence was that he had the right to do these things under the Mi'kmaq treaties of 1760–61. A divided court (with Binnie writing the judgment and McLachlin the dissent) found in Marshall's favour, working from trial and provincial appeal court decisions that relied heavily on competing evidence about historical practices and actions. However, the decision also included more general language that was widely regarded as a dramatic expansion and protection of treaty rights across the country. The impact was most pronounced on Canada's East Coast, where serious and sometimes violent confrontations between Aboriginal peoples and the rest of the population broke out.

One immediate result was an application by the West Nova Fishermen's Coalition (which had been an intervener in the original appeal) for a rehearing of *Marshall 1* and for a stay of judgment pending the rehearing. *Marshall 2* is on the face of it a simple denial of the motion for a rehearing, but in the process the court effectively revisits and clarifies the earlier decision in a way that constrains its implications for Aboriginal and treaty rights, both for the Mi'kmaq immediately involved and more generally.[45] The response from First Nations communities was disappointment, even anger, directed at a Supreme Court that had seemed at first to boldly vindicate treaty rights and then to retreat, allegedly under government pressure.

Since Supreme Court decisions do not often provoke angry public reaction, and since the Supreme Court itself even more rarely implicitly revisits earlier decisions to cope with that reaction, the case was a highly unusual one and (we cannot help thinking) at least mildly embarrassing to the court. We think this explains why *Marshall 1* was a divided panel with the normal attribution of a majority judgment, whereas *Marshall 2* responded to the institutional challenge with a *By the Court* decision.

The Minor Trio: *Chaulk, Christie,* and *Lameman*

Chaulk is an unusual inclusion, not only because of its brevity but also because it was not a substantive appeal at all, but rather an appeal from an unsuccessful application for leave to appeal.[46] At its core was an argument that the Supreme Court's procedures for dealing with such applications was in violation of the procedure laid down in recent amendments to the *Supreme Court Act.* The alleged problem had to do with the interaction between two sections of the *Supreme Court Act* (sections 41 and 45), which could be interpreted as suggesting that section 41(3) excluded appeals on indictable offences from the procedure laid out in the earlier subsections, whereas section 45's back-references to section 41 seemed to suggest that such appeals then fell under the "oral hearing" alternative of section 45(1)c. The wider implications were twofold: 1) it cast into doubt the way the court had handled similar applications in recent months; and 2) it would as a practical matter create significant workload and scheduling issues for the justices on the court. Although the court conceded that a "strictly literal approach" to the reading of the statute made the argument credible, following it to its logical conclusion would lead to a "highly implausible, indeed absurd" result. It therefore retreated to a "Parliament could not possibly have intended" argument, and laid out a better understanding of the interaction between sections 41 and 45 grounded in a broader consideration of both the *Supreme Court Act* and the *Criminal Code.* The wider implications make it plausible to treat this as a minor example of the institutional set.

Christie involved a challenge to a provincial tax on the purchase price of legal services (ostensibly to fund legal aid).[47] Lawyer Dugald Christie's argument was that the net effect of the tax was to make it impossible for low-income litigants to pursue their claims. (Since the tax was levied on the lawyer, to be recovered from clients, and since many of Christie's own clients were unable to pay their bills on time, this had the further effect of driving lawyers like Christie out of business altogether.) The taxing provisions therefore violated a fundamental constitutional right, grounded in the principles of the rule of law, for effective access to the courts; "effective" implied and therefore included legal services. His argument persuaded the chambers judge at first hearing, and also a majority of a divided British Columbia Court of Appeal, but it was unanimously rejected by the Supreme Court. The court was not persuaded that the generalized right to have a lawyer (beyond the narrower set of criminal proceedings referenced by section 10 of the Charter) is an established element of the rule of law.

Lameman involved an attempt by persons who claimed to be descendants of the Papaschase First Nation in Alberta to sue the provincial government under an 1889 agreement involving the surrender of their reserve lands in what is now Southeast Edmonton.[48] The critical issues before the Supreme Court, however, arose from the fact that a chambers judge had granted the government's application for summary dismissal on a number of grounds, including the fact that the claims were time-barred by the Alberta *Limitations of Actions Act*.[49] A divided Court of Appeal would have allowed the action to proceed with respect to most of the issues involved. The question before the Supreme Court (there being no notice of any constitutional question) was purely and simply whether the Court of Appeal was correct in overturning the chamber judge's discretionary decision, and a unanimous Supreme Court said that it was not.

If *By the Court* as a response style for federal references can carry an overtone of institutional confidence and strength, the overtones of at least some of this "institutional defensive set" are rather different. *Truscott* in particular conjures up the image of a beleaguered court establishing a defensive wall, and *Marshall 2* is transparently a procedurally unique salvage effort for a decision (or at least a set of reasons for judgment) that has worked out badly. We will follow up on this thought in the next chapter.

Accidentally *By the Court:* The *"faut de mieux"* Cases

Our general assumption has been that *By the Court* represents a deliberate choice by the justices on the panel to present a decision under this unusual rubric rather than the conventional author-attributed format, and our purpose in this chapter has been to discover useful generalizations in the context of the content of those decisions. In the process, however, we discovered a small number of *By the Court* decisions that resulted from unusual circumstances such that the normal judgment-assignment and judgment-attribution procedures were short-circuited. These were, in a sense, "accidental" *By the Court* decisions, taking this form for internal and procedural reasons because there was no better alternative. The four examples of this phenomenon that we wish to identify are products of the Dickson court.

There were several reasons Brian Dickson's years as chief justice were unusually challenging. First, his court had to deal with the "first wave" of decisions on the newly entrenched *Canadian Charter of Rights and Freedoms.* This meant that decisions had to be made without the established precedential background that normally framed the process, and that the reasons for those decisions would carry unusual weight for subsequent Charter decisions. Both of these implications called for more careful attention than usual and led to delays in issuing decisions.

Second, these delays were caused by the fact that a number of the judges were careful and meticulous drafters in any event, a tendency aggravated by the special challenges of the early Charter cases; they tended to resist (and were sometimes annoyed by) Dickson's attempts to move things along.[50] Given the increasing caseload in general, and the increasing constitutional caseload in particular, this more methodical approach to careful drafting would have become particularly problematic.

Third, there was a series of interruptions in the service of the justices. Willard Estey's full-year secondment to head a committee of inquiry into the failure of two Western Canadian banks was one example, but an unusual cycle of poor health on the part of several of the justices was a more serious and ongoing problem. Julien Chouinard was diagnosed with cancer in late 1986 and passed away two months later. Estey was out of action at the same time with a blood clot problem. This was followed by serious and debilitating illnesses for Jean Beetz and Gerald Le Dain in late 1988.[51] This complicated the assignment of panels to hear appeals and slowed the delivery of reasons for reserved judgments.

Fourth, the Dickson court saw an unusually large number of retirements and appointments, a total of seven in six years (with Le Dain filling Laskin's seat, La Forest replacing Roland Ritchie, Claire L'Heureux-Dubé replacing Chouinard, John Sopinka replacing Estey, Charles Gonthier replacing Beetz, Peter Cory replacing Le Dain, and Beverley McLachlin replacing William McIntyre). In addition to the need to accommodate a vacant seat while waiting for a replacement, it is likely that it took some time for the new judges to become fully integrated with the institution and its practices.

The result was that the normal process of assigning a lead author and circulating the draft judgment for feedback from other members of the panel simply broke down on several occasions. This was clearly what happened in the four cases shown in Table 9.5, and we have our suspicions about a couple of others.

The purest example is *Healy*.[52] After a standard *By the Court* beginning ("judgment delivered by THE COURT"), the actual text begins, "We adopt the reasons for judgment written and circulated by our late and much respected Justice Chouinard during the Fall Term. The reasons

Table 9.5 The "accidental" set of *By the Court* decisions

Case	*Citation*	*Words*	*Subject*
Québec (A.G.) v Healy	[1987] 1 SCR 158	6,972	First Nations
Canadian Pacific Ltd. v Paul	[1988] 2 SCR 654	8,529	First Nations
Ford v Quebec (Attorney General)	[1988] 2 SCR 712	24,634	Language/ Charter
Devine v Quebec (Attorney General)	[1988] 2 SCR 790	9,277	Language/ Charter

follow." The *By the Court* format notwithstanding, there is an attributed solo author, but under such circumstances that it could not be handled in the usual fashion. The case had been argued in late October 1986, the writing of a united panel was assigned to Chouinard, and draft reasons were circulated "during the Fall Term" – which must mean within four to six weeks, which seems remarkable. However, during the Christmas break, Chouinard was diagnosed with cancer with only months to live, and he passed away on February 6, a month before the delivery of the judgment on March 5. Since there is no mention in that opening sentence of revisions to accommodate feedback from the other members of the panel, it must be presumed that these were not significant.

The major language decisions of *Ford* and *Devine* seem to be among the prime examples suggesting that the anonymity of *By the Court* is deliberately used for prominent and controversial decisions.[53] Certainly the cases enjoyed a high profile at a politically critical time. They involved Quebec's "sign law" legislation that soured the attempts at constitutional reconciliation through the Meech Lake Accord and the Charlottetown referendum, the more so for its use of the often-criticized section 33 "notwithstanding" (or *non obstante*) clause of the *Canadian Charter of Rights and Freedoms.*[54] If *Blaikie* and *Forest* mark the revival of *By the Court,* then *Ford* and *Devine* seem cut from the same cloth.[55]

In fact however, *Ford* and *Devine* are actually the product of circumstances similar to those described for *Healy.*[56] The oral arguments for this pair of cases had been heard in November 1987 (unusually allotted several successive days). At his request, Le Dain had been assigned the drafting of the reasons for judgment and had circulated a version during the summer of 1988, only to be incapacitated with a "major depressive illness" in the late summer; by the fall he was hospitalized and completely unable to function.[57] With Le Dain's poor health as well as Estey's retirement several months earlier, the initial seven-judge panel for these controversial cases was approaching the point where there might need to be a rehearing, embarrassing for the court at the best of times but all the more so with such high-profile cases.[58] A further problem was that the circulation of the draft reasons for judgment had demonstrated the need for major revisions; with Le Dain clearly unable to undertake this, the work of revision fell to Antonio Lamer and Bertha Wilson. The judgment was handed down in mid-December, but Le Dain's condition prevented him from signing his name to the final version, either as attributed author (possibly misleading given the extensive revisions) or even as a fully participating panel member (since he was in no shape to read and respond to the lengthy reasons). For this reason, the *Supreme Court Reports* indicate that he "did not participate in the judgment," a statement that is both technically correct and profoundly misleading. The absence of a *Healy*-style first sentence is presumably explained partly by the difficulty in finding a brief explanation that would adequately cover the ground, and partly by the fact that the extensive revisions meant that the final judgment was no longer the draft reasons that had been circulated in early summer.

Canadian Pacific Ltd. v Paul (handed down the same day as *Ford* and *Devine*) seems to be a strong candidate for addition to this list.[59] Again, a seven-judge panel had been reduced to five by Estey's retirement and Le Dain's incapacity, although in this case the delay was more protracted given that the oral argument had been heard more than eighteen months earlier. The most likely initial author of the reasons is Estey, but he had to be listed as "did not participate" because more than six months had elapsed since his retirement and, under the *Supreme Court Act*, he could no longer participate in the decision. At first glance, it is puzzling that this could have taken so long – this was a unanimous judgment of moderate length that did not involve a constitutional element. Sharpe and Roach provide a strong hint of a possible explanation. Estey was adamant, despite Dickson's pleas, that he would carry out his long-standing intention to retire after ten years of service on the court. He assured Dickson that he would deal promptly with the reserved judgments from the twenty-five pending panels on which he had sat, but "[his] assurances proved to be unreliable."[60] For this particular case, then, it may be that Estey was slow to respond to feedback from his colleagues, resulting in a judgment initially written by him but possibly revised to some extent to respond to the concerns of others, and then delivered so late that it could not be attributed to him.

Given that December 15, 1988, was the only time that the Supreme Court has ever handed down four different *By the Court* judgments in a single day, and given that we have just finished presenting good reasons for thinking that three of them (*Ford, Devine,* and *Paul*) were *faut de mieux* contrivances rather than deliberate uses of the *By the Court* device, it is tempting to make a similar argument with respect to the fourth of these cases, namely, *Clark v Canadian National Railway Co.,* but there is reason to hesitate.[61] Although the delay is comparable to that in *Paul* (nineteen months from oral argument to judgment), the seven-judge panel had suffered only a single attrition (Le Dain) and therefore was not threatened by the four-judge rule. Further, the lead author of the unattributed reasons seems to have been the chief justice, rather than a panel member who was for some reason unable to complete the reasons. Finally, unlike in *Paul,* there is a more credible constitutional subject matter, since this was a federalism case where the final result hinged on an explicit reversal of an earlier Supreme Court precedent.

There is also reason to wonder about four more of the Dickson court's *By the Court* decisions. The first is *A.G. (Que.) v Carrières Ste-Thérèse Ltée,* a rather straightforward administrative law case centring on simple statutory interpretation.[62] The only question was whether a particular type of departmental order could be signed by the deputy minister or whether it required the signature of the minister. The court decided that on a careful reading of the statute, the answer was the latter, which meant that *Carrières Ste-Thérèse* was successful in its challenge to the order. This does not seem on the face of it to raise any major issues, and certainly none with constitutional implications, although it is worth noting that this particular decision has been cited no less than ten times by the Supreme Court.

The second is *Lamb v Lamb,* a family law case dealing with the division of assets and the making of a support order.[63] The appellant had raised federalism issues, arising from an alleged inconsistency between the federal *Divorce Act* and the provincial *Family Law Reform Act,* but the court dealt with this in a single paragraph of the relatively short reasons: "The provisions in the two statutes are not mutually exclusive. Indeed, they do not even deal with the same subject matter." That said, there seemed to be enough at stake for attorney generals of six provinces to appear as interveners.

The third is *Air Canada v City of Dorval,* a simple case of municipal law without constitutional overtones (the critical issue is whether the council of the City of Dorval proceeded by way of resolution on a matter that should have been dealt with through a bylaw), reserved for only a modest period (four and a half months), and delivered by an intact seven-judge panel.[64] Equally curious, this is one of only four *By the Court* decisions delivered by a panel that did not include the chief justice.[65] It is clear that something unusual was happening, but it is not clear that that unusualness detracts from what may still have been a deliberate choice.[66]

The fourth case, *R v Wigman,* was a criminal case involving the *Kienapple* principle (that is, a person cannot be charged for a second offence arising out of the same incident).[67] It had been complicated by a second oral argument hearing after a three-month adjournment to allow lawyers on both sides to speak to a relevant case that had been decided while this case was pending. The decision itself is of moderate length and addresses no constitutional issues, although there was a delay of fourteen months from the second oral argument and a single member of the seven-judge panel (Chouinard) had died in the meantime. The leading author of the unattributed reasons was presumably Lamer (since he was the most experienced in criminal law matters), so this is not another example like *Healy.* Although we have no idea why the choice was made to deliver this decision *By the Court,* we have no reason not to treat it as a deliberate choice.

Selective Choice: The "Proactive" Set of Cases

The previous sections of this chapter have categorized more than half of the Supreme Court's *By the Court* decisions in terms of three distinct sets – the federal reference case set, the judicial-institutional set, and the *faut de mieux* set. For lack of a clear "trigger" element comparable to those found in the first three sets, we will call the remaining half the "proactive" set. Table 9.6 shows a list of these cases.

There is no clear single focus (reflecting the fact that it is essentially a residual list), but there is some distinct clustering. Several of the earlier cases – *Blaikie 1, Forest, Blaikie 2,* and *Protestant Schools* – can be understood as part of a larger "constitutional and language" package, playing off this aspect of the broader constitutional challenge of Quebec within Canada. Some of these did take the form of federal references (specifically, the

Table 9.6 The "proactive" set of *By the Court* decisions

Chief justice	*Case*	*Citation*	*Subject*
Cartwright	*Bd. of Transport Commissioners*	[1968] SCR 118	Federalism
Laskin	*Att. Gen. of Quebec v Blaikie et al. [Blaikie 1]*	[1979] 2 SCR 1016	Federalism/language
	Attorney General of Manitoba v Forest	[1979] 2 SCR 1032	Federalism/language
	Attorney General of Quebec v Blaikie et al. [Blaikie 2]	[1981] 1 SCR 312	Federalism/language
Dickson	*Attorney General of Quebec v Quebec Association of Protestant School Boards et al. [Protestant Schools]*	[1984] 2 SCR 66	Charter/language
	A.G. (Que.) v Carrières Ste-Thérèse Ltée	[1985] 1 SCR 831	Administrative law
	Lamb v Lamb	[1985] 1 SCR 851	Family law
	Air Canada v City of Dorval	[1985] 1 SCR 861	Municipal law
	R v Wigman	[1987] 1 SCR 246	Criminal law
	Clark v Canadian National Railway Co.	[1988] 2 SCR 680	Federalism
	Irwin Toy Ltd. v Quebec (Attorney General)	[1989] 1 SCR 927	Charter
	Tremblay v Daigle	[1989] 2 SCR 530	Charter
Lamer	*Sinclair v Quebec (Attorney General)*	[1992] 1 SCR 579	Federalism/language
	Reza v Canada	[1994] 2 SCR 394	Charter
	Libman v Quebec (Attorney General)	[1997] 3 SCR 569	Charter

McLachlin	*R v Latimer*	2001 SCC 1	Charter
	United States v Burns	2001 SCC 7	Charter
	Suresh v Canada (Minister of Citizenship and Immigration)	2002 SCC 1	Charter
	Ahani v Canada (Minister of Citizenship and Immigration)	2002 SCC 2	Charter
	R v Powley	2003 SCC 43	First Nations/Métis
	R v Blais	2003 SCC 44	First Nations/Métis
	Solski (Tutor of) v Quebec (Attorney General)	2005 SCC 14	Charter/language
	Gosselin (Tutor of) v Quebec (Attorney General)	2005 SCC 15	Charter/language
	Okwuobi v Lester B. Pearson School Board; Casimir v Quebec (Attorney General); Zorrilla v Quebec (Attorney General)	2005 SCC 16	Charter/language
	Canada (Justice) v Khadr	2008 SCC 28	Charter
	BCE Inc. v 1976 Debentureholders	2008 SCC 69	Corporate law
	Canada (Prime Minister) v Khadr	2010 SCC 3	Charter
	Carter v Canada (Attorney General)	2015 SCC 5	Charter
	R v Smith	2015 SCC 34	Charter
	R v Cody	2017 SCC 31	Charter

string of Manitoba language references that stretched over several chief justices) that drew *By the Court* responses, so this might reflect a conscious decision to deal with all the cases of this sort in the same distinctive way. Perhaps the same can be said of the Lamer court's decision in *Sinclair*, which takes exception to legislative procedural steps taken by the Quebec legislature that the Supreme Court characterized as trying to evade the implications of section 133 of the *Constitution Act 1867.* The citations to judicial authority in *Sinclair* are to the Manitoba language cases. *Ford* and *Devine* would at first glance seem to be part of the same subset, but instead of reinforcing the presumption of a consistent deliberate strategy, they undermine it by representing attempts to salvage judgments that would have been attributed in the normal way had Le Dain not been hospitalized. Perhaps the *Solski/Gosselin/Okwuobi* trio in 2005 can be thought of as a late addition to this same language set. In all, then, this accounts for nine *By the Court* judgments, five of which fold into two sets of companion decisions.

The second major subset clearly comprises Charter cases. Even omitting the two sets of language cases with Charter overtones (*Protestant Schools* and the *Solski/Gosselin/Okwuobi* trio), this still accounts for twelve of the proactive cases, including almost all of the post-1989 examples (we will look more closely at these in the next chapter). Together, the language cases and the Charter cases include all but a handful of the cases on our proactive list. As we have already indicated, *Ste-Thérèse, Lamb, Dorval,* and *Wigman* are difficult to explain. They are unusual in that they did not involve constitutional issues, and *Dorval* is unusual again for being delivered by a panel that did not include the chief justice. Although *Clarke* was a federalism decision involving the explicit repudiation of a much earlier precedent, it was not in any sense a major decision. The remaining cases are considerably more interesting: the *Powley/Blais* companion cases of 2003 (dealing with the constitutional status of the Métis in Ontario and Manitoba) are the only *By the Court* decisions to have made a major contribution to the First Nations case law, and *BCE* is the first deliberate use of *By the Court* to deliver a major decision on a non-constitutional issue.[68]

Our "proactive" label begs the question, however. Our first three categories are marking out fairly specific territory with some sense of a category boundary, whereas this is a list with no clear centre of gravity, no sense of why these cases are included but others are not. Since good typologies should not conclude with a large "miscellaneous" set (although, we hasten to add, not totally miscellaneous because the focus on constitutional cases remains), we are still left with the question of "why these cases?" that we will address in the next chapter.

Why These Cases? 10

A typology is not in itself an explanation, so all of the foregoing discussion takes us to the most critical question: Why these cases? If *By the Court* is the answer, what was the question? We will present four possible explanations, rejecting (reluctantly) the drama of the first and concluding with the dramatic and original fourth that will call for a much more extended treatment than the others.

The Triumphalist Explanation

The first explanation, and the one that embodies by far the strongest and most ambitious vision of *By the Court,* is what we will call the "triumphalist" position: it would see this selective anonymous unanimity as the judgment presentation style that the modern Supreme Court of Canada has deliberately developed and consciously uses for its most important constitutional decisions, simultaneously achieving emphasis and heightening attention. In the purest form of the device, this requires the qualifier "provided unanimity within the panel could be achieved." We have been treating "joint authorship by all the members of the majority of the panel" as a functional equivalent that is sometimes, albeit more rarely, used even when unanimity is not quite achieved.

The way that *By the Court* so clearly replaced *seriatim* decisions as the preferred judgment style for federal reference questions goes a considerable way to making this a credible suggestion. The reference question device is a uniquely Canadian practice that is outside the "normal" functions of a common law national high court but one that has been used often enough and on sufficiently important questions to establish it as a significant aspect of the practice and evolution of Canadian federalism. Beyond this easy and obvious beginning, however, the generalization of "*By the Court* = major constitutional decision" becomes very difficult to defend.

For one thing, it is clear that many transparently important constitutional decisions have not taken this form, even when the panel has been unanimous and even when there might have been a good reason for the court to treat the decision as having special significance. For example, the Dickson court's *Skapinker* case was arguably the Supreme Court's first Charter decision, but although it was unanimous, it was not delivered anonymously.[1] *Hunter v Southam* is one of the iconic Charter decisions, and *Oakes* is still the leading case for the meaning of the Charter's "reasonable limits" in section 1, but both judgments were attributed to the chief justice alone rather than to "THE COURT."[2] *Mahe* explored the implications of the minority language education rights in the Charter, and *Sparrow* was the court's first case dealing with the scope and application of section 35 (Aboriginal and treaty rights) under the *Constitution Act, 1982*, but these were not *By the Court* either.[3] And the *General Motors* decision in 1989 finally breathed some life and content into the long dormant "second branch" of the federal trade and commerce power from the 1881 Judicial Committee of the Privy Council decision in *Parsons*, but again this was a solo judgment by the chief justice.[4] There is nothing here that justifies the conclusion that the court was working from a new protocol requiring that major constitutional decisions be delivered by means of this anonymous format.

Similarly, the Lamer court may have provided us with the poster-child of the *By the Court* set in the *Quebec Secession Reference*, but in the *Quebec Sales Tax* reference it also delivered the only unanimous decision on a federal reference question in the last fifty years that was attributed to a specific judge rather than to "THE COURT."[5] *Law* was an extremely ambitious (and ultimately less than fully successful) attempt to deal with diverging ways in which the court had been dealing with equality rights cases under section 15 of the Charter by establishing an elaborate new framework for section 15 claims, but the unanimous judgment was authored solely by Frank Iacobucci.[6] The *Remuneration Reference* established a dramatic new understanding of and basis for judicial independence, but it did so in a judgment written by Chief Justice Antonio Lamer.[7] And *UFCW v KMart* arguably marks the turning point when the Supreme Court began to listen more sympathetically to trade unions and their freedom of association claims under section 2 of the Charter, but once again it did so with solo-attributed rather than anonymous reasons.[8]

Finally, the McLachlin court handed down a number of major constitutional decisions that could have been, but were not, *By the Court*. The *Insite* case frustrated the federal government's intention of ending the "safe injection sites" policy in Vancouver.[9] *Bedford* dramatically expanded the meaning of section 7 of the Charter ("security of the person") in the immediate context of the rights of sex workers and in a way that invalidated the relevant *Criminal Code* provisions.[10] *Daniels* firmly established, over the arguments to the contrary of the national government, that the meaning of "Indians" in section 91.24 of the *Constitution Act 1867* included the Métis and "non-status Indians."[11] *Tsilhqot'in* set down elements of a test for establishing Aboriginal title in the context of unresolved land claims.[12] And *Withler* began to provide the new framing for section 15 equality rights necessitated by the court's recently expressed reservations about *Law*.[13]

These lists could be expanded, but they suffice to demonstrate that the claim that *By the Court* is the Supreme Court's mode of choice for major constitutional cases simply cannot be sustained. We are particularly struck by the "dog that didn't bark" in the *By the Court* lists – that is, major cases dealing with Aboriginal issues. Constitutional law in Canada today is something of a three-legged stool, the legs being federalism, the Charter, and Aboriginal rights. Federalism cases dominate the use of *By the Court* and Charter cases have also been reasonably numerous, but apart from the *Powley/Blais* companion cases on Métis rights and the unique salvage effort of *Marshall 2,* Aboriginal matters have not drawn this form of judicial response.[14] Since the importance of these issues is beyond dispute, the suggestion that major constitutional decisions are *By the Court* decisions is unsustainable.

Nor is the other side of our proposed equation particularly convincing, because not all *By the Court* decisions seem to be particularly important. Indeed, as our earlier puzzlement demonstrated, a certain number of them do not seem to raise any constitutional issues at all, and it is perplexing that they were delivered in this style. Our general claim remains: *By the Court* is a uniquely Canadian device that our Supreme Court has used for a subset of its major constitutional decisions, but that subset is clearly not defined in any simple way by "more important." The notion of triumphalism does not provide a workable framework for exploring the subject, although we cannot deny having found it profoundly tempting.

The "Hot Potatoes" Explanation

A more satisfactory framework for a reasonable number of *By the Court* decisions is the notion that it is the court's response to a case that puts it in an unusually problematic corner. *Truscott,* which we have identified as the paradigmatic lead example of *By the Court,* is beyond question such an example, for reasons we have elaborated on in Chapter 7.[15] Although the content of that decision may not have provided a permanently satisfactory escape from the dilemma (as demonstrated by the Ontario Court of Appeal reference case of 2007), it served at least temporarily to take the Supreme Court out of the spotlight, which may have been enough to give it a place in institutional memory as a way of dealing with comparable tight corners in later years.[16]

The pair of 1979 language cases that we have earlier described as providing the until recently conventional account of the origins of *By the Court* would also qualify as good examples, despite the brevity of their supporting reasons.[17] The direct challenge to the flagship legislative initiative of a recently elected separatist government in Quebec could not help but be politically explosive (potentially the Canadian equivalent to the United States Supreme Court's *Dred Scott* decision in the lead-up to the American Civil War), especially given the anticipation of a sovereignty referendum. Sirota has suggested that *By the Court* might sometimes function as a "blame diffusion" strategy, where a collective judgment prevents the focused attacks that might be directed toward a single individual.[18] A judgment by a non-Quebec judge might have provided easy ammunition for a separatist critique, but a judgment by a Quebec judge would definitely have exposed that individual to personal attacks.

The *Patriation Reference* is another clear candidate for the "hot potato" list, because it put the Supreme Court right in the middle of a major high-profile disagreement between the federal government on the one hand, and most of the provincial governments on the other.[19] The question of whether the Supreme Court is "biased" in favour of the national government in federal-provincial disputes is one that tends to materialize whenever a provincial government feels particularly aggrieved about a recent constitutional decision, and this was certainly the case in the *Patriation* context, with the usually moderate government of Saskatchewan furious about a pair of recent Supreme Court decisions on natural resources.[20] In the event, the Supreme Court can be thought of as "splitting the difference" between the two sides, finding that there was no legal requirement for provincial agreement before an amendment request to the British Parliament, but there was a conventional requirement for some level of such agreement. Peter Russell admired the court's "bold statecraft" footwork but was critical of its "questionable jurisprudence."[21] For present purposes, the point is that the case generated not one but two sets of reasons for judgment – one on the legal issue, the other on the conventional issue – and both took the form of jointly authored judgments by all the members of the majority; we are treating this as the form that *By the Court* takes when it is confronted by a dissent. The delicacy of the court's deliberations in the *Patriation Reference* are transparently mirrored by the *Quebec Secession Reference*, especially in the light of concerns that an unsympathetic handling of the question by the Supreme Court might conceivably trigger a third sovereignty referendum.[22]

In Chapter 9, we treated four *By the Court* judgments as an administrative convenience when the "real" author of the reasons could not be attributed in the normal way: *Healy* (Julien Chouinard had died before the decision was handed down), *Paul* (Willard Estey had drafted the reasons but not completed them within six months of his retirement), and the companion cases of *Ford* and *Devine* (Gerald Le Dain had drafted the reasons for both decisions but was hospitalized before the revised reasons could be handed down).[23] The fact that this last pair of cases involved Quebec's controversial but popular sign law would already seem to have made these cases "hot potato" candidates comparable to *Blaikie*, but nothing in Sharpe and Roach's biography of Dickson suggests that this was in the works before Le Dain went into hospital because of a breakdown caused by overwork and severe depression. However, a recent CBC radio program presented a different angle, signalled by its subtitle, "How Depression Cost Gerald Le Dain His Supreme Court Post."[24] In the CBC account, it also cost him the attribution of these two major decisions. The suggestion is that Dickson was very concerned that the immediate decisions and the Supreme Court itself not be tagged with the stigma of mental illness (which was then how severe depression was often regarded), and pressured Le Dain very strongly to resign rather than take some time off to recover and return, and also that he shifted the attribution of the reasons for judgment from Le Dain to *By the Court*, both decisions over some opposition from members of the court.

The *Same-Sex Marriage Reference* can also be seen as presenting a particular challenge for the court, because it was at the time a major point of contention between the governing Liberals and the opposition Conservatives.[25] The reference would have had the double effect of taking the issue out of the next election campaign (because of the impropriety of debating something that was already before the courts), and ultimately recruiting the court for the government side of the issue when the legislation was introduced. Ultimately, the court simply declined to answer the core question (whether the existing opposite-sex definition of marriage was consistent with the Charter), a very unusual manoeuvre that highlights the problematic nature of the case.[26]

The "hot potatoes" aspect obviously overlaps with the "institutional defensive" category described in the previous chapter. *Marshall 2* and the *Nadon* case are particularly strong examples, and the recusal pair of *Wewaykum* and *Mugesera* raise an issue that strikes a nerve with judges that might not be so obvious to the general public.[27] It would also explain a number of decisions – most obviously but not only the pair of *Khadr* cases – that raised the question of the balance between individual rights on the one hand and national security interests on the other, with the search for such a balance complicated by global tensions.[28]

Knopff has suggested a further subset of these "special treatment" cases, suggesting that *By the Court* is a device that the court uses for explicitly overruling an earlier precedent of some ongoing significance.[29] The particular example that he mentions is *Burns*.[30] Dealing with an American extradition request involving the possibility of a death penalty, the court found that the Minister of Justice was constitutionally bound "to ask for and obtain" an assurance that the death penalty would not be imposed, although the court had explicitly rejected this position a decade earlier in *Kindler* and *Ng*.[31] Another example in the same vein is *Carter*, which explicitly (and surprisingly casually) reversed the twenty-year-old precedent in *Rodriguez* to find that the *Criminal Code* prohibition against physician-assisted suicide unjustifiably infringed section 7 of the Charter.[32] Although it might be stretching the point, the same description applies to *Clark*, as mentioned above.[33]

The Federalism Explanation

An obvious set of *By the Court* cases is the one that focuses on federalism issues. This, too, we can think of as having been clearly signalled from the very beginning: after the ultimate "hot potato" use of a joint judgment in *Truscott* in May 1967, the court followed up in November with the *Offshore Mineral Rights Reference*.[34] The connection of *By the Court* with federalism is by no means a new idea. Bzdera made this argument in 1993 with his suggestion that the anonymous unanimous style is typical of the way that national high courts in federal countries accomplish their centralizing tendencies.[35] It is clear, as we have demonstrated, that the style is unique to Canada, and also that it is used for decisions (such as the *Securities Act Reference*) that undermine as well as those that reinforce the central government's position, but there is definitely a Canadian link between anonymous unanimous decisions and federalism cases.[36]

It important to stress that in its own way the use of *By the Court* for the *Offshore Mineral Rights Reference* is just as unexpected and innovative as *Truscott*. Given the very special circumstances of *Truscott,* the uniquely embarrassing corner in which the court found itself being second-guessed in any earlier decision, the unfamiliar problem of an unusually agitated public opinion, and the atypical trial-like nature of the proceedings, it was entirely plausible to think that the joint judgment device might vanish into history as a one-off. Instead, the new chief justice (whom we have credited with the stratagem in the first place) used it again to hand down an advisory opinion six months later. This has real overtones of a deliberate institutional manoeuvre for the Supreme Court in a strategically advantageous position vis-à-vis the federal government – and this is not the kind of description that one would have applied to the Supreme Court of fifty years ago, the one that Cheffins famously described, only one year earlier, as "a quiet Court in an unquiet country."[37]

As mentioned in the previous chapter, the reference power is all but unique to Canada, but it has been employed in this country frequently enough that its use is not exceptional. The *Offshore Mineral Rights Reference* was the eleventh federal reference since the end of the Second World War and there had been an equal number of appeals on references by provincial governments to their respective courts of appeal. The *Offshore Mineral Rights Reference* itself was significant, but not unusually so, and not in such a way as to present the court with an unusually sensitive or potentially embarrassing challenge. There is therefore something much more calculated in this second use of a joint judgment (this time unanimous).

The third joint judgment occurred only two weeks later, in the *Board of Transport Commissioners* case.[38] This was also a constitutional case at a time when the court did not normally hear many such cases – two in a single month was unusual at the time – but again it does not seem to have been a significant constitutional case, nor did it have any aspects that created a special or unusual problem for the court. Nor, on the face of it, was it a reference question but rather an appeal from a lower court decision. There is therefore some reason to take this as an institutional hint that *By the Court* was going to be used not just for federalism references but for federalism cases more generally (and this at a time when federalism issues comprised almost all the admittedly limited constitutional caseload). Obviously, as we conceded when we abandoned the "triumphalist" thesis, this did not happen. Perhaps we are simply reading too much into a single example, or perhaps the combination of John Robert Cartwright's short chief justiceship and the small number of constitutional cases prevented such a new practice from becoming firmly established. What clearly survived, as shown in the previous chapter, was the use of *By the Court* for federal references; only briefly did it appear that the practice would extend to provincial references as well.

To be sure, a number of the federal government's reference questions have already made it to the "hot potato" list, but this is overlap rather than complete duplication. Neither the *Assisted Human Reproduction Act Reference* nor the *Securities Act Reference* seems to have been potentially embarrassing for the court – which is not to deny that the first was very challenging or that the second surprised the national government in a way that contributed to the bad feelings that boiled over after the *Nadon* case in 2014.[39]

The "New Collegiality" Explanation

To the foregoing we would add one further set, namely, those cases that resulted from the "new collegiality" practices of Chief Justice Beverley McLachlin after 2000. This is an extremely significant development that goes beyond the *By the Court* phenomenon while at the same time simultaneously embracing and transforming it. In Chapter 3, we teased readers with the idea that perhaps one day the Supreme Court's "one judgment, one author" decision-delivery style that emerged in the late 1960s might be replaced by something else. *By the Court* was clearly not that moment: for one thing, it was born at the same time as the "one judgment, one author" style itself; for another, its use was much too infrequent and sporadic to qualify. But the McLachlin court's new collegiality has a much stronger claim to being considered as possibly the beginning of something genuinely new and different.

Beyond "One Judgment, One Author": McLachlin's New Collegiality

In a CBC interview as she was retiring from the Supreme Court, McLachlin was asked about her time as chief justice and what she thought she had accomplished. She responded that she was proud to have led a court that was more united and more collegial than it had been in the past. Her summary of the eighteen years significantly echoed the comments she had made almost a decade earlier, when it was her first decade as chief justice that was being acknowledged and honoured. The fact that this has been such a running theme of her leadership makes it all the more important as a point of analysis.

Up to a point, the "more united" part of the claim is straightforward and easily validated. Where the Lamer court had achieved full unanimity in barely 40 percent of its reserved decisions, the McLachlin court was able to do so almost 60 percent of the time.[40] With a minor proviso – "more united" should also take into account how many judges were in the minority in the divided decisions, as well as the extent to which the outside-the-majority judges were themselves united or divided – this amply justifies her claim and her satisfaction.

But what about the "collegiality" claim, which seems to be a further claim rather than simply an echo of the first. What would validate a claim of greater collegiality? One factor is surely the absence of a persisting central cleavage on the court. For example, not only was a good proportion of the Lamer court's significant decisions made by a divided panel but there was also a tendency for one set of judges to be on the majority side of those divisions and another set to be in the minority. This is the "gang of five" motif that frequently figures in descriptions of the Lamer court, pointing to the set of judges (Antonio Lamer, John Major, John Sopinka, Frank Iacobucci, and Peter Cory) who tended to dominate especially the five-year "natural court" period that centred the Lamer decade.[41] But there is no sign of any such persisting cleavage on the McLachlin court. Even if one divides McLachlin's tenure into subperiods to examine the steadily shifting membership of the court from the thirteen new appointments, no comparable judgment-dominating subset emerges.

There is a second aspect of this heightened collegiality, however, in the form of a persistent practice of pervasive cooperation beyond the earlier norm for the Supreme Court of Canada itself and beyond anything that exists on comparable courts. This practice is the co-authorship of judgments. This goes far beyond the *By the Court* phenomenon that attracted us in the first place, but for reasons that we will expand on later, we think that it has to some extent simply absorbed (and therefore altered) the earlier practice of *By the Court.*

To reiterate: the long-standing practice for the Supreme Court of Canada, as for other comparable courts in the common law tradition, is for a set of reasons for judgment to be attributed to a specific individual judge. Whether it involves a unanimous decision or a majority or plurality decision, the Supreme Court's standard format for the last fifty years has been "the judgment was delivered by X," where X is one of the judges in the majority; we labelled this the "single judgement, single author" era.

For some time, this apparent solo authorship has been softened by a "circulate and revise" process within the panel. The person assigned to write the majority or unanimous judgment prepares a draft and circulates it for critical comment by other members of the panel.[42] All indications are that all the judges take this very seriously and the critical comments can be extensive. The expectation then is that the initial writer will consider those comments carefully and undertake revisions addressing them, which are then recirculated; this process can go through more than one iteration.[43] This gives a strongly collegial dimension to what is typically presented as a solo effort, such that the named judge should really be thought of as a lead author rather than a genuinely solo author in the most literal sense, but with this qualification the attribution remains meaningful and can be taken seriously.

An increasing number of the court's recent decisions are taking a different form, however. Consider, for example, the recent case of *Clyde River (Hamlet) v Petroleum Geo-Services Inc.* in the summer of 2017.[44] This major case involved the notion of the "honour of the Crown" and what it implied in terms of consultation with Aboriginal communities prior to actions that impacted Aboriginal or treaty rights. It was a unanimous decision by a nine-judge panel, and the 6,500-word judgment was delivered "by Karakatsanis and Brown." But why "Karakatsanis and Brown"? Why not Karakatsanis? Or Brown? Nor was this an isolated event: the decision in a companion case handed down the same day was also co-authored by this same pair of judges.[45] The next day, the reasons for judgment in a completely unrelated case were jointly authored by Wagner and Gascon, with jointly authored separate concurring reasons by Brown and Rowe.[46] And a day later, there was another completely unrelated case, again with a judgment jointly authored by Wagner and Gascon.[47] That is no less than five sets of co-authored reasons in three days, four of them judgments, involving three different pairs of judges who together make up a majority of the members of the court. Extend the count to the entirety of the McLachlin court, and the number of co-authored judgments rises to 121 and the number of co-authored minority reasons to 68.[48]

We cannot quite say that the McLachlin court invented this mode of judgment presentation. The first example seems to have been the 1985 case of *John v The Queen,* with a joint decision by Estey and Lamer for a unanimous seven-judge panel that briefly (1,500 words) allowed an appeal by applying the *Kienapple* principle.[49] It does not appear that the case has ever been subsequently cited by the Supreme Court, and there is no reason why it should have taken this unusual form. A dozen examples in the next dozen years followed before a major change in 1998 and 1999 – sixteen co-authored decisions in two years – signalled an emerging new practice of joint two-judge authorship of unanimous or majority reasons. The new reality of multiple examples in sequential years justifies describing this as an "emerging practice," in contrast with the earlier "sporadic examples."

But if the McLachlin court did not invent the practice, it certainly normalized it. After a slow start, with only two such decisions in 2000, there were eleven in 2002 and twelve in 2003, and there was never a year since then in which the McLachlin court did not deliver several co-authored judgments. For the McLachlin court as a whole, co-authorships account for about one-ninth of all reserved decisions, and this share was rising over the closing years of her chief justiceship.

In the early years after 2000, the leader in this practice was clearly Iacobucci; in the middle years of the McLachlin court, it was Louis LeBel and to some extent McLachlin herself; toward the end of the McLachlin years it was Richard Wagner. More significant, however, is the fact that every single one of the twenty-two judges who served on the McLachlin court was involved more than once. It is also striking that there is today remarkably little clustering in the partnerships that underpin the shared authorships. In the early years (1998–99), Iacobucci and Cory clearly anchored the practice – take away all the examples in which one or both of them were involved and the Lamer court count is reduced by 80 percent. On the McLachlin court, however, the co-authorship partnerships have been far more diverse; there have been forty-four different two-judge pairings and three different three-judge groupings. Co-authorship has become a court-pervasive and court-uniting phenomenon; it is not something that is characteristic of only one part of its membership, and it is not something that works in such a way as to reflect or reinforce enduring cleavage.

An obvious caveat about attaching importance to this new practice is the question of whether it is perhaps directed toward the more routine end of the caseload. This is not the case, however. In terms of the type of law for which co-authored decisions are used, the most frequent is constitutional cases, and a further breakdown into the three major elements of the constitutional caseload – Charter, federalism, and Aboriginal issues – reveals that it is equally likely to be used for all three of them. More than one constitutional decision in every six, compared with one in every ten for private law cases and one in every twenty for criminal law cases, have been delivered by joint authorship.

A very practical measure of the significance of a judicial decision is how frequently it is subsequently cited by the court itself. Many – perhaps most – Supreme Court decisions are never cited in this way, but a smaller number of them provide a solid anchor point for subsequent decisions that is acknowledged in a string of citations. The immediately obvious problem in establishing this is the fact that some of the McLachlin court decisions were handed down more than fifteen years ago while others were delivered much more recently. The drastically uneven time periods over which citations have been accumulated makes a simple citation count unhelpful. Our solution was to count "citations per year," dividing the number of accumulated citations by the length of time for which they have been available to be cited. This is not a perfect measure: as has been demonstrated elsewhere, there is a steady year-by-year erosion of the citation frequency of even the most significant Supreme Court decisions, so the per-year count slightly favours more recent decisions over older ones.[50] However, because the erosion rate of citations by the

Table 10.1 Frequency of joint judgments, by subsequent citation frequency

Cite rank per year	*By the Court*	*Joint*	*Solo*	*Total*	*By the Court (%)*	*Joint (%)*	*Solo (%)*
0	21	15	159	195	10.8	7.7	81.5
0.01–0.5	22	38	373	433	5.1	8.8	86.1
0.51–1.0	5	24	197	226	2.2	10.6	87.2
1.01–2.0	3	25	107	135	2.2	18.5	79.3
>2.0	2	14	29	45	4.4	31.1	64.4
Total	53	116	865	1,034*	5.1	11.2	83.7

Notes: * = excludes decisions between January 1, 2017, and July 31, 2017, none of which had accumulated any citations as of the June 30, 2017, cut-off date for the database.

McLachlin court is very low, this factor is less critical than it might have been.

On this measure of importance, it clearly is not the case that the use of co-authorships is tilted toward the less important side of the caseload spectrum – quite the contrary, as shown in Table 10.1. To make the point as dramatically as possible: the most frequently cited decision of the McLachlin court was *Dunsmuir v New Brunswick,* co-authored by Michael Bastarache and LeBel; the second was *Housen v Nikolaisen,* co-authored by Iacobucci and Major; the third was *Bell ExpressVu Limited Partnership v Rex,* also co-authored by Iacobucci and Major; and the fourth was *R v Grant,* co-authored by McLachlin and Louise Charron.[51] And perhaps the court's most recent highly controversial decision, ramping up the standards implied by the Charter's guarantee of "trial within a reasonable time" is the 2016 decision in *R v Jordan,* co-authored by Michael Moldaver, Andromache Karakatsanis, and Russell Brown.[52] Seven of the top twelve, and thirteen of the top twenty-five, most frequently cited decisions were co-authored.

The co-authorship of judicial reasons was an established practice of the McLachlin court in a way that was not true of any prior court. Its use was tilted toward the most significant parts of the caseload, and it generated decisions that tended to be cited more often than the more numerous solo-authored judgments. This combination of novelty, caseload selection, and lasting impact made the emergence of co-authorship one of the major stories of the McLachlin court. Moreover, it is an increasing factor, rather than steady-state or decreasing, within the Supreme Court reserved decision caseload. To look at it from the point of view of the individual justice: during the closing years of the McLachlin chief justiceship, the average member of a Supreme Court panel was more likely to take part in a judgment by co-authorship or *By the Court* than to write solo-authored reasons. This remarkable fact solidly anchored the collegiality of which McLachlin was so proud.

What does this practice have to do with *By the Court*? McLachlin herself has spoken of *By the Court* in terms that suggest it should to some extent be seen as part of this new tendency. In an interview reported in the *Toronto Star,* she said that on a number of occasions, when she had been assigned the writing of the judgment, she found the comments of her colleagues so helpful that she not only incorporated them in her own reasons but extended credit for those reasons by using the rubric of "THE COURT."[53] Although she herself did not make the extension, something of the sort may well apply to the broader phenomenon of co-authorship, with both of these shared attribution styles emerging from the circulate-and-revise process rather than through a conscious decision at the post-hearing judicial conference. On the one hand, McLachlin's comment makes the choice of *By the Court,* at least for her court, somewhat more casual and occurring later in the process than we had been assuming; on the other hand, it provides a clear link to a new and expanding significant change to the court's deliberation and judgment delivery process. *By the Court* has a starting date thirty years earlier, but it seems to have been caught up in this new development. But only, we would add, to some extent because, even more so than co-authorship generally, *By the Court* still retains the very strong focus on constitutional cases that has characterized it since 1967.

Together, co-authored judgments and *By the Court* judgments made up over one-sixth of the court's reserved judgments over the eighteen years of McLachlin's tenure as chief justice, including a disproportionate share of the most frequently cited decisions. We think that this justifies a claim we could not realistically make of *By the Court* alone, but now make for the combination of these two not-single-author judgment styles:

there is a real signal here that we are moving beyond the "single judgment, single author" style that has characterized our Supreme Court since the 1960s toward an institutional judgment presentation style that is more collegial and less focused on a single individual. We will expand on this development and its implications in the concluding chapter.

PART 4
Conclusion

The Meaning and Future of the *By the Court* Format

11

Our empirical investigation of the *By the Court* phenomenon has led to the following conclusions:

- *Origins* – *By the Court* is a practice that is both original and unique to the Supreme Court of Canada. It emerged in the late 1960s, initially as a response to an embarrassing challenge to the status of the court.
- *Content* – With regard to content, the centre of gravity of *By the Court* is constitutional law, more specifically the constitutional law of Canadian federalism.
- *Provenance* – With regard to provenance, the centre of gravity of *By the Court* is the constitutional reference by the federal government.
- *Timing* – With regard to timing, the centre of gravity of *By the Court* has been the McLachlin court.
- *Extent* – Beyond these fairly specific confines, there has been some wider use of *By the Court* (dealing, for example, with some Charter issues), but this has been occasional rather than regular, and haphazard rather than systematic.

These parameters make *By the Court* an important dimension of the transformation of the Supreme Court of Canada into a national institution with a major role in national governance, a part it has come to play only in recent decades. To recognize *By the Court* as the court's preferred response to a federal reference establishes the device as significant, given that this unusual procedure has been an important element in the constitutional evolution of Canadian federalism.[1] That reference cases decided *By the Court* have been joined by a comparable number of constitutional decisions on federalism issues that have been brought before the court by the normal appeal process raises the importance of the practice, as does the fact that it sometimes reaches further, to other constitutional issues such as the Charter when those cases have some particularly challenging or problematic aspect.

But what is the broader frame within which we should be looking at this phenomenon?

We take it as axiomatic that agreement, let alone unanimity, is not easily achieved on a collegial panel court. The Supreme Court is a body of nine experienced and committed professionals, each with his or her own prioritized set of legal and professional principles and values. On any save the most straightforward of cases, no two justices would write reasons for judgments in precisely the same way, with precisely the same implications for the future of the law. To some extent, persuasion will soften some of these initial differences, and negotiation will soften others.[2] Even on the most collegial of courts, however, some differences will remain, and the critical question is how significant those differences must be before a notional threshold is met and collegiality yields to candour.[3] Short of that threshold, nuanced differences between the preferred positions of individual justices will give way to a set of compromises presented as if they were themselves preferred positions. And of course that threshold itself will vary, responding to a variety of considerations but generally in such a way as to be higher for constitutional matters.

Within this frame, it would seem at first glance that the easiest explanation for the ebb and flow of agreement and disagreement would be the personalities of the judges within a small and intensely interactive group.[4] This impact of personality can play out down two different tracks: the first is the influence of the chief justice, and the second is the extent to which the specific mix of individuals on the court do or do not get along.[5] We would reject this personalities approach, and prefer to treat the balance between institutional solidarity and individual outspokenness as a function of broader institutional contexts and expectations. As Henderson has suggested, any persisting change in the way that a body like the Supreme Court does its business should be understood not as a product of whim or idiosyncrasy but as a rational institutional response to changing social circumstances, and specifically as a reaction to immediate threats or opportunities.[6] There are times when the court needs to speak with clarity and focus; there are other times when the court needs to "let many flowers blossom," such that different voices within the court are acknowledging a diversity of points of view in the broader society. The Quebec secession threat called for the first; the early years of the Charter required instead an initial openness to a variety of possible solutions that gradually yielded to a clearer central direction. There is no level of disagreement (how many non-unanimous decisions, how many fragmented decisions, how frequently the notional average justice is willing to write or to sign minority reasons) that is simply and universally the "right" level for common law national high courts in general, or for any specific national high court. Rather, the current balance between unanimity and division is the way that the functions of a national high court decision play out in immediate circumstances.

McCormick has elsewhere reflected on the role of national high courts, evaluating the relative performance of the Canadian and American Supreme Courts with respect to recent high-profile constitutional decisions, specifically the *Quebec Secession Reference* for the former and *Bush v Gore* for the latter.[7] He suggested such an evaluation should be done in terms of nine different functions of a national high court decision, grouped according to three different elements:

Element 1: The Decision Trilogy

- *Proposition 1* – A national high court decision should clearly resolve the immediate case (the Issue Resolution principle).

- *Proposition 2* – A national high court decision should provide clear guidance to lower courts (and legislatures and public officials) on how to deal with related and/or ancillary questions (the Guidance principle).
- *Proposition 3* – A national high court decision should settle the major legal/constitutional issues directly involved in the immediate case (the Principle Resolution principle).

Element 2: The Persuasion Trilogy

- *Proposition 4* – A national high court decision should reconcile the loser (and the broader interests implicitly represented by the loser as a party to the immediate dispute) to the results (the Reconciliation principle).
- *Proposition 5* – A national high court decision should be consistent in its reasons and its invocation of principle with the tenor and direction of its own earlier decisions (the Consistency principle).
- *Proposition 6* – A national high court decision should educate citizens about legal principles and constitutional matters (the Citizen Education principle).

Element 3: The Caution Trilogy

- *Proposition 7* – A national high court decision should accurately record, and do sympathetic justice to, the major issues and the value-arguments presented by both sides (the Issue Fairness principle).
- *Proposition 8* – A national high court decision should set the foundation for, rather than prematurely limit the scope of, future evolution of doctrine and practice on grand legal and constitutional issues (the Future Openness principle).
- *Proposition 9* – A national high court decision should adopt a tone and a style that maintain and enhance the stature and reputation of the tribunal itself (the Status-Maintenance principle).

The nine propositions are not just amenable to classification in terms of the three elements (decision, persuasion, caution) suggested but can

Figure 11.1 Schematic representation of the functions of a national high court decision

Value/target	*Litigants*	*Lower courts and government*	*Public*
Decision	Issue-resolution	Guidance	Principle-clarity
Persuasion	Reconciliation	Consistency	Education
Caution	Issue-fairness	Issue openness	Status-maintenance

also be unfolded in a different way as targeted to three different audiences – the immediate parties or litigants (Propositions 1, 4, and 7), the lower courts and governmental bureaucracies and leaders (Propositions 2, 5, and 8), and the general public (Propositions 3, 6, and 9). This can be schematically represented as shown in Figure 11.1.

This is a complicated set of requirements that pulls national high courts in several different directions. Proposition 3 calls for focused precision and tight argument, and Proposition 2 builds on it, but Proposition 8 implies a preference for an intentional element of open-textured ambiguity; it is difficult to serve both at once. Proposition 1 requires, and Proposition 3 implies, a clear-cut result with a definite winner and loser, a position victorious and a position rejected; Proposition 4 suggests instead a "something for everybody" outcome with a touch of "split the difference." Proposition 5 implies a degree of rigidity (or at least its appearance), while Proposition 8 requires conscious adaptability and flexibility. Proposition 6 calls for brevity and eloquent language, while Proposition 2 requires length and technical language. Even Propositions 1 and 3, in many ways the most obvious, may sometimes conflict; as the cliché has it, hard cases make bad law. (At the same time, of course, even relatively "easy" cases may carry their own dangers. It is a general problem of judiciaries as decision-making bodies that their knowledge of social issues is derived from a deep knowledge of a narrow and skewed sample of human experiences; the immediate case may or may not be such as to imply a more general rule.) Propositions 1, 2, 3, and 6 suggest the desirability of a unanimous court, but Proposition 7 (and possibly 4, and by implication perhaps 8 as well) points to the importance of minority opinions, both dissents and the much-maligned separate concurrences. And Proposition 9 almost looks like a way of rewarding the court for evading Propositions 1 and 3, even to the extent of possibly punishing it for taking them too seriously; indeed, its call for pragmatic calculation is at some variance with the high value and principle of most of the rest of the propositions.

This is the obstacle course through which the court must find its way, with the further complication that not only are the nine principles not necessarily of equal importance, but their relative importance changes from one field of law to another, from one time to another, and even from one case to another, depending on the immediate social and political context. McCormick saw consistency as the primary value, but on further reflection we would revisit that suggestion by proposing instead the value of status maintenance. Or, to use a different word for the same idea, and one that links to an excellent recent book: reputation.[8]

Reputation is enormously important to the courts because of their profoundly limited leverage, given that they have neither tax-and-spend powers nor a bureaucracy (or a police force) to enforce their will. In the standard phrase from the American literature, they control neither the purse nor the sword. Only through the words in their written decisions can they wield any influence, and the most relevant consideration in how much impact those words will have with how wide an audience is reputation, which Garoupa and Ginsburg define "simply as the stock of judgments about an actor's past behavior."[9] (As George and Gulati suggest, this is a rather thin definition for this central concept, and seems to cry out for a clearer idea of what sorts of decisions in what sorts of contexts, and in the eyes of what sorts of publics, we are talking about, but it provides a useful starting point.[10]) The currency of the judicial world, they suggest, is persuasion and reputation, or as they sum it up even more bluntly, "reputation is power."[11]

Both individual courts within the system and the judicial system as a whole must build and maintain a solid and positive reputation, which contributes to what Gibson, Caldeira, and Baird have referred to as "diffuse support."[12] On the one hand, it is this generalized and diffuse support that enables the institution to survive a certain number of relatively unpopular decisions and yet still be able to carry public opinion with it. On the other hand, like a bank account that can be overdrawn, such support can be shattered in a moment by a spectacularly "bad" decision. The obvious American example would be *Dred Scott,* which held that no black person could be a citizen of the United States, and that slavery could not be prohibited in American territories.[13] This is widely regarded in the academy as the worst decision that the US Supreme Court ever handed down and as a precipitating factor (to call it a cause would be putting it too strongly) of the American Civil War.[14] As a practical matter, it took the US Supreme Court a generation to regain the stature within the national political system that it had squandered in that single moment.

Reputation has two dimensions, partly complementary and partly competitive: the individual reputation of specific judges, and the collective reputation of the judiciary. The civil law/common law distinction is one exemplification of these two alternatives.[15] The civil law has a career judiciary and a cultivated appearance of anonymity and unanimity – panels are pervasive, but judgments are never authored and there are no minority reasons.[16] This is a judiciary that relies heavily on its collective reputation, because individual faces and voices have no opportunity to present themselves and would not be welcomed if they did.[17] Conversely, the individual judges in a common law judiciary are appointed only later in a career, after some degree of professional success, with their selection based on individual qualities and achievements (a "recognition judiciary"). Once in office, that individuality is simultaneously reflected and promoted by the practice of signed judgments and the writing of signed minority reasons, although the collective reputation of the judiciary as a whole remains a consideration that somewhat constrains judicial behaviour in the quest for individual reputation, because it underpins that reputation.

But individuals come with specific attributes and doctrinal preferences that can be identified and either celebrated or condemned by different audiences. Among other things, a focus on individualized performances has the potential for identifying, or can be characterized as reflecting, ideological divisions within the judiciary. The very performances (authored judgments, powerful minority reasons) that judges rely on to enhance individual reputations can reveal the judiciary – and even the highest court itself – to be a shifting battleground of ideological preferences, not something that stands above the partisan political struggle but simply that same politics translated into a different forum. The most obvious example is the contemporary United States Supreme Court, which is seen as having been drawn into the nation's ongoing "culture wars." It is now widely regarded as consisting of two balanced ideological factions on either side of the current "swing justice," who thereby exercises enormous discretion and power. From the "O'Connor court" to the "Kennedy court" to (after the death of Antonin Scalia) an evenly divided four-to-four court waiting for a new appointment that might well signal the emergence of a new "swing justice" – this is, arguably, where the judicial politics of a recognition judiciary can take us.[18]

Judgment delivery format becomes a way of ratcheting this process up or down. The strong institutional preference for majority judgments goes some distance, and a preference for unanimity goes even further, toward promoting collective reputation by containing individual reputation. On the one hand, it constrains the "splendid freedom" of utterly candid solo reasons that can attract and reinforce individual reputation; on the other hand, even solo-authored unanimous reasons have been softened by the persuasive give and take that keeps the other signatures on side.[19] (The swing phenomenon shows that movement within panels after the post-hearing judicial conference is much more frequent than one might have assumed, making the willingness to consider negotiated revision a real concern.[20]) The current Supreme Court of Canada practice of co-authorship has similar implications: not only must two judges have negotiated a common position even more intensively than with the regular circulate-and-revise process but after the fact we cannot be sure which parts of the judgment belong to which member of the pair.[21] But *By the Court* is the most dramatic flourishing of collective reputation, with important decisions that are attributed to the institution itself, without any specific justice or justices accepting one iota of individual responsibility, whether for credit or blame.

This consideration does not imply that every judgment should be unanimous. Given the complexity of the law and the fact that the Supreme Court caseload is necessarily skewed toward the problematic and the previously unexplored, this is hardly a credible target. It is also true, given the multiple functions of a national high court, that the ideologically fraught issues that come before the court are often such that there must be some degree of accommodation of the losers, in the form of minority reasons showing that the loser's argument was heard sympathetically by at least part of the court. Restricting *By the Court* to a focused subset of the caseload is therefore a sensible strategy – constitutional law, especially federalism issues, and especially federal references.

This notion of a conscious court policy of sometimes contributing anonymously to a collective rather than an individual reputation may explain what is otherwise a mystery. The justices are accomplished individuals of experience and principle who have accepted appointment to the court and have assumed the responsibilities and pressures of its workload in order to make their own contribution to the evolution of Canadian law. That contribution is shaped by values, principles, and priorities that may be similar but are not identical for any pair of those justices, and so the attributed authorship of the judgment in significant cases is the way they live up to these expectations. Yet *By the Court* involves individuals who do the work only to eschew the credit of attribution, denying themselves the visible fingerprints on the law that would normally be their professional legacy. An emerging commitment to a collective reputation that competes with this pursuit of individual reputation is a credible explanation. By the same token, however, it must often be a hard sell to the individual justice or justices who have toiled over the drafting, and this may explain its restrained and somewhat sporadic use.

The emergence and expansion of the co-authorship practice represents a smaller step but one that is very much headed in the same direction with some of the same implications. Joint authorship represents a midpoint between the individual emphasis of solo attribution (even if that is constrained to some extent by the circulate-and-revise process) and the institutional emphasis of anonymous unanimity. The more extended history of *By the Court* still means that it has to be understood on its own terms, but the emergence of co-authorship suggests that it has become part of a broader phenomenon that now embraces a considerably larger, growing share of the caseload. Co-authorship raises some of the same lingering questions as *By the Court* always did: What is really going on behind the curtain? Was there really a lead author all the time, such that the Supreme Court's biographers have always been on the right track when they try to tease out who was actually doing the writing? Was there a genuine meeting of minds (all nine of them for *By the Court,* two or three of them for co-authorships) so that the reasons carry much the same authenticity as solo authorship, or were there differences that were papered over by careful drafting but that may emerge in the future?[22] This is the price of a continuing shift away from individualism to a more overtly institutional positioning.

This has been accompanied by another intriguing development, which we might call "the vanishing of the names." The major weapon in the court's persuasive arsenal is the citation of prior judicial decisions, and recent decades have seen a steady increase in the proportion of citations to prior decisions of the Supreme Court itself. Sometimes these citations provide the name of the specific judge who wrote the reasons (and, as noted above, until recently all judgments and reasons were attributed to a specific individual) and sometimes they do not. The Laskin court identified the writing judge in 39.8 percent of its citations, the Dickson court in 44.5 percent, and the Lamer court in 40.5 percent. For the McLachlin court, this same figure fell by a third, to 26.4 percent; even more to the point, it was 32.2 percent for the first five years of McLachlin's tenure as chief justice but only 20.4 percent for the last five years. Again, it is entirely appropriate to identify McLachlin herself as a leader in this process. During the first five years of her tenure, she named the writing judge in only 22.2 percent of her citations, which at the time made her a lonely outlier by a considerable margin. During her last five years on the court, this proportion of named citations dropped only slightly (to 19.2 percent), but this put her right in the middle of the judges on her court, which strongly suggests that the practice will survive her departure.

Not all citations are of the same type, of course. Some quote directly from an earlier decision or discuss it at length, some simply point to a single case as support for a particular statement or proposition, and some involve an American "string style" of citation that can list half a dozen or more cases to back up an idea. The proportion of all citations that involve direct quotation from the earlier judgment has not changed much over time – 30.1 percent for Lamer and 29.2 percent for McLachlin – but the likelihood that a direct quotation would be attributed to a specific named judge has fallen considerably. This happened 85 percent of the time for the Lamer court; it now (over the last five years) has fallen to less than 50 percent for the McLachlin court.

Citations are how the court links its decision in the immediate case to its own past, and to a steadily increasing extent this is being done in ways that point much less often to specific individual judges from earlier courts or the current court and much more often to an institutional product – "in such and such a case, the court decided" or "in an earlier case, the court said." A Supreme Court decision from twenty-five or thirty years ago was something of a historical survey of the great names from the history of the court – Duff and Rand and Laskin and Dickson walked side by side with Lamer and Sopinka and La Forest and Iacobucci, and almost every judicial decision directly referenced several of them by name. Not so with more recent decisions. Again, the swing is from individual reputation to institutional and collective reputation, and although it may be gradual and not yet complete, it has been persistent and cumulative.

What we have described are perhaps only modest steps away from the practices of the past toward a significantly different mode of judicial self-presentation. But all of them take us in the same direction, and modest steps are how institutions undertake change when they have solid practical and functional reasons for being reluctant to change. *By the Court* is arguably the most dramatic and high-profile of these changes, and the one that has the longest pedigree, but the importance it enjoys in its own right is enhanced by the fact that it has recently become part of this more broad-based shift.

Conclusion

We would like to close by considering what we will call "the Strangelove Problem." Our reference, of course, is to the 1964 movie *Dr. Strangelove or: How I Learned to Stop Worrying and Love the Bomb,* starring Peter Sellers in multiple roles. In the movie, an unhinged US Air Force general launches a first-strike nuclear attack on the Soviet Union, and the United States and the Soviet Union cooperate in trying to turn back (or, as a last resort, shoot down) the bombers, almost but not quite succeeding. The turning point is the discovery that the Soviet Union, fearing that it is losing the arms race, has set up a "doomsday device" that will automatically trigger a massive radioactive explosion that will end life on the planet. As Dr. Strangelove points out to the Russian ambassador, the whole point of having such a doomsday device is lost if you don't make sure everybody knows you have it.[23]

The same observation applies to the Supreme Court's use of *By the Court.* Surely the whole point of adopting a judgment delivery device for selected constitutional cases as a strategy for investing more heavily in the collective reputation of the Supreme Court and less in potentially corrosive individual reputations is completely wasted if nobody knows that you have adopted it and why. How can this have come about?

Part of the blame must lie with the court-watching academic community, which has exhibited a remarkable lack of curiosity about an unusual device that it sometimes casually notices for specific cases. Peter Hogg, whose *Constitutional Law of Canada* is arguably the major academic authority – cited by the Supreme Court more often than any other academic source – repeatedly acknowledges in a footnote that a particular decision was delivered *By the Court,* but with no indication of what significance (if any) we should attach to this fact.[24] It baffles us that law and political science professors have failed to take note of such an unusual emergent practice, and that there was no academic literature on the subject before the project of which this book is the final product.[25]

The Supreme Court itself is also partly to blame, however. For one thing, it has diluted the impact of the new practice by using the identical label for the routine formulaic (often as brief as a single twelve-word sentence) dismissal of appeals by right; we identified 160 uses of *By the Court* by the McLachlin court, a large majority of which exemplified this ongoing "minor tradition."[26] As a result, *By the Court* signals both "minor routine case" and "major constitutional case," a confusing juxtaposition. For another, the court has been less than consistent in its use of the device. We cannot say that "all major constitutional decisions are *By the Court*" or that "all *By the Court* decisions are major constitutional cases," but only that some major constitutional decisions account for some of the cases on the *By the Court* list. Furthermore, the court has never given any clear public or professional statement about the practice, in terms of when it uses the device and what significance attaches to it. We know from recent direct inquiry to the court that there is nothing along this line, either in the form of a policy directive from the court or a speech by the chief justice, nor has any *By the Court* decision (*Healy* aside) provided any explanation of why it was being used in the immediate case.[27] Even the biographies of Chief Justices Bora Laskin and Brian Dickson have treated the practice as something to be penetrated to identify the "real" author, rather than as a practice that calls for understanding on its own terms. Such an official statement might make it more likely that the practice will survive in a consistent way into the next chief justiceship and beyond.

"The next chief justiceship" is a critical consideration. It is obvious that chief justices make a difference – Gérald Fauteux completely ignored John Robert Cartwright's innovation, Laskin seems to have been reluctant passenger rather than deliberate leader, Dickson's use ("accidental" examples aside) was modest, and Antonio Lamer (*Quebec Secession Reference* aside) seemed unenthusiastic, while McLachlin has been the most persistent user.[28] The McLachlin court seemed to show an increase and consolidation with respect to *By the Court,* but what will happen now that McLachlin has gone? Has the practice become something that the court as an institution is comfortable with as the response of choice to certain kinds of challenging constitutional cases, or is it something that the McLachlin court was doing only because the chief justice encouraged it? The obvious answer is the clichéd "time will tell." But given that McLachlin has been succeeded by Richard Wagner, it is worth noting that he has been the Supreme Court's most frequent and prolific co-author to date. We have presented the McLachlin court as employing the most developed form to date of *By the Court,* and simultaneously developing a broader co-authorship practice that is in some sense a reflection of the same kind of institutional shift. We now leave hanging the question of whether this is but one step in a longer journey or a historic high-water mark.

Notes

Preface

1 *Attorney-General of Quebec v Blaikie et al.*, [1979] 2 SCR 1016 [*Blaikie*]; *Attorney-General of Manitoba v Forest*, [1979] 2 SCR 1032 [*Forest*].

Chapter 1: What Are *By the Court* Decisions?

1 Peter McCormick and Marc Zanoni, "The First 'By the Court' Decisions: The Emergence of a Practice on the Supreme Court of Canada" (2014) 38 Man LJ 1; Peter McCormick, "'By the Court' – the Untold Story of a Canadian Judicial Innovation" (2016) 53 Osgoode Hall LJ 1048; Peter McCormick, "*Nom de Plume:* Who Writes the Supreme Court's 'By the Court' Judgments?" (2016) 39 Dal LJ 77.

2 Some reviewers object to the use of the term "anonymity" when a panel declines to identify the lead author. It is not anonymous, they tell us, when all the judges have jointly signed the reasons, making them all equally identified authors. This objection is not entirely fanciful: the French judges' union has recently demanded that the anonymity of their non-attributed unanimous reasons be enhanced by not publishing the names of the judges serving on the panel, ratcheting secrecy up another notch. See Leonid Sirota, "Judges in Masks" (February 17, 2017), *Double Aspect* (law blog), online: https://doubleaspect.blog. Our position is that not being told which Supreme Court justice took the lead in writing the reasons is inscrutable enough and unusual enough to be labelled "anonymity," and we will use the term in this sense throughout this book.

3 *Reference re Secession of Quebec*, [1998] 2 SCR 217.

4 Alternatively, when biographers do notice that no specific author has been identified, they assure us that the subject of their book is really the author – when Girard, for example, tells us that a non-attributed major decision is clearly written in Laskin's distinctive style, or when Sharpe and Roach assure us that their access to the judge's private papers enables them to state with assurance that Dickson was the actual author. Philip Girard, *Bora Laskin: Bringing Law to Life* (Toronto: Osgoode Society for Canadian Legal History/University of Toronto Press, 2005); Robert Sharpe and Kent Roach, *Brian Dickson: A Judge's Journey* (Toronto: University of Toronto Press, 2003). For them, *By the Court* is not a deliberate choice in its own right that needs to be understood and explained but an inexplicably curious obscuring manoeuvre.

5 We will return to this idea in Chapter 4, explaining why we are not persuaded that it is the origin or the inspiration for our own court's distinctly different practices.

6 See Peter McCormick, "Structures of Judgment: How the Modern Supreme Court of Canada Organizes Its Reasons" (2009) 32 Dal LJ 35.

7 Starting twenty years ago, the attribution has increasingly been to a pair or even a trio of judges rather than to one alone; see Peter McCormick, "Sharing the Spotlight: Co-authored Reasons on the Modern Supreme Court of Canada" (2011) 34 Dal LJ 165. We will attach considerable importance to this development in our concluding chapters.

8 *R v Sheppard*, [2002] 1 SCR 869, 2002 SCC 26.

9 The Supreme Court itself records statistics on judgments that are "unanimous as to outcome" – that is, separate concurrences do not count – but we are using the term "unanimous" in the stricter sense of "univocal," the term suggested by Alan Paterson in *Final Judgment: The Last Law Lords and the Supreme Court* (Oxford: Hart, 2013). In contrast, in the United States Supreme Court, the apparently similar signal of a *per curiam* judgment is typically accompanied by the fragmentation of multiple reasons and more recently by an equal division that denies either set of reasons precedential authority.

10 *R v Aitkens*, 2017 SCC 14; *R v Peers*, 2017 SCC 13.

11 Ira P. Robbins, "The Supreme Court's Misuse of Per Curiam Opinions" (October 5, 2012), *SCOTUSblog* (blog), online: www.scotusblog.com/.

12 Interveners have become more frequent during the tenures of recent chief justices and now appear in approximately one-third to one-half of the cases heard by the Supreme Court. The presence of interveners – most commonly, federal or provincial attorneys-general – is therefore a reasonable indicator of some degree of case significance.

McCormick has shown that most Supreme Court decisions are never subsequently cited by the court, and most cases that are cited are cited only once or twice; see Peter McCormick, "Precedent by the Numbers: The Laskin Court" (Paper presented at the Midwest Political Science Association Annual Meeting, Chicago, April 2012). "Several citations" is therefore a much higher threshold than it might appear.

13 *Attorney-General of Manitoba v Forest*, [1979] 2 SCR 1032. A second omission would have been *Ahani v Canada*, 2002 SCC 2, the companion case to *Suresh v Canada*, 2002 SCC 1.

14 See, e.g., Elaine Mak, *Judicial Decision-Making in a Globalised World: A Comparative Analysis of the Changing Practices of Western Highest Courts* (Oxford: Hart, 2013).

15 With one striking and very recent British exception, discussed in Chapter 5.

16 *Re: Objection by Quebec to a Resolution to Amend the Constitution*, [1982] 2 SCR 793.

17 *Reference re Securities Act*, 2011 SCC 66.

18 *Ford v A.-G. (Quebec)*, [1988] 2 SCR 712; *Devine v A.G. (Quebec)*, [1988] 2 SCR 790.

19 *Daigle v Tremblay*, [1989] 2 SCR 530.

20 *United States v Burns*, 2001 SCC 7.

21 *Marshall 2: R v Marshall*, [1999] 3 SCR 533; *Marshall 1: R v Marshall*, [1999] 3 SCR 456.

22 *Re: Authority of Parliament in Relation to the Upper House*, [1980] 1 SCR 54; *Reference re Senate Reform*, 2014 SCC 32.

23 *Patriation Reference: Re: Resolution to Amend the Constitution*, [1981] 1 SCR 753; *Re: Exported Natural Gas Tax*, [1982] 1 SCR 1004; *Nadon* case: *Reference re Supreme Court Act, ss. 5 and 6*, 2014 SCC 21.

24 *Carter v Canada (Attorney General)*, 2016 SCC 4.

Chapter 2: The Supreme Court of Canada Takes to the Constitutional Stage

1 *Severn v The Queen* (1878) 2 SCR 70; *City of Fredericton v The Queen* (1880) 3 SCR 505; *Citizens' and The Queen Insurance Cos. v Parsons* (1880) 4 SCR 215.

2 The practice of an "appellate committee" within the King's Privy Council seems to date back to the seventeenth century, and by 1833 non-lawyer members were excluded and the bulk of the membership was made up of current or previous members of the House of Lords, supplemented after 1895 by provisions for senior justices from Australia, South Africa, and Canada to serve as well. For the history and practices of the Judicial Committee, see Loren P. Beth, "The Judicial Committee: Its Development, Organization and Procedure" (1975) 3 PL 219; and Loren P. Beth, "The Judicial Committee of the Privy Council and the Development of Judicial Review" (1976) 24 Am J Comp L 22.

3 To this day, it continues to refer to itself as "the board" rather than as a court.

4 *Seriatim* means "one after the other," the point being that all or almost all the members of the panel present their own free-standing and independent judgments, rather than organizing themselves into a majority bloc and possibly confronting dissenting reasons. We will explore the notion of *seriatim* in Chapter 3. After 1966, amendments to the relevant legislation opened up the possibility of minority

reasons in the Judicial Committee of the Privy Council, which are still unusual but do occur.

5 See James G. Snell and Frederick Vaughan, *The Supreme Court of Canada: History of the Institution* (Toronto: University of Toronto Press, 1985).

6 (1881), 7 AC 96 (PC).

7 [1989] 1 SCR 641.

8 (1882), 7 AC 829 (PC).

9 (1887), 12 AC 575 (PC).

10 *Attorney General of Ontario v Attorney General of Canada*, [1896] AC 348.

11 See W.H. McConnell, "The Judicial Review of Prime Minister Bennett's 'New Deal'" (1968) Osgoode Hall LJ 39.

12 The situation was complicated by the fact that although the Conservative government of R.B. Bennett had framed the constitutional challenges, by the time the cases were heard by the Judicial Committee it was the Liberal government of Mackenzie King that was defending them in London.

13 *Radio Reference: Reference re Regulation and Control of Radio Communication* [1932] AC 304; *Labour Conventions Reference: Canada (Attorney-General) v Ontario (Attorney General)*, [1937] UKPC 6, [1937] AC 326. The question is not whether or not Canada could now enter into treaties on its own behalf – clearly it could – but rather whether the existence of a valid treaty necessarily gave the federal government the jurisdiction to carry out its commitments under the treaty even if those would override the s 91/s 92 division of legislative authority. The *Labour Conventions Reference* stands for the principle that such treaties did not validate such an expansion of jurisdiction.

14 *Supreme Court Act*, RSC 1985, c S-26, s 52.

15 Bora Laskin, "The Supreme Court of Canada: A Final Court of and for Canadians" (1951) 29 Can Bar Rev 1038. Almost thirty years later, it was Chief Justice Bora Laskin who declared that Judicial Committee decisions were no longer binding precedent for the Supreme Court of Canada in *Re: Agricultural Marketing Act*, [1978] 2 SCR 1198.

16 Only in the 1970s did the Supreme Court adopt a policy of reporting every single decision; in earlier years, a certain amount of selectivity was involved in deciding whether a case was significant enough to be reported. Arguably, however, the primary effect would be to reduce the total count of reported cases but not the count of constitutional cases, which would be considerably more likely to pass the selection process. See Anne Roland, "Official Law Reporting in Canada" (Paper presented at the Second International Symposium in Official Law Reporting, New York City, 2004).

17 Because the *Supreme Court Reports* did not report every single judgment during this time period, but deliberately selected the more significant cases for reporting, we think that this exaggerates the proportion of constitutional cases for these decades – constitutional cases (many of which were federal reference cases) are

much more likely to pass the significance threshold, so that count is reasonably accurate, but the total count is reduced by the omission of non-constitutional cases.

18 In practice, the "notional one-ninth" is not a realistic presentation of the way that the judgment-delivery workload is divided, especially for constitutional cases, with some judges having considerably more, and a set of judges considerably less, than this equal share. See Peter McCormick, "Judgment and Opportunity: Decision Assignment on the McLachlin Court" (2015) 38 Dal LJ 271.

19 *Insite: Canada (Attorney General) v PHS Community Services Society*, 2011 SCC 44; *Reference re Securities Act*, 2011 SCC 66 [*Securities Act Reference*]; *Reference re Senate Reform*, 2014 SCC 32.

20 When political scientists refer to "cooperative federalism," they are referring to the 1950s and 1960s, when the federal government used conditional grants under the federal spending power to entice provinces to enact parallel policies with built-in national standards and transferability by means of conditional grant programs, normally paying one-half of all the costs of delivering such programs. This is not at all what the Supreme Court is suggesting; "accommodative federalism" might be a more apt description.

21 The notion receives only a passing mention in the *Securities Act Reference, supra* note 19, but it is more closely described in cases such as *Quebec (Attorney General) v Canadian Owners and Pilots Association*, 2010 SCC 39; *Saskatchewan (Attorney General) v Lemare Lake Logging Ltd.*, 2015 SCC 53; and *Alberta (Attorney General) v Moloney*, 2015 SCC 51. However, the court split rather spectacularly 5-4 on how to apply the notion to Quebec's demand for information from the defunct federal firearms registry in *Quebec (Attorney General) v Canada (Attorney General)*, 2015 SCC 14.

22 *R v Morgentaler*, [1988] 1 SCR 30.

23 *Andrews v Law Society of British Columbia*, [1989] 1 SCR 143. "So-called" because they are not in fact *numbered* in the constitutional document, which is what "enumerated" would lead one to expect.

24 *Egan v Canada*, [1995] 2 SCR 513; *Vriend v Alberta*, [1998] 1 SCR 493.

25 *Rodriguez v British Columbia (Attorney General)*, [1993] 3 SCR 519; *Carter v Canada (Attorney General)*, 2015 SCC 5.

26 *Constitution Act, 1982*, being Schedule B to the *Canada Act 1982* (UK), 1982, c 11. Somewhat curiously, governments do not normally cooperate with this, and a search of websites such as CanLII will still turn up the current version of the statutes, including the offending sections of constitutionally challenged statutes.

27 *R v Big M Drug Mart Ltd.*, [1985] 1 SCR 295.

28 The critical case that introduced suspended invalidation as a Charter remedy (although without applying it in the immediate case) was *Schachter v Canada*, [1992] 2 SCR 679.

29 See Bruce Ryder, "Suspending the Charter" (2003) 21 Sup Ct L Rev (2d ser.) 267.

30 The case was *R v Latimer,* 2001 SCC 1, but its treatment is perplexing. The notion of a "constitutional exemption" is listed as one of the six issues before the court, but the ultimate conclusion is that it was "not necessary" to answer this question.

31 In *Kingstreet Investments Ltd. v New Brunswick (Finance),* 2007 SCC 1, Bastarache J condemned the idea for raising problems of "horizontal equity" and failing to ensure that "all similarly situated persons are treated the same." The following year, McLachlin CJ in *R v Ferguson,* 2008 SCC 6, was even blunter, saying that constitutional exemptions "buy flexibility at the cost of undermining the rule of law." *Carter* decision: *Carter v Canada (Attorney General)* 2016 SCC 4.

32 See Peter McCormick, *The End of the Charter Revolution: Looking Back from the New Normal* (Toronto: University of Toronto Press, 2015).

33 *Calder v Attorney-General of British Columbia,* [1973] SCR 313.

34 *R v Van der Peet,* [1996] 2 SCR 507; *R v N.T.C. Smokehouse Ltd.*, [1996] 2 SCR 672; *R v Gladstone,* [1996] 2 SCR 723; *Delgamuukw v British Columbia,* [1997] 3 SCR 1010.

35 *Tsilhqot'in Nation v British Columbia,* 2014 SCC 44.

36 The court steered clear of the question of Aboriginal self-government most notably in *R v Pamajewon,* [1996] 2 SCR 821. Regarding its accomplishment through the treaty process, see, e.g., Jennifer E. Dalton, "Aboriginal Self-Determination in Canada: Protections Afforded by Judiciary and Government" (2006) 21 CJLS 11; and Timothy Dickson, "Self Government by Side Agreement?" (2004) 49 McGill LJ 420.

37 *R v Marshall,* [1999] 3 SCR 456.

38 *R v Marshall,* [1999] 3 SCR 533. The central issue of these and other cases is whether or not an individual Aboriginal right to hunt or fish or otherwise exploit natural resources can legitimately be expanded to include the right of an Aboriginal community to engage in commerce with respect to those resources. Generally, the court has treated this as a question of whether the specific Aboriginal community at the time of European contact was engaged in practices that amounted to commercial exploitation of the resource in question.

39 *Daniels v Canada (Indian Affairs and Northern Development),* 2016 SCC 12; *Constitution Act (An Act for the Union of Canada, Nova Scotia, and New Brunswick, and the Government thereof; and for Purposes connected therewith) 1867,* 30 and 31 Vict., c. 3 (originally known as the *British North America Act*).

40 *Reference re Remuneration of Judges of the Provincial Court of Prince Edward Island; Reference re Independence and Impartiality of Judges of the Provincial Court of Prince Edward Island,* [1997] 3 SCR 3.

41 *Reference re Secession of Quebec,* [1998] 2 SCR 217.

42 *Canada (House of Commons) v Vaid,* 2015 SCC 30.

43 *Reference re Supreme Court Act, ss. 5 and 6,* 2014 SCC 21.

44 *Extradition Treaty between Canada and the United States of America,* Can TS 1976 No 3; *United States v Burns,* 2001 SCC 7.

Chapter 3: Why Decision Presentation Formats Matter

1 Nuno Garoupa and Tom Ginsburg, *Judicial Reputation: A Comparative Theory* (Chicago and London: University of Chicago Press, 2015) at 3.

2 James L. Gibson, Gregory A. Caldeira, and Vanessa Baird, "On the Legitimacy of National High Courts" (1998) 92 American Political Science Rev 343.

3 Although some federal and state court judges in the United States have indeed used verse (although not, to our knowledge, rap) to present decisions. See the "Parody and Verse in Opinions" list on the University of Washington law school website, https://lib.law.washington.edu/content/guides/judhumor.

4 A case in point is the controversy that Justice Russell Brown recently provoked, in his decision in *Canada v Igloo Vikski Inc.*, 2016 SCC 38, when his opening paragraph echoed – with casual whimsy but appropriate acknowledgment – both Justice Denning's famous "cricket case" dissent and Ken Dryden's book *The Game* before proceeding to a more standard exposition and analysis. This earned Justice Brown an accusation of "judicial arrogance" on one of Canada's leading law blogs: Alice Woolley, "The Problem of Judicial Arrogance" (October 20, 2016), *Slaw* (blog), online: www.slaw.ca.

5 As a result, and as one might expect, there is not much of a literature on the subject. We would acknowledge Rudolph Delson, "Typography in the U.S. Reports and Supreme Court Voting Protocols" (2001) 76 NYUL Rev 1203; William D. Popkin, *Evolution of the Judicial Opinion: Institutional and Individual Styles* (New York: New York University Press, 2007); and Chris Hanretty, "The Structure of Supreme Court Judgments: Eleven Ways to Leave One's Mark" (2013) 2 Cambridge J Intl & Comparative L 41. Peter McCormick examines the question in the Canadian context in "Structures of Judgment: How the Modern Supreme Court of Canada Organizes Its Reasons" (2009) 32 Dal LJ 35 [McCormick, "Structures of Judgment"].

6 McCormick "discovered" the most recent major shift only when student research assistants grumbled that database coding of Supreme Court decisions was much more difficult for earlier years than for the 1990s, which had been the starting point for that particular project. The explanation for the difference was a major change in the format for the presentation of Supreme Court decisions, such that the "new" style did, and the "old" style did not, routinely display in an accessible way all the information that McCormick was interested in coding.

7 Michael J. Gerhardt, *The Power of Precedent* (Oxford: Oxford University Press, 2008) at 62.

8 For an explanation and defence of the minimalist approach, see Cass R. Sunstein, *One Case at a Time: Judicial Minimalism on the Supreme Court*, rev. ed. (Cambridge, MA: Harvard University Press, 2001).

9 See Virgilio Afonso da Silva, "Deciding without Deliberating" (2013) 11 Int'l J Const L 557.

10 For an account of this episode and Laskin's position on it, see Philip Girard, *Bora Laskin: Bringing Law to Life* (Toronto: Osgoode Society for Canadian Legal History/ University of Toronto Press, 2005) at 187.

11 See Peter McCormick, "Duets, Not Solos: The McLachlin Court's Co-authorship Legacy" (2018) 41 Dal LJ 479.

12 Five was the *maximum* size of a Supreme Court panel before the court was expanded from six justices to seven in 1927, and it remained the *normal* size of a panel for some time after that. Under Laskin and subsequent chief justices, there has been a steady tendency toward an expanded use of larger panel sizes of seven and nine.

13 There is currently some debate within the English legal profession as to whether the new Supreme Court of the United Kingdom should, as its Law Lords predecessor did, follow a *seriatim* practice, and this section of our discussion reflects this conversation. See Alan Paterson, *Final Judgment: The Last Law Lords and the Supreme Court* (Oxford: Hart, 2013).

14 Josh Friedman, Book Review of *Dissent and the Supreme Court* by Melvin Urofsky (Pantheon, 2015), *Columbia Magazine* (Winter 2015–16), online: http://magazine.columbia.edu.

15 See Michael J. Gerhardt, *The Power of Precedent* (Oxford: Oxford University Press, 2008) at 62. "There was, in effect, no precedent until a later majority declared what it was."

16 Barry Friedman, Andrew Martin, Thomas B. Bennett, and Susan Navarro Smelcer, "Divide and Concur: Separate Opinions and Legal Change" (2017) 103 Cornell L Rev 817 at 820.

17 *Ibid.*

18 *Ibid.*

19 See Claire L'Heureux-Dubé, "The Length and Plurality of Supreme Court of Canada Decisions" (1990) 28 Alta L Rev 581.

20 Within this tradition, any set of reasons written by any judge, whether or not it was on the prevailing side of a divided court, was labelled a judgment. This point will be expanded on below.

21 Peter Hogg and Ravi Amarnath, "Why Should Judges Dissent?" (2017) 67 UTLJ 128.

22 Rebecca Gill, "Consensus or Ambivalence: Why Court Traditions Matter" (June 29, 2011), online: Social Science Research Network, https://ssrn.com/abstract=1881961.

23 [1954] SCR 127.

24 *MacDonald v Vapor Canada Ltd.*, [1977] 2 SCR 134 at 165.

25 Or to the appealed-from decision of a provincial court of appeal that has not adopted a format or standard descriptions that comparably embody the judgment/reasons distinction.

26 This pitches it perhaps a little too strongly, because, as McCormick has demonstrated, the dissents and separate concurrences of post-1970 decisions of the court are in fact cited and quoted approvingly by the current court, sometimes to the eclipse of the majority judgment from which they separated themselves. See Peter McCormick, "Second Thoughts: Supreme Court Citations of Dissents and Separate Concurrences, 1949–1996" (2001) 81 Can Bar Rev 369.

27 See Peter McCormick, "Judgment and Opportunity: Decision Assignment on the McLachlin Court" (2015) 38 Dal LJ 271 [McCormick, "Judgment and Opportunity"].

28 On post-hearing conferences, see Hogg and Amarnath, *supra* note 21 at 128. This is a much less routine accomplishment than one might expect; neither the Australian High Court nor the Supreme Court of the United Kingdom has achieved it, despite several attempts.

Pinpointing the emergence of the "judgment/reasons" distinction is complicated by the fact that it was only when two or more judges were joining that the *Supreme Court Reports* at the time typically used any label at all to introduce the text; for solo reasons, which were common, we simply find the name of the judge followed by the reasons.

29 "Problematic handful" refers to cases where the panel has divided in such a way that there is no single set of reasons that draws even the qualified support of a majority of the panel. Most such plurality outcomes permit the identification of a "judgment," but a small number do not. We have been able to identify only a single case – *Comité paritaire de l'industrie de la chemise v Potash*, [1994] 2 SCR 406 – that was reported with two separate judgments, an apparent logical impossibility explained by the fact that two of the judges on the nine-judge panel signed both sets of reasons.

30 Before 2005, the publication sequencing was directed by the seniority of the writer of the reasons, such that a dissent could be, and frequently was, published first among the reasons if it was written by a senior justice.

31 See Ian Greene et al., *Final Appeal: Decision-Making in Canadian Courts of Appeal* (Toronto: James Lorimer, 1998) at 121.

32 The strictness of the protocol also enables us to identify those occasions when the initial writer for the majority has lost so much support that the judgment is actually written by a colleague who was initially presenting minority reasons – this is the only way that a judgment can begin with "I have read the reasons." See Peter McCormick, "'Was It Something I Said?' Losing the Majority on the Modern Supreme Court of Canada 1984–2011" (2012) 50 Osgoode Hall LJ 93.

33 See McCormick, "Structures of Judgment," *supra* note 5.

34 Da Silva, *supra* note 9.

35 John Alder, "Dissents in Courts of Last Resort: Tragic Choices?" (2000) 20 Oxford J Legal Stud 221 at 235.

36 The more so because the *Supreme Court Reports* are the official reporting service for the Supreme Court and operate under the ultimate supervisory authority of the chief justice. This was an insider's label, not an outsider's imposition.
37 Gill, *supra* note 22.
38 The appearance in the mid-1990s and expansion under McLachlin of a judgment delivery style where two (and, more recently, occasionally three) judges from the majority present themselves as joint co-authors of the reasons might be thought of as a modest further step in the same direction. For a discussion of the co-authorship phenomenon see Peter McCormick, "Sharing the Spotlight: Co-Authored Reasons on the Modern Supreme Court of Canada" (2011) 34 Dal LJ 165.
39 Or, as a slightly amusing reversal of the question of which judges on the Supreme Court are the most significant, we can search for the most insignificant justice. See David P. Currie, "The Most Insignificant Justice: A Preliminary Inquiry" (1983) 50 U Chicago L Rev 466, and a comparably tongue-in-cheek response by Frank H. Easterbrook, "The Most Insignificant Justice: Further Evidence" (1983) 50 U Chicago L Rev 481.
40 See McCormick, "Judgment and Opportunity," *supra* note 27.
41 See Peter McCormick, "What Supreme Court Cases Does the Supreme Court Cite?" (1996) 7 Sup Ct L Rev (2d ser.) 452.
42 Mitchel de S.-O.-l'E. Lasser, *Judicial Deliberations: A Comparative Analysis of Judicial Transparency and Legitimacy* (Oxford: Oxford University Press, 2009).
43 Although the desire for a good professional reputation is an element of judicial behaviour that should not be overlooked. See, e.g., Richard A. Posner, *Cardozo: A Study in Reputation* (Chicago: University of Chicago Press, 1993). See also Richard A. Posner, "What Do Judges and Justices Maximize?" (1993) 3 Sup Ct Econ Rev 1: "A significant element of the judicial utility function is reputation, both with other judges, especially ones on the same court – one's colleagues – and with the legal profession at large." "Threat of searing professional criticism": Richard A. Posner, *The Federal Courts: Challenge and Reform* (Cambridge, MA: Harvard University Press, 1999) at 349.
44 Ruth Bader Ginsburg, "Remarks on Writing Separately" (1990) 65 Wash L Rev 133 at 139.
45 Ira P. Robbins, "Hiding behind the Cloak of Invisibility: The Supreme Court and Per Curiam Opinions" (2012) 86 Tul L Rev 1215.
46 For an example of the first approach, see Robert Sharpe and Kent Roach, *Brian Dickson: A Judge's Journey* (Toronto: University of Toronto Press, 2003). For an example of the second approach, see Girard, *supra* note 10.
47 Not necessarily indefensible because, for example, courts are routinely more parsimonious about what they report and how they report it for family law decisions

and national security decisions. Leonid Sirota, "Says Who, Again?" (January 10, 2017), *Double Aspect* (blog), online: doubleaspect.blog.

Chapter 4: Originality

1 Paul Weiler, *In the Last Resort: A Critical Study of the Supreme Court of Canada* (Toronto: Carswell, 1974).
2 See, e.g., Anne-Marie Slaughter, "A Global Community of Courts" (2001) 44 Harv Int'l LJ 191; and Anne-Marie Slaughter, "Judicial Globalization" (2000) 40 Va J Int'l L 1103.
3 "Role of the JCPC," online: Judicial Committee of the Privy Council, http://www.jcpc.uk.
4 See Terence Ingman, *The English Legal Process,* 13th ed. (Oxford: Oxford University Press, 2011) at 98.
5 Curiously, the actual published decision for a number of cases in the late 1870s and early 1880s does not include an attributed author, giving a tantalizing impression of a genuine forerunner for *By the Court.* This appears to be a temporary reporting quirk, however, rather than a genuine change in practice. Historians such as John Saywell in his *The Lawmakers: Judicial Power and the Shaping of Canadian Federalism* (Toronto: University of Toronto Press, 2002) have no hesitation in precisely identifying from the accounts of the day the specific solo authors of a string of these "no visible author" decisions. See in particular Saywell's c 5, which deals with this period.
6 See, e.g., F.M. Greenwood, "Lord Watson, Institutional Self-Interest, and the Decentralization of Canadian Federalism in the 1890s" (1974) 9 UBC L Rev 244; Frederick Vaughan, *Viscount Haldane: "The Wicked Step-Father of the Canadian Constitution"* (Toronto: Osgoode Society for Canadian Legal History/University of Toronto Press, 2010). See also David Schneiderman's very critical book review, "Haldane Unrevealed" (2012) 57 McGill LJ 597.
7 *Cukurova Finance International Limited and Cukurova Holding A.S. v Alfa Telecom Turkey Ltd,* [2013] UKPC 2 (January 30, 2013) at para 1, online: British and Irish Legal Information Institute, http://www.bailii.org.
8 *Cukurova Finance International Limited and Cukurova Holdings A.S. v Alfa Telecom Turkey Limited,* [2013] UKPC 25.
9 This is no longer remotely true. The McLachlin court cites previous Supreme Court cases over ten times as often as it cites all English courts combined. See Peter McCormick, "American Citations and the McLachlin Court: An Empirical Study" (2009) 47 Osgoode Hall LJ 83.
10 Ian Bushnell, "The Use of American Cases" (1986) 35 UNBLJ 157 at 160.
11 Editorial Comment, "The Use of American Legal Literature" (1943) 21 Can Bar Rev 57; J.M. MacIntyre, "The Use of American Cases in Canadian Courts" (1966) 2 UBC L Rev 478 at 479–80.

12 Gérard V. La Forest, "The Use of American Precedents in Canadian Courts" (1994) 46 Me L Rev 211 at 217.

13 Claire L'Heureux-Dubé, "The Dissenting Opinion: Voice of the Future?" (2000) 38 Osgoode Hall LJ 495 at 500–1. Embarrassingly, her footnote reference for this comment is an earlier article by McCormick, who now recants such a suggestion.

14 F.L. Morton, ed., *Law, Politics and the Judicial Process in Canada,* 1st ed. (Calgary: University of Calgary Press, 1984); *Brown v Board of Education of Topeka,* 347 US 483 (1954).

15 *Bush v Gore,* 531 US 98 (2000).

16 See Stephen L. Wasby, Steven Peterson, James Schubert, and Glendon Schubert, "The Per Curiam Opinions: Its Nature and Functions" (1992) 76 Judicature 29; Laura Krugman Ray, "The Road to *Bush v Gore:* The History of the Supreme Court's Use of the Per Curiam Opinion" (2000) 79 Neb L Rev 518 [Ray, "Road to *Bush v Gore*"]; and Michael C. Gizzi and Stephen L. Wasby, "Per Curiams Revisited: Assessing the Unsigned Opinion" (2012) 96 Judicature 110.

17 John Council, "Who Wrote for the Majority in Controversial Abortion Decision?" *Texas Lawyer* (June 10, 2015), online: *Texas Lawyer,* www.texaslawyer.com; Ira P. Robbins, "The Supreme Court's Misuse of Per Curiam Opinions" (October 5, 2012) *SCOTUSblog* (blog), online: www.scotusblog.com.

18 Robbins, *ibid.*

19 See the "Stat Pack" on *SCOTUSblog* (blog), online: www.scotusblog.com.

20 Constance Baker Motley, "*Brown v Board of Education* and Its Legacy" (1992) 61 Fordham L Rev 1, fn 39 at 16. "Eleven words or less": Jeff VanDam, "The Per Curiam Cases: How the Post-*Brown* Court Changed America in Eleven Words or Less," online: Social Science Research Network, http:ssrn.com/abstract=2264397. "Without any discursive explanation": see, e.g., Dennis J. Hutchinson, "Unanimity and Desegregation: Decisionmaking in the Supreme Court, 1948–1958" (1979) 68 Geo LJ 1.

21 Alexander Bickel and Harry H. Wellington, "Legislative Purpose and the Judicial Process: The Lincoln Mills Case" (1957) 71 Harv L Rev 1 at 3–4.

22 Wasby et al., *supra* note 16.

23 Ray, "Road to *Bush v Gore,*" *supra* note 16 at 561.

24 *Ibid.* at 542.

25 Laura Krugman Ray, "Circumstance and Strategy: Jointly Authored Supreme Court Opinions" (2012) 12 Nev LJ 727 [Ray, "Circumstance and Strategy"].

26 Frankfurter signed the all-justice opinion and also wrote a separate concurrence. As a general rule, judges on common law panel courts do one or the other, but "one signature per decision" is a general expectation rather than a firm protocol. For the Supreme Court of Canada one can also assemble a list of several dozen "double signature" decisions.

27 Ray, "Circumstance and Strategy," *supra* note 25 at 748.

28 These are cases where the full court of nine judges was able to hear oral arguments, but the panel was reduced to eight by Scalia's death. Unlike the Supreme Court of Canada, the US Supreme Court does not set panels of varying sizes, but given the persistent cleavages on the American court, it would be just as problematic to decide which justice would be left off any particular smaller panel.

29 American practice is to use the term "opinion," whereas Canada uses the term "judgment."

30 The case is *Moir v Huntington* (1891) 19 SCR 363.

31 *R v Morgentaler*, [1988] 1 SCR 30. Jury nullification is the idea that a jury can simply ignore the statute to reach an outcome that it prefers, and that a lawyer can directly suggest this to the jury in his or her summation.

32 See, e.g., Mitchel de S.-O.-l'E. Lasser, *Judicial Deliberations: A Comparative Analysis of Transparency and Legitimacy* (Oxford: Oxford University Press, 2009).

Chapter 5: Uniqueness

1 For example, both the United States Supreme Court and the Supreme Court of Canada started off with a strong preference for the *seriatim* – everybody writes – style of judgment delivery, and the reasonable assumption is that this was largely because of the example of the similar practice by the highly regarded House of Lords. On the other hand, both the US Supreme Court and the Supreme Court of Canada gradually abandoned the practice even though it persisted in the House of Lords.

2 It is echoed by some, but by no means all, of the Circuit Courts of Appeal in the federal court system.

3 Rudolph Delson, "Typography in the U.S. Reports and Supreme Court Voting Protocols" (2001) 76 NYUL Rev 1203. Delson's speculation is that this emerged as a stylistic accommodation of the increasing length of Supreme Court decisions, rather than specifically to deal with the sharp increase in minority reasons.

4 The case was *Williams v Taylor*, 529 US 362 (2000).

5 Which is not to deny that the actual practice of conferencing and circulating drafts to draw responses and suggestions for revisions may in fact be very similar between the two courts. The point is that the way they choose to present the outcome is subtly but importantly different.

6 Pamela C. Corley, Amy Steigerwalt, and Artemus Ward, *The Puzzle of Unanimity: Consensus on the United States Supreme Court* (Stanford, CA: Stanford Law Books, 2013).

7 John Alder, "Dissents in Courts of Last Resort: Tragic Choices?" (2000) 20 Oxford J Legal Stud 221.

8 *Cukurova Finance International Limited and Cukurova Holding A.S. v Alfa Telecom Turkey Ltd*, [2013] UKPC 2 (January 30, 2013) at para 1, online: British and Irish Legal Information Institute, www.bailii.org.

9 *Cukurova Finance International Limited & Cukurova Holdings A.S. v Alfa Telecom Turkey Limited*, [2013] UKPC 25.

10 Rosa Raffaelli, *Dissenting Opinions in the Supreme Courts of the Member States* (Brussels: European Parliament/Policy Department, 2012) at 29, online: European Parliament, www.europarl.europa.edu.

11 The style of the United States Supreme Court is different again – an "opinion" (we would say "judgment") of the court is indicated as authored by a specific individual, and others sign on (or not) to specific "parts" of that majority opinion. See Delson, *supra* note 3.

12 See, e.g., John T. Saywell, *The Lawmakers: Judicial Power and the Shaping of Canadian Federalism* (Toronto: University of Toronto Press, 2002).

13 *R. (on the application of Miller and another) (Respondents) v Secretary of State for Exiting the European Union (Appellant)*, [2017] UKSC 5.

14 Erin F. Delaney, "Judiciary Rising: Constitutional Change in the United Kingdom" (2014) 108 Nw UL Rev 543.

15 *Reference re Supreme Court Act, ss. 5 and 6*, 2014 SCC 21.

16 *Re: Resolution to Amend the Constitution*, [1981] 1 SCR 753.

17 This is an ongoing issue in Australia and has been the subject of at least one Royal Commission (in 1927). At one time, the High Court seemed to have such a jurisdiction under the *Judiciary Act*, but it decided in 1921 that the relevant section was itself unconstitutional – *Re Judiciary and Navigation Acts* (1921), 29 CLR 257. See John M. Williams, "Advisory Opinions: 'A Well Covered Harbor'" (2010) 22 Bond L Rev 169; Helen Irving, "Advisory Opinions, the Rule of Law, and the Separation of Powers" (2004) 4 Macquarie UL Rev 105; and John M. Williams, "Re-thinking Advisory Opinions" (1996) 7 Pub L Rev 205.

18 Comments based on statistics generated by the authors from the year-by-year decision database, online: Australasian Legal Information Institute, www.austlii.edu.au.

19 Reginald S. Sheehan, Rebecca D. Gill, and Kirk A. Randazzo, *Judicialization of Politics: The Interplay of Institutional Structure, Legal Doctrine and Politics on the High Court of Australia* (Durham, NC: Carolina Academic Press, 2012) at 142.

20 "The practice of the High Court has varied from informal conferences among the justices after the hearing of a case to the circulation of draft judgments without any conference taking place." Cosmas Moisidis, "Achieving the World's Best Practice in the Writing of Appellate Judgments" (2001) 66 L Institute J 30. See also Susan Kiefel (Justice, HCA), "Reasons for Judgment: Objects and Observations" (Speech delivered on May 18, 2012, and published in 2014: 88 Aust LJ 554).

21 Since minority reasons, concurring and dissenting, are often attributed to solo judges, this reveals both a style of writing and a minority position on some issues that later becomes a majority position, and both are strong hints as to the authorship of later reasons.

22 Zoe Robinson, "A Comparative Analysis of the Doctrinal Consequences of Interpretive Disagreement for Implied Constitutional Rights" (2012) 11 Wash U Global Studies L Rev 97.

23 Andrew Lynch, "The Gleeson Court on Constitutional Law: An Empirical Analysis of Its First Five Years" (2003) 26 UNSWLJ 32; Rebecca Gill, "Consensus or Ambivalence: Why Court Traditions Matter" (June 29, 2011), online: Social Science Research Network, https://ssrn.com/abstract=1881961; Rosalind Dixon and Tom Ginsburg, "Introduction" in Tom Ginsburg and Rosalind Dixon, eds., *Comparative Constitutional Law* (Cheltenham, UK, and Northampton, MA: Edward Elgar, 2011) at 11.

24 An earlier court established in 1841 had also been named "the Supreme Court of New Zealand" but it was a trial court, initially with only a single judge, and after 1957 its decisions could be appealed to the Court of Appeal. It was renamed "the High Court" in 1980.

25 The legislation says five or six justices, but in practice it has always been five. Perusing its decision list on the New Zealand Legal Information Institute at www.nzlii.org gives a different impression of the court's caseload, with 150–200 entries per year, but almost all of these deal with applications of various kinds – applications for leave to appeal, or extensions of deadlines, or submission of new evidence, or "recall" (i.e., reconsideration of a prior decision on an appeal or application), or review of awards of costs, or review of decisions of the registrar; almost all of these are dealt with by a panel of three judges (rarely four, almost never five). The count indicated is for actual appeals allowed or dismissed, which is always by the full court of five justices.

26 Stephen Gardbaum, "The New Commonwealth Model of Constitutionalism" (2001) 49 Am J Comp L 79. Mark Tushnet has made the same distinction in terms of "strong-form" and "weak-form" judicial review; see Mark Tushnet, *Weak Courts, Strong Rights: Judicial Review and Social Welfare Rights in Comparative Constitutional Law* (Princeton, NJ: Princeton University Press, 2009).

27 "Historical Background of the Constitutional Court," online: South African History Online, www.sahistory.org.za/historical-background-constitutional-court. The newness is also signalled by the judges' specially designed green robes.

28 A significant Canadian influence is worth noting: "[J]udgments of the Canadian courts relating to their Charter were particularly helpful in dealing with cases concerning the new South African Bill of Rights." Johann Kriegler, "The Constitutional Court of South Africa" (2003) 36 Cornell Int'l LJ 363.

29 "Constitutional Court of South Africa," online: Constitutional Court of South Africa, www.constitutionalcourt.org.za.

30 "Condonation" means letting a case go ahead even though some requirement or deadline has been violated. Regarding "direct access," in addition to its appellate jurisdiction, the Constitutional Court can, under unusual circumstances, hear a constitutional case on an original hearing basis.

31 *Hlophe v Premier of Western Cape Province*, [2012] ZACC 4.
32 *Justice Alliance of South Africa v President of the Republic of South Africa*, [2011] ZACC 23.
33 *Residents of Joe Slovo Community, Western Cape, v Thubelisha Homes*, [2009] ZACC 16.
34 In a slightly different context, Robinson refers to this as "polyvocality" – there is no single court that speaks with a single voice, but rather a shifting set of small, separate panels, each of which may have a slightly (or sometimes a starkly) different interpretation of the law. See Nick Robinson, "Structure Matters" (2013) 61 Am J Comp L 173.
35 André Bzdera, "Comparative Analysis of Federal High Courts: A Political Theory of Judicial Review" (1993) 26 Can J Political Science 27. He provides no footnote reference for this assertion, and a closer reading suggests that it is really the unanimity of the decisions, not their anonymity, that he wishes to emphasize.

Chapter 6: Early History

1 This chapter is a very condensed version of Marc Zanoni's master's thesis at the University of Lethbridge; see Marc Zanoni, *An Early History of the "By the Court" Decisions on the Supreme Court of Canada* (MA thesis, University of Lethbridge, 2015), online: University of Lethbridge, http://www.uleth.ca.
2 The case was *Martley v Carson*, (1886) 13 SCR 439, decided on March 26, 1886, and reported on May 17, 1886. It dealt with a motion to dismiss an appeal on the grounds of excessive delay, and the decision is presented without further explanation as "By the court: motion refused with costs."
3 James G. Snell and Frederick Vaughan, *The Supreme Court of Canada: History of the Institution* (Toronto: University of Toronto Press, 1985).
4 The relevant section of the *Supreme Court Act* is s 17, which provides that "the Registrar or the Deputy Registrar, as the chief justice directs, shall report and publish the judgments of the Court." Anne Roland, "Official Law Reporting in Canada" (Paper presented at the Second International Symposium in Official Law Reporting, New York City, 2004).
5 Readers may have noticed the escape hatch "as the chief justice directs," which would seem to make selective reporting a possibility, but it does not appear from the early accounts that this section of the *Supreme Court Act* was read in this way. In the mid-twentieth century, the *Supreme Court Reports* did adopt a practice of not reporting some of the less important cases, although it is curious that the private reporters published some of the cases that the *Supreme Court Reports* omitted.
6 Snell and Vaughan, *supra* note 3 at 74.
7 *Shaw v The Canadian Pacific Railway Company*, (1892) 16 SCR 703. The juxtaposition of "1892" and "[vol] 16" is very curious, because vol 16 came out in 1889, and by 1892 decisions were being published in vol 21. We concede that this may be a

typographical error that is now deeply embedded in the records, and the appearance of a three-year delay may actually just be a mistake.

8 *Great North Western Telegraph Co. v The Montreal Telegraph Co.,* (1891) 20 SCR 170.

9 *Bickford v Hawkins,* (1891) 19 SCR 362.

10 The archival evidence that was reviewed for this project also verified this point.

11 McCormick recalls reading that in the early years after Confederation, the Minister of Justice had a support staff consisting of six full-time (and one part-time) employees.

12 Snell and Vaughan, *supra* note 3.

13 *Reference re Secession of Quebec,* [1998] 2 SCR 217.

14 The fact that these files could be accessed through an unlocked and unguarded door is a further aspect that would make anyone who was interested in such historical material shudder.

15 Anne Roland, "Official Law Reporting in Canada" (Paper presented at the Second International Symposium in Official Law Reporting, New York City, 2004).

16 *Ibid.*

17 In this sense, they were not quite the counterpart of the summaries that now appear as part of the headnotes for every Supreme Court decision, part of the introduction to the actual judicial reasons. Under current practice, a summary is provided for each of the separate reasons, whereas we are describing a process that generated an amalgamated summary.

18 There was, of course, a similar selection process for the commercial law reports, working with somewhat different criteria and deadlines, so that although the *Supreme Court Reports* was the most complete record, the *Dominion Law Reports* reported (at least in summary) some of the cases it omitted, and some of the third-party unattributed decisions in the *Supreme Court Reports* were reported with attribution in the *Dominion Law Reports* (and vice versa). In order to keep the data manageable, we have limited our data collection to the *Supreme Court Reports.*

19 And, to repeat our point from Chapter 3, the court had not yet evolved a "majority practice" that identified one of the sets of reasons as a "judgment" to which the others were simply minority reasons indicating reservations on the part of individual judges. This format did not emerge until the late 1960s. "Summarize the judgment" was not an available strategy when any set of reasons, even those dissenting from the outcome, were considered to be "judgments" when the precedential implications were evaluated.

20 And – again repeating a point from Chapter 4 – they were not published under a *per curiam* label, which was used for very different purposes.

21 Snell and Vaughan, *supra* note 3 at 108.

22 *A.E. Hamilton v G.H. Evans,* [1923] SCR 1.

23 The pronoun itself is also worth noting. For judgments – even unanimous decisions – the normal style of the Supreme Court of Canada is the singular pronoun

"I" (unlike the US Supreme Court, where even opinions of the court specifically attributed to a solo author always use the plural "we"). Until the emergence of co-authorships in the mid-1990s, the court used the plural pronoun only for *By the Court* decisions, so this unpromisingly brief decision is in this sense a noteworthy first.

24 *City of Toronto v Prince*, [1934] SCR 414, [1934] 3 DLR 81 [*Prince*].

25 *Brooks v The King*, [1927] SCR 633

26 *McLean v The King*, [1933] SCR 688, [1934] 2 DLR 440.

27 *Prince*, *supra* note 24.

28 *Fiset v Morin*, [1945] SCR 520, [1945] 3 DLR 800.

29 For example, of the 1,202 decisions handed down by the Laskin court, only 46 have been cited more than 20 times. See Peter McCormick, "Precedent by the Numbers: The Laskin Court" (Paper presented at the Midwest Political Science Association Annual Meeting, Chicago, April 2012).

Chapter 7: Emergence

1 This chapter is a revised and shortened version of an earlier article: Peter McCormick and Marc Zanoni, "The First 'By the Court' Decisions: The Emergence of a Practice of the Supreme Court of Canada" (2015) 38 Man LJ 159. We thank the *Manitoba Law Journal* for its permission to use this revised version.

2 *Attorney-General of Quebec v Blaikie et al.*, [1979] 2 SCR 1016 [*Blaikie*]; *Attorney-General of Manitoba v Forest*, [1979] 2 SCR 1032 [*Forest*].

3 We cannot help thinking that the judges must have heaved a sigh of relief when the Quebec case argued in June 1979 was joined in the docket by the Manitoba case argued in October 1979, allowing a symmetrical response rather than what might otherwise have appeared to be a heavy-handed response targeted on Quebec alone.

4 Not to mention a third referendum that seemed to be looming on the horizon during the Quebec provincial election in 2014, although that spectre was exorcised when the Parti Québécois government went down to a crushing defeat, at least partly because of the referendum question.

5 *Dred Scott v Sandford*, 60 US 393 (1857). The other two are *Plessy v Ferguson*, 163 US 537 (1896), and *Lochner v New York*, 198 US 45 (1908); some would add to this list *Korematsu v U.S.* 323 US 214 (1944).

6 *Re: Authority of Parliament in Relation to the Upper House*, [1980] 1 SCR 54; *Attorney-General of Quebec v Blaikie et al.*, [1981] 1 SCR 312; *Re: Objection by Quebec to a Resolution to Amend the Constitution*, [1982] 2 SCR 793. Somewhat misleadingly, the *Superior Court Reference* was indexed as *McEvoy v Attorney General of New Brunswick*, [1983] 1 SCR 704.

7 These comments are based on a lengthy telephone conversation between McCormick and former Chief Justice Brian Dickson shortly before Dickson's death.

8 See Peter McCormick, "Choosing the Chief: Duality, Seniority and Beyond" (2013) 47 J Can Studies 5.

9 See Philip Girard, *Bora Laskin: Bringing Law to Life* (Toronto: Osgoode Society for Canadian Legal History/University of Toronto Press, 2005), c 18, *passim*, both for its acceptance of the "seniority tradition" and for the professional reaction to the choice of Laskin. The implications of the appointment in terms of doctrinal direction were crystal-clear – Professor Laskin, as he was before he became Justice Laskin, was a consistent champion of constitutional law ideas favouring civil liberties and of a vigorous interpretation of federal powers within the federal system.

10 "Canada has never had a chief justice who dissented as frequently, and freely, as Laskin": *ibid.* at 453. See also Peter McCormick, "Assessing Leadership on the Supreme Court of Canada: Toward a Typology of Chief Justice Performance" (1993) 4 Sup Ct L Rev (2d ser.) 409.

11 More correctly, they *almost* fit, because they are actually about a year early. Lamer was not appointed until 1980, and one cannot even nudge the date earlier by (slightly less plausibly) considering Julien Chouinard's 1979 replacement of Yves Pratte as the turning point, because the critical *Blaikie* panel still included Pratte, who had resigned by the time the decision was handed down.

12 Ralph Lerner, "The Supreme Court as Republican Schoolmaster" (1967) Sup Ct Rev 127; and Christopher L. Eisgruber, "Is the Supreme Court an Educative Institution?" (1992) 67 NYUL Rev 961. Mark Tushnet is skeptical; see "Style and the Supreme Court's Educational Role in Government" (1994–95) 11 Const Commentary 215.

13 [1968] SCR 118, decided on November 20, 1967.

14 [1967] SCR 792, decided on November 7, 1967.

15 [1967] SCR 309, decided on May 4, 1967.

16 It may seem curious that there was not an appeal by right for a death sentence, but under the wording of the *Criminal Code* at the time, there was none. The *Code* was amended shortly afterward, at least partly in response to the outcry over the *Truscott* case, so that from then on there would be an appeal by right in such a case.

17 Isabel LeBourdais, *The Trial of Steven Truscott* (Toronto: McClelland and Stewart, 1966).

18 The juxtaposition of "1967" and "Minister of Justice" immediately suggests a powerful name from recent Canadian political history – namely, Pierre Elliott Trudeau – but the reference question was submitted to the Supreme Court some months before Trudeau assumed the Justice portfolio.

19 There were real similarities to the earlier case of *R v Coffin*, [1956] SCR 191, a federal reference after the court dismissed an application for leave to appeal, although in that case only a single Supreme Court justice had been involved in the decision on the application.

20 We could not find a list of the names of the judges on the application panel in any of the writings about the *Truscott* case, but the registrar of the Supreme Court of Canada was kind enough to provide us with this information.

21 It may be that the government was reluctant simply to issue a full pardon in such controversial circumstances because this would have meant a degree of political involvement in a purely legal case that would compromise the justice system. We fail to see how the reference question itself was not a comparably dangerous challenge to the court, and one that in our opinion the court ultimately failed to meet, to its lasting discredit. LeBourdais had recommended, and internal memos now show us that the members of the court fully agreed, that it was not the best body to deal with this question, and that an independent committee or commission of some sort, whatever its findings, would have better served the cause of justice.

22 Truscott was paroled in 1969 and his parole restrictions ended in 1974. In 2001, he made an application under more recent provisions of the *Criminal Code* to have his conviction reviewed. This led to an inquiry that resulted in the Kaufman Report in 2004, followed by a reference to the Ontario Court of Appeal. See "Executive Summary – Report to the Minister of Justice Prepared by the Honourable Fred Kaufman," online: Department of Justice, https://www.justice.gc.ca/eng/rp-pr/cj-jp/ccr-rc/sec690-art690/exec.html. That court found unanimously that the trial resulting in Truscott's conviction was not valid and that its decision should be set aside (*Re Truscott*, 2007 ONCA 575).

23 Frederick Vaughan, *Aggressive in Pursuit: The Life of Justice Emmett Hall* (Toronto: University of Toronto Press, 2004). There is some suggestion that the initial split on the court was much more even, with as many as four judges prepared to dissent from the ultimate outcome. In the end, they did not, and left Hall in isolation.

24 We presume that the chief justice will write for the court on cases of particular significance, and conversely that a judgment delivered by the chief justice will tend to give a decision a higher profile. Both these presumptions may not have been as justified at that time as they are today.

25 It is also possible, and is hinted at in Vaughan's biography of Hall (*supra* note 23), that the other members of the majority might have had some reservations about assigning this responsibility to their faltering chief, and the novel format was adopted as a way around this. The suggestion is intriguing. We have been framing *By the Court* throughout as a confident gesture of institutional strength, projecting unusual solidarity on significant issues, but in Vaughan's account this transitional example could be seen as the product of institutional weakness, with a harassed court labouring under a faltering chief justice in the face of an embarrassing dissent.

26 We hesitate to treat the *Truscott Reference* as the first *By the Court* because it is missing two features central to our treatment of this practice: it was not unanimous, and it was not a constitutional case. We prefer to think of it as a transition to *By*

The Court, a kind of halfway stepping point that made the new practice possible without itself being a complete example.

27 Technically, the court delivers "opinions" on reference questions and "judgments" on appeals, so although *Reference re: Offshore Mineral Rights,* [1967] SCR 792 [*Offshore Mineral Rights Reference*] could be a "joint opinion," *The Queen v Board of Transport Commissioners,* [1968] SCR 118, should have labelled itself a "joint judgment."

28 *Offshore Mineral Rights Reference, ibid.*

29 Ronald I. Cheffins, "The Supreme Court of Canada: A Quiet Court in an Unquiet Country" (1966) 4 Osgoode Hall LJ 259.

30 Vaughan, *supra* note 23.

31 It seems hardly controversial to describe this moment in the Supreme Court's history as not just challenging but also humiliating and embarrassing, not least because it culminated forty years later in a unanimous decision by a panel of Canada's strongest provincial Court of Appeal that Truscott should not have been found guilty, although it stopped just short of saying that he could not possibly have committed the crime. This must stand as a repudiation without precedent, a retroactive shaming of an earlier age and an earlier Supreme Court.

32 Justice Charles Gonthier's judgment for the court in *Reference re Quebec Sales Tax,* [1994] 2 SCR 715, is the only counter-example since 1967.

33 A colleague who interviewed the justices asked about the *By the Court* device, and was told by one of the justices that this came about when there was an appeal from a particularly objectionable court of appeal decision – wanting to make an unusually sharp retort in an unusually obvious way, the Supreme Court hit upon this combination of anonymity and unanimity. Although this description does not match the circumstances of either 1967 or 1979, it is interesting that it would have emerged as an institutional self-understanding of the device.

34 For a full expansion of this argument, see McCormick and Zanoni, *supra* note 1.

35 Vaughan, *supra* note 23.

36 *Reference re Supreme Court Act, ss. 5 and 6,* 2014 SCC 21.

Chapter 8: Inventory and Chronology of Decisions

1 Frederick Vaughan, *Aggressive in Pursuit: The Life of Justice Emmett Hall* (Toronto: University of Toronto Press, 2004).

2 *Juvenile Delinquents Act,* RSC 1952, c 160; *Motor Vehicle Act,* RSBC 1960, c 253; *Summary Convictions Act,* RSBC 1960, c 373.

3 *Canadian Bill of Rights,* SC 1960, c 44.

4 Twelve if one includes cases under the 1960 *Canadian Bill of Rights,* but we have already indicated that we are not persuaded by this inclusion.

5 *Reference re Remuneration of Judges of the Provincial Court of Prince Edward Island; Reference re Independence and Impartiality of Judges of the Provincial Court of Prince Edward Island,* [1997] 3 SCR 3.

6 For an extended discussion of that string of cases, see Peter McCormick, "New Questions about an Old Concept: The Supreme Court of Canada's Judicial Independence Jurisprudence" (2004) 37 Can J Political Science 839.

7 For favourable comment on the decision, see Jeffrey Bone, "The Supreme Court Revisiting Corporate Accountability" (n.d.) Alta L Rev Online Supplement, online: Alberta Law Review, www.albertalawreview.com. For criticism, see, e.g., Edward Waitzer and Johnny Jaswal, "Peoples, BCE and the Good Corporate 'Citizen'" (2009) 47 Osgoode Hall LJ 439.

Chapter 9: A Typology of Decisions

1 An earlier version of this chapter appeared as "'By the Court' – The Untold Story of a Canadian Judicial Innovation" (2016) 53 Osgoode Hall LJ 1048.

2 Or "advisory opinion," the two terms being effectively interchangeable. Section 53 of the *Supreme Court Act* uses the label "references by Governor in Council" but then describes it as "referring certain questions for opinion."

3 This almost uniquely Canadian practice is also seriously underexplored. The best catalogue and historical review is a thirty-year-old article in an American law journal: James L. Huffman and MardiLyn Saathoff, "Advisory Opinions and Canadian Constitutional Development: The Supreme Court's Reference Jurisdiction" (1990) 74 Minn L Rev 1251. We acknowledge and welcome a recent PhD dissertation on the subject: Kate Puddister, *Inviting Judicial Review: A Comprehensive Analysis of Canadian Appellate Reference Cases* (PhD dissertation, McGill University, 2015), online: McGill Library, http://digitool.library.mcgill.ca/.

4 The story is actually a bit more convoluted. The Australian Constitution was amended in 1910 to include a reference power, but on the first occasion when it was exercised a decade later, the Australian High Court rejected that amendment as itself unconstitutional because it violated the principle of the separation of powers. See Helen Irving, "Advisory Opinions, the Rule of Law, and the Separation of Powers" (2004) 4 Macquarie UL Rev 105. For advocacy of the establishment of such a power, see John M. Williams, "Re-thinking Advisory Opinions" (1996) 7 Pub L Rev 205; and John M. Williams, "Advisory Opinions: 'A Well Covered Harbor'" (2010) 22 Bond L Rev 169.

5 *Supreme Court of Pakistan Annual Report,* May 2014–May 2015, online: Supreme Court of Pakistan, www.supremecourt.gov.pk; Deepaloke Chatterjee, "Presidential References and the Precedential Value: A Constitutional Analysis" (2009) 21 National Law School of India Review 175.

6 *Ontario (Attorney General) v Canada (Attorney General),* [1912] AC 571.

7 Equally, if circumstances should evolve such that the government for tactical reasons wishes to delay the court's response – for example, the *Reference re Same-Sex Marriage* – it can file supplementary questions that have the effect of turning the clock back.

8 *Reference re Secession of Quebec,* [1998] 2 SCR 217.

9 Mark Tushnet, "Policy Distortion and Democratic Debilitation: Comparative Illustration of the Countermajoritarian Difficulty" (1995) 94 Mich L Rev 245.

10 For example, the Ontario government's *Reference Re Bill 30*, [1987] 1 SCR 1148.

11 For example, *Reference re Securities Act*, 2011 SCC 66 [*Securities Act Reference*]. As the example shows, this manoeuvre can backfire spectacularly.

12 For example, *Attorney-General for Manitoba v. Manitoba Egg and Poultry Association et al.*, [1971] SCR 689.

13 Huffman and Saathoff, *supra* note 3. We think they overcount by four: they have "double-counted" three reference cases by including one motion, one application for intervener status, and one order as well as the court's actual judgment; and they include one supposed reference from 1874, the year before the Supreme Court was established. At the same time, they omit one: *Attorney-General for Manitoba v. Manitoba Egg and Poultry Association et al.*, [1971] SCR 689.

14 Two of which were references to the Federal Court of Appeal, subsequently appealed to the Supreme Court. For our present purposes, "references by the federal government" is a more important element than "first decided in a court of appeal and then appealed to the Supreme Court."

15 The *Supreme Court Act* allows for appeals from provincial references but does not specifically identify them as "appeals by right." In practice, it seems that although there must be an application for leave to appeal, this is never refused.

16 Two of the recent cases were actually references to the Federal Court of Appeal in 2012 that were then appealed to the Supreme Court. For present purposes, we think it is more important that these were reference cases by the federal government than that they were second-look references on appeal from a lower court of appeal.

17 See Claire L'Heureux-Dubé, "The Length and Plurality of Supreme Court of Canada Decisions" (1990) 28 Alta L Rev 581.

18 This six-to-three division of the panel almost replicates the split on the convention question of the *Patriation Reference*, with Estey and Lamer changing sides. Even more recently, the decision on the federal government's motion to extend the deadline for the suspended finding of invalidity regarding physician-assisted dying took a similar form: majority reasons jointly attributed to five judges (Abella, Karakatsanis, Wagner, Gascon, and Côté) confronting a "dissent in part" by four judges (McLachlin, Cromwell, Moldaver, and Brown). See *Carter v Canada (Attorney General)* 2016 SCC 4. We do not include this on our lists because it was a response to a motion, not a reference case or a decision on appeal, and because the reasons (both majority and minority) are so short.

19 Mathen also picks up on this use of *By the Court* (although she uses the *per curiam* label): "A joint opinion is a very blunt message, only delivered in the context of a serious power struggle or challenge to a court's authority." Carissima Mathen, "The Shadow of Absurdity and the Challenge of Easy Cases: Looking Back on the Supreme Court Act Reference" (2015) 71 Osgoode Hall LJ 161.

20 *Reference re: Steven Murray Truscott*, [1967] SCR 309.

21 *Reference re Supreme Court Act, ss. 5 and 6*, 2014 SCC 21, [2014] 1 SCR 433.

22 Only six, because the challenge to *Nadon* had reduced the court to eight active members and Justice Rothstein had recused himself on the grounds that he had been appointed to the Supreme Court from the Federal Court of Appeal.

23 This question was before the court because in addition to the question of whether Nadon was qualified under s 6, the Supreme Court was also asked whether Parliament had the power to amend that section of the *Supreme Court Act* to provide an interpretive gloss to s 6 that would have answered the question in the federal government's favour.

24 *Constitution Act, 1982*, being Schedule B to the *Canada Act 1982* (UK), 1982, c 11.

25 As, for example, when it amended the *Supreme Court Act* in 1999 to narrow (but not quite to do away with) the category of "appeals by right," which meant that the Supreme Court would not have complete control of its own docket in the way that the United States Supreme Court does.

26 For a recent consideration of the issue of Supreme Court recusal and its importance to the judicial system, see Louis Virelli, *Disqualifying the High Court: Supreme Court Recusal and the Constitution* (Lawrence: University Press of Kansas, 2016).

27 It is possible that this different appearance for an anonymous and unanimous judgment was intended to highlight the fact that the specific judge who was the subject of recusal concerns was not part of the panel rendering the decision.

28 *Wewaykum Indian Band v Canada*, 2003 SCC 45, [2003] 2 SCR 259.

29 *Wewaykum Indian Band v Canada*, 2002 SCC 79, [2002] 4 SCR 245.

30 *Mugesera v Canada (Minister of Citizenship and Immigration)*, 2005 SCC 40, [2005] SCR 91.

31 *Mugesera v Canada (Minister of Citizenship and Immigration)*, 2005 SCC 40, [2005] SCR 100.

32 For a consideration of the dozen cases and the evolution of doctrine within them, see Peter McCormick, "New Questions about an Old Concept: The Supreme Court of Canada's Judicial Independence Decisions" (2004) 37 Can J Political Science 839; and Peter McCormick, *Judicial Independence and Judicial Governance in the Provincial Courts* (Toronto: Canadian Association of Provincial Court Judges, 2004).

33 *Reference re Remuneration of Judges of the Provincial Court of Prince Edward Island; Reference re Independence and Impartiality of Judges of the Provincial Court of Prince Edward Island*, [1997] 3 SCR 3.

34 One curious consequence of this decision was to take the judicial independence cases out of the category of "*Charter* decisions" and into the broader category of "constitutional law." All these cases between 1984 and 1997, but none of the cases since, have listed Charter issues in the headnotes.

35 [1997] 3 SCR 391.

36 See Peter McCormick, "Judicial Councils for Provincial Judges in Canada" (1986) 6 Windsor YB Access Just 160.

37 *Mackin v New Brunswick (Minister of Finance); Rice v New Brunswick,* 2002 SCC 13, [2002] 1 SCR 405; *Ell v Alberta* 2003 SCC 35, [2003] 1 SCR 857. McCormick was involved in the *Ell* case at the trial level as an expert witness.

38 *Provincial Court Judges' Assn. of New Brunswick v New Brunswick (Minister of Justice); Ontario Judges' Assn. v Ontario (Management Board); Bodner v Alberta; Conférence des juges du Québec v Quebec (Attorney General); Minc v Quebec (Attorney General)* 2005 SCC 44, [2005] 2 SCR 286.

39 See, e.g., Jeffrey Goldsworthy, "The Preamble, Judicial Independence and Judicial Integrity" (2000) 11 Const Forum Const 60; and Tsvi Kahana, "The Constitution as a Collective Agreement: Remuneration of Provincial Court Judges in Canada" (2003–04) 29 Queen's LJ 445.

40 *R v Ahmad,* 2011 SCC 6.

41 In ss 96 through 100 of the *Constitution Act, 1867.*

42 *Re Residential Tenancies Act,* [1981] 1 SCR 714, is probably the central case, although *Attorney General of Quebec v. Grondin,* [1983] 2 SCR 364, displays the problem of the actual pre-1867 practice's variation from one colony to another. *Sobeys Stores v. Yeomans and Labour Standards Tribunal (NS),* [1989] 1 SCR 238, is an important clarification, establishing a "blended historical test" to deal with this.

43 There is a further complication in that it may be under the authority of the provincial attorney general that the prosecution is proceeding in the first place, whereas it is under the authority of the federal attorney general that the application to constrain disclosure is put before the Federal Court. That was not the central concern in this case, however.

44 *R v Marshall,* [1993] 3 SCR 456.

45 *R v Marshall,* [1999] 3 SCR 533.

46 *R v Chaulk (Application),* [1989] 1 SCR 369.

47 *British Columbia (Attorney General) v Christie,* 2007 SCC 21.

48 *Canada (Attorney General) v Lameman,* 2008 SCC 14.

49 *Limitations of Actions Act,* RSA 1980, c L-15, s 4.

50 See, e.g., Robert Sharpe and Kent Roach, *Brian Dickson: A Judge's Journey* (Toronto: University of Toronto Press, 2003) at 431. "Le Dain's painstaking work habits made him very slow with his judgments."

51 *Ibid.* at 375.

52 *Québec (A.G.) v Healy,* [1987] 1 SCR 158.

53 *Ford v Quebec (Attorney General),* [1988] 2 SCR 712; *Devine v Quebec (Attorney General),* [1988] 2 SCR 790.

54 Which the actual decision deftly sidestepped by finding that the legislation offended the Quebec *Charter of Human Rights and Freedoms,* RSQ c-12.

55 *Attorney-General of Quebec v Blaikie et al.,* [1979] 2 SCR 1016 [*Blaikie*]; *Attorney-General of Manitoba v Forest,* [1979] 2 SCR 1032 [*Forest*].

56 See Sharpe and Roach, *supra* note 50 at 427–32. There is no suggestion that these decisions would have had the *By the Court* format had Le Dain been able to follow through with the revisions himself.

57 *Ibid.* at 431.

58 Estey's retirement date took him beyond the six-month period during which the *Supreme Court Act* allows retired judges to continue to be part of the panel. The *Supreme Court Act* provides that although five judges is the minimum for hearing an appeal, a judgment can still be delivered by a panel that has been reduced to four participating judges, but only with the consent of both parties.

59 [1988] 2 SCR 654.

60 Sharpe and Roach, *supra* note 50 at 428. The situation was aggravated by the fact that Estey had given a number of media interviews immediately after his retirement that were critical of many of his colleagues and highly deprecatory of the implications of the Charter.

61 [1988] 2 SCR 680.

62 [1985] 1 SCR 831.

63 [1985] 1 SCR 851.

64 [1985] 1 SCR 861.

65 The others were *Forest, supra* note 55, in 1979, *Reza v Canada*, [1994] 2 SCR 394, and *R v Cody*, 2017 SCC 31.

66 It is also striking that these three cases are almost sequential in the *Supreme Court Reports*, although they were not all handed down on the same day.

67 [1987] 1 SCR 246.

68 *Marshall 2* might be considered as a counter-example of a contribution to First Nations case law, but, as indicated above we think that this was more a judicial salvage effort for an earlier decision that had created significant problems. It has the further complication that it was technically a simple dismissal of an application for a rehearing to which was appended some clarification.

Chapter 10: Why These Cases?

1 *Law Society of Upper Canada v Skapinker*, [1984] 1 SCR 357. Some would give the Laskin court's decision in *Westendorp v the Queen*, [1983] 1 SCR 43, pride of place as the Supreme Court's first Charter decision, but it was not delivered *By the Court* either.

2 *Hunter et al. v Southam Inc.*, [1984] 2 SCR 145; *R v Oakes*, [1986] 1 SCR 103.

3 *Mahe v Alberta*, [1990] 1 SCR 342; *R v Sparrow*, [1990] 1 SCR 1075.

4 *General Motors of Canada Ltd. v City National Leasing*, [1989] 1 SCR 641; *Citizens' Insurance Company of Canada v Parsons*, (1881) 7 App.Cas. 96.

5 *Reference re Secession of Quebec*, [1998] 2 SCR 217; *Reference re Quebec Sales Tax*, [1994] 2 SCR 715.

6 *Law v. Canada (Minister of Employment and Immigration)*, [1999] 1 SCR 497.
7 *Reference re Remuneration of Judges of the Provincial Court of Prince Edward Island; Reference re Independence and Impartiality of Judges of the Provincial Court of Prince Edward Island*, [1997] 3 SCR 3.
8 *U.F.C.W., Local 1518, v KMart Canada Ltd.*, [1999] 2 SCR 1083.
9 *Canada (Attorney General) v PHS Community Services Society*, 2011 SCC 44.
10 *Canada (Attorney General) v Bedford*, [2013] 3 SCR 1101.
11 *Daniels v Canada (Indian Affairs and Northern Development)*, 2016 SCC 12.
12 *Tsilhqot'in Nation v British Columbia*, 2014 SCC 44.
13 *Withler v Canada (Attorney General)*, 2011 SCC 12. The court's reservations were expressed in *R v Kapp*, 2008 SCC 41.
14 *R v Powley*, 2003 SCC 43; *R v Blais*, 2003 SCC 44; *R v Marshall*, [1993] 3 SCR 533.
15 *Reference re: Steven Murray Truscott*, [1967] SCR 309.
16 *Re Truscott*, 2007 ONCA 575.
17 *Attorney-General of Quebec v Blaikie et al.*, [1979] 2 SCR 1016; *Attorney-General of Manitoba v Forest*, [1979] 2 SCR 1032.
18 Leonid Sirota, "Says Who?" (July 4, 2013) *Double Aspect Law Blog*, online: www.doubleaspect.blog.
19 *Re: Resolution to Amend the Constitution*, [1981] 1 SCR 753.
20 The two cases were *Canadian Industrial Gas & Oil Ltd. v Government of Saskatchewan et al.*, [1978] 2 SCR 545, and *Central Canada Potash Co. Ltd. et al. v Government of Saskatchewan*, [1979] 1 SCR 42. Peter Hogg responded to this general charge, and specifically to the pair of cases that prompted Saskatchewan's unusual vocal complaint, in "Is the Supreme Court of Canada Biased in Constitutional Cases?" (1979) 57 Can Bar Rev 721.
21 Peter Russell, "The Supreme Court Decision: Bold Statecraft Based on Questionable Jurisprudence" in Peter Russell et al., eds., *The Court and the Constitution: Comments on the Supreme Court Reference on Constitutional Amendment* (Kingston, ON: Queen's University Institute of Intergovernmental Relations, 1982).
22 *Reference re Secession of Quebec*, [1998] 2 SCR 217.
23 *Québec (A.G.) v Healy*, [1987] 1 SCR 158; *Canadian Pacific Ltd. v Paul*, [1988] 2 SCR 654; *Ford v Quebec (Attorney General)*, [1988] 2 SCR 712; *Devine v Quebec (Attorney General)*, [1988] 2 SCR 790.
24 Michael Enright, "One Judge Down," The Sunday Edition/CBC Radio One (January 14, 2018), online: www.cbc.ca.
25 *Reference re Same-Sex Marriage*, 2004 SCC 79.
26 See John McEvoy, "Separation of Powers and the Reference Power: Is There a Right to Refuse?" (1988) 10 Sup Ct L Rev 429; and John McEvoy, "Refusing to Answer: The Supreme Court and the Reference Power Revisited" (2005) 29 UNBLJ 29.
27 *R v Marshall*, *supra* note 14; *Reference re Supreme Court Act, ss. 5 and 6*, 2014 SCC 21 [*Nadon*]; *Wewaykum Indian Band v Canada*, 2003 SCC 45; *Mugesera v Canada (Minister of Citizenship and Immigration)*, 2005 SCC 40.

28 *Canada (Justice) v Khadr*, 2008 SCC 28; *Canada (Prime Minister) v Khadr*, 2010 SCC 3.
29 Rainer Knopff, "Charter Reconsiderations" (2012) 21 National Magazine 38.
30 *United States v Burns*, 2001 SCC 7.
31 *Kindler v Canada (Minister of Justice)*, [1991] 2 SCR 779; *Reference Re Ng Extradition (Can.)*, [1991] 2 SCR 858.
32 *Carter v Canada (Attorney General)*, 2015 SCC 5; *Rodriguez v British Columbia*, [1999] 3 SCR 519.
33 *Clark v Canadian National Railway Co.*, [1988] 2 SCR 680.
34 *Reference re: Offshore Mineral Rights*, [1967] SCR 792.
35 André Bzdera, "Comparative Analysis of Federal High Courts: A Political Theory of Judicial Review" (1993) 26 Can J Political Science 27.
36 *Reference re Securities Act*, 2011 SCC 66.
37 Ronald I. Cheffins, "The Supreme Court of Canada: The Quiet Court in an Unquiet Country" (1966) 4 Osgoode Hall LJ 259.
38 *The Queen v Board of Transport Commissioners*, [1968] SCR 118.
39 *Reference re Assisted Human Reproduction Act*, 2010 SCC 61; *Securities Act Reference*, *supra* note 36; *Nadon*, *supra* note 27.
40 Full unanimity equates to "univocality," with all the judges signing on to a single set of reasons for the outcome. The Supreme Court keeps a record of the proportion of judgments that are "unanimous as to outcome" – meaning that separate concurrences do not matter – but we are not convinced by this implicit trivialization of what can often represent significant disagreement. See Peter McCormick, "Standing Apart: Separate Concurrence and the Supreme Court of Canada 1984–2006" (2008) 53 McGill LJ 137; and Peter McCormick, "The Choral Court: Separate Concurrences on the McLachlin Court 2000–2004" (2005–06) 37 Ottawa LJ 1.
41 "Natural court" refers to one with a stable membership, without any departures or arrivals.
42 As to when this started, the most plausible answer would connect it to the beginning of the practice of a post-oral argument conference at which the responsibility for writing the draft judgment could be assigned, i.e., in the late 1960s under the leadership of Chief Justice Cartwright.
43 These writing concessions are not simply a matter of courtesy but also of making sure that the initial majority on whose behalf the judgment is being written is not itself divided by those reasons, such that what started as a set of dissenting or separately concurring reasons becomes the "new" judgment. For a consideration of this possibility, and ways of identifying it when it has taken place, see Peter McCormick, "'Was It Something I Said?' Losing the Majority on the Modern Supreme Court of Canada, 1984–2011" (2012) 50 Osgoode Hall LJ 93.
44 2017 SCC 40.
45 *Chippewas of the Thames First Nation v Enbridge Pipelines Inc.*, 2017 SCC 41.

46 *Quebec (Attorney General) v Guérin*, 2017 SCC 42.
47 *Uniprix inc. v. Gestion Gosselin et Bérubé inc.*, 2017 SCC 43.
48 Co-authorship has become frequent and regular enough that the lawblog of Osgoode Hall Law School (thecourt.ca) has begun to take note of it in its annual summaries of the court's activities. See, e.g., Richard Haigh, "The Supreme Court by Numbers 2: The McLachlin Years" (July 26, 2016), *theCourt.ca* (blog), online: www.thecourt.ca.
49 *John v The Queen*, [1985] 1 SCR 476. *Kienapple* principle: *Kienapple v R.*, [1975] 1 SCR 729, which bars multiple convictions for a single criminal act.
50 See Peter McCormick, *The End of the Charter Revolution: Looking Back from the New Normal* (Toronto: University of Toronto Press, 2015).
51 *Dunsmuir v New Brunswick*, 2008 SCC 9; *Housen v Nikolaisen*, 2002 SCC 33; *Bell ExpressVu Limited Partnership v Rex*, 2002 SCC 42; *R v Grant*, 2009 SCC 32.
52 2016 SCC 27.
53 Tonda MacCharles, "Chief Justice Beverley McLachlin Ready to Write New Chapter with Novel," *Toronto Star* (June 15, 2017).

Chapter 11: The Meaning and Future of the *By the Court* Format

1 James L. Huffman and MardiLyn Saathoff, "Advisory Opinions and Canadian Constitutional Development: The Supreme Court's Reference Jurisdiction" (1990) 74 Minn L Rev 1251.
2 See, e.g., Forrest Maltzman, James F. Spriggs II, and Paul Wahlbeck, *Crafting Law on the Supreme Court: The Collegial Game* (New York: Cambridge University Press, 2000).
3 See, e.g., David L. Shapiro, "In Defense of Judicial Candor" (1987) 100 Harv L Rev 731; and Scott C. Idleman, "A Prudential Theory of Judicial Candor" (1995) 75 Tex L Rev 1307.
4 "Small group theory" has been a staple of the social science study of the courts for decades, the earliest example probably being Eloise Snyder's "The Supreme Court as a Small Group" (1958) 36 Social Forces 232.
5 The question of "getting along" may be simply one of personality – as in the sense of "the person you would least like to be stuck in an elevator with" – or one of judicial ideology. See Benjamin Alarie and Andrew Green, "Should They All Just Get Along? Judicial Ideology, Collegiality, and Appointments to the Supreme Court" (2007) 58 UNBLJ 73.
6 M. Todd Henderson, "From 'Seriatim' to Consensus and Back Again: A Theory of Dissent" (2007) Sup Ct Rev 283.
7 Peter McCormick, "The Political Jurisprudence of Hot Potatoes: A Comparison of the *Secession Reference* and *Bush v Gore*" (2002) 13 NJCL 271 at 287; *Reference re Secession of Quebec*, [1998] 2 SCR 217; *Bush v Gore*, 531 US 98 (2000).
8 Nuno Garoupa and Tom Ginsburg, *Judicial Reputation: A Comparative Theory* (Chicago and London: University of Chicago Press, 2015).

9 *Ibid.*

10 Tracey E. George and Mitu Gulati, "Courts of Good and Ill Repute: Garoupa and Ginsburg's *Judicial Reputation: A Comparative Theory*" (Book review, May 23, 2016), online: Social Science Research Network, www.ssrn.com.

11 Garoupa and Ginsburg, *supra* note 8 at 180, 184.

12 James L. Gibson, Gregory A. Caldeira, and Vanessa Baird, "On the Legitimacy of National High Courts" (1998) 92 American Political Science Rev 343.

13 *Dred Scott v Sandford,* 60 US 393 (1857).

14 As Ehrlich put it, "American legal and constitutional scholars consider the Dred Scott decision to be the worst ever rendered by the Supreme Court." Walter Ehrlich, "*Scott v Sandford*" in Kermit L. Hall, ed., *The Oxford Companion to the Supreme Court of the United States* (New York: Oxford University Press, 1992) at 761. Currie described it as "bad policy, bad judicial politics, and bad law." David P. Currie, *The Constitution in the Supreme Court: The First Hundred Years, 1789–1988* (Chicago: University of Chicago Press, 1985) at 264. For something of a reappraisal, see Mark A. Graber, *Dred Scott and the Problem of Constitutional Evil* (Cambridge and London: Cambridge University Press, 2006).

15 George and Gulati, *supra* note 10, object to the simplification involved in this two-model framing. For them, the purest form of a "recognition judiciary" is represented by the elected judges of many American states, with the US federal "Article III" judiciary therefore as the middle element of a trichotomy.

16 And if the French judges' union has its way, the anonymity will be ratcheted up another notch by not publishing the names of the judges who served on the panel. See Leonid Sirota, "Justice in Masks" (February 17, 2017), *Double Aspect* (law blog), online: https://doubleaspect.blog.

17 There will of course be an "individual reputation" factor within the judiciary itself – the apparent simplicity of identifying the two dimensions of reputation has to be qualified by an awareness of the different audiences and publics within which they operate, but this complication does not undercut the basic point of the argument.

18 See, e.g., Nancy Maveety, *Queen's Court: Judicial Power in the Rehnquist Era* (Lawrence: University Press of Kansas, 2008); Kenneth M. Murchison, "Four Terms of the Kennedy Court: Projecting the Future of Constitutional Doctrine" (2009–10) 39 U Balt L Rev 1.

19 The phrase "splendid freedom" is Scalia's; see A. Scalia, "The Dissenting Opinion" (1994) 19 J Sup Ct History 33.

20 See Peter McCormick, "'Was It Something I Said?' Losing the Majority on the Modern Supreme Court of Canada 1984–2011" (2012) 50 Osgoode Hall LJ 93.

21 See Peter McCormick, "Sharing the Spotlight: Co-Authored Reasons on the Modern Supreme Court of Canada" (2011) 34 Dal LJ 165.

22 The McLachlin court's most frequently cited decision is *Dunsmuir v New Brunswick,* [2008] 1 SCR 190, on standards of review; it is also one of the most widely discussed

and seriously criticized of the court's recent decisions. For this reason, Leonid Sirota's *Double Aspect* law blog and Paul Daly's *Administrative Law Matters* law blog jointly celebrated the decision's tenth anniversary with a symposium of twenty-one lawyers, judges, and academics analyzing and critiquing the decision. These pieces were posted between February 13 and March 9, 2017, concluding with comments from *Dunsmuir*'s two co-authors. But these final comments were not themselves co-authored – Bastarache and LeBel wrote separate, and intriguingly non-identical, explanations of the decision.

23 In the movie, the answer is that they were waiting until the Soviet premier's birthday celebration the following week to make the announcement. It seems rather late in the day to suggest a comparable reason for the silence about *By the Court.*

24 See Peter McCormick, "Do Judges Read Books, Too? Academic Citations by the Supreme Court of Canada" (1998) 9 Sup Ct L Rev (2d ser.) 463.

25 Our attitude here is not one of "aren't we smarter than everybody else" but, quite the contrary, one of marvel that this book came into being only because a graduate student's thesis project wound up disproving most of what his supervisor thought he knew about the subject.

26 The formulaic minimum, frequently achieved, is: "The appeal is dismissed for the reasons given in the court below."

27 *Québec (A.G.) v Healy,* [1987] 1 SCR 158.

28 *Reference re Secession of Quebec,* [1998] 2 SCR 217.

Bibliography

Alarie, Benjamin, and Andrew Green. "Should They All Just Get Along? Judicial Ideology, Collegiality, and Appointments to the Supreme Court" (2007) 58 UNBLJ 73.

Alder, John. "Dissents in Courts of Last Resort: Tragic Choices?" (2000) 20 Oxford J Legal Stud 221.

Beth, Loren P. "The Judicial Committee: Its Development, Organization and Procedure" (1975) 3 PL 219.

–. "The Judicial Committee of the Privy Council and the Development of Judicial Review" (1976) 24 Am J Comp L 22.

Bickel, Alexander M., and Harry H. Wellington. "Legislative Purpose and the Judicial Process" (1957) 71 Harv L Rev 1.

Bone, Jeffrey. "The Supreme Court Revisiting Corporate Accountability" (n.d.) Alta L Rev Online Supplement. Online: Alberta Law Review, www.albertalawreview.com.

Bushnell, Ian. "The Use of American Cases" (1986) 35 UNBLJ 157.

Bzdera, Andrew. "Comparative Analysis of Federal High Courts: A Political Theory of Judicial Review" (1993) 26 Can J Political Science 27.

Chatterjee, Deepaloke. "Presidential References and the Precedential Value: A Constitutional Analysis" (200) 21 National Law School of India Review 175.

Cheffins, Ronald I. "The Supreme Court of Canada: A Quiet Court in an Unquiet Country" (1966) 4 Osgoode Hall LJ 259.

Corley, Pamela C., Amy Steigerwalt, and Artemus Ward. *The Puzzle of Unanimity: Consensus on the United States Supreme Court* (Stanford, CA: Stanford Law Books, 2013).

Council, John. "Who Wrote for the Majority in Controversial Abortion Decision?" *Texas Lawyer* (June 10, 2015). Online: *Texas Lawyer,* www.texaslawyer.com.

Currie, David P. *The Constitution in the Supreme Court: The First Hundred Years, 1789–1988* (Chicago: University of Chicago Press, 1985).

–. "The Most Insignificant Justice: A Preliminary Inquiry" (1983) 50 U Chicago L Rev 466.

Da Silva, Virgilio Afonso. "Deciding without Deliberating" (2013) 11 Int'l J Const L 557.

Dalton, Jennifer E. "Aboriginal Self-Determination in Canada: Protections Afforded by Judiciary and Government" (2006) 21 CJLS 11.

Delson, Rudolph. "Typography in the U.S. Reports and Supreme Court Voting Protocols" (2001) 76 NYUL Rev 1203.

Dickson, Timothy. "Self Government by Side Agreement?" (2004) 49 McGill LJ 420.

Dixon, Rosalind, and Tom Ginsburg. "Introduction" in Tom Ginsburg and Rosalind Dixon, eds. *Comparative Constitutional Law* (Cheltenham, UK, and Northampton, MA: Edward Elgar, 2011).

Easterbrook, Frank H. "The Most Insignificant Justice: Further Evidence" (1983) 50 U Chicago L Rev 481.

Editorial Comment. "The Use of American Legal Literature" (1943) 21 Can Bar Rev 57.

Eisgruber, Christopher L. "Is the Supreme Court an Educative Institution?" (1992) 67 NYUL Rev 961.

Enright, Michael. "One Judge Down." The Sunday Edition/CBC Radio One (January 14, 2018). Online: CBC, www.cbc.ca.

Friedman, Barry, Andrew Martin, Thomas B. Bennett, and Susan Navarro Smelcer. "Divide and Concur: Separate Opinions and Legal Change" (2017) 103 Cornell L Rev 817.

Friedman, Josh. Book Review of *Dissent and the Supreme Court* by Melvin Urofsky (Pantheon, 2015). *Columbia Magazine* (Winter 2015–16). Online: *Columbia Magazine,* https://magazine.columbia.edu/.

Gardbaum, Stephen. "The New Commonwealth Model of Constitutionalism" (2001) 49 Am J Comp L 79.

Garoupa, Nuno, and Tom Ginsburg. *Judicial Reputation: A Comparative Theory* (Chicago and London: University of Chicago Press, 2015).

George, Tracey E., and Mitu Gulati. "Courts of Good and Ill Repute: Garoupa and Ginsburg's *Judicial Reputation: A Comparative Theory*" (Book review, May 23, 2016). Online: Social Science Research Network, www.ssrn.com.

Gerhardt, Michael J. *The Power of Precedent* (Oxford: Oxford University Press, 2008).

Gibson, James L., Gregory A. Caldeira, and Vanessa Baird. "On the Legitimacy of National High Courts" (1998) 92 American Political Science Rev 343.

Gill, Rebecca. "Consensus or Ambivalence: Why Court Traditions Matter." *SSRN Electronic Journal* (June 29, 2011). Online: Social Science Research Network, www.ssrn.com.

Ginsburg, Ruth Bader. "Remarks on Writing Separately." (1990) 65 Wash L Rev 133.

Girard, Philip. *Bora Laskin: Bringing Law to Life* (Toronto: Osgoode Society for Canadian Legal History/University of Toronto Press, 2005).

Gizzi, Michael C., and Stephen L. Wasby. "Per Curiams Revisited: Assessing the Unsigned Opinion" (2012) 96 Judicature 110.

Goldsworthy, Jeffrey. "The Preamble, Judicial Independence and Judicial Integrity" (2000) 11 Const Forum Const 60.

Graber, Mark A. *Dred Scott and the Problem of Constitutional Evil* (Cambridge and London: Cambridge University Press, 2006).

Greenwood, F.M. "Lord Watson, Institutional Self-Interest, and the Decentralization of Canadian Federalism in the 1890s" (1974) 9 UBC L Rev 244.

Haigh, Richard. "The Supreme Court by Numbers 2: The McLachlin Years" (July 26, 2016). *theCourt.ca* (blog). Online: www.thecourt.ca.

Hanretty, Chris. "The Structure of Supreme Court Judgments: Eleven Ways to Leave One's Mark" (2013) 2 Cambridge J Intl & Comparative L 41.

Henderson, M. Todd. "From 'Seriatim' to Consensus and Back Again: A Theory of Dissent" (2007) Sup Ct Rev 283.

Hogg, Peter. "Is the Supreme Court of Canada Biased in Constitutional Cases?" (1979) 57 Can Bar Rev 721.

Hogg, Peter, and Ravi Amarnath. "Why Should Judges Dissent?" (2017) 67 UTLJ 128.

Huffman, James L., and MardiLyn Saathoff. "Advisory Opinions and Canadian Constitutional Development: The Supreme Court's Reference Jurisdiction" (1990) 76 Minn L Rev 1251.

Hutchinson, Dennis J. "Unanimity and Desegregation: Decisionmaking in the Supreme Court, 1948–1958" (1979) 68 Geo LJ 1.

Idleman, Scott C. "A Prudential Theory of Judicial Candor" (1995) 75 Tex L Rev 1307.

Ingman, Terence. *The English Legal Process.* 13th ed. (Oxford: Oxford University Press, 2011).

Irving, Helen. "Advisory Opinions, the Rule of Law, and the Separation of Powers" (2004) Macquarie UL Rev 105.

Kahana, Tsvi. "The Constitution as a Collective Agreement: Remuneration of Provincial Court Judges in Canada" (2003–04) 29 Queen's LJ 445.

Kiefel, Susan (Justice, HCA). "Reasons for Judgment: Objects and Observations." (Speech delivered on May 18, 2012, and published in 2014: 88 Aust LJ 554).

Knopff, Rainer. "Charter Reconsiderations" (2012) 21 National Magazine 38.

La Forest, Gérard V. "The Use of American Precedents in Canadian Courts" (1994) 46 Me L Rev 211.

Laskin, Bora. "The Supreme Court of Canada: A Final Court of and for Canadians" (1951) 29 Can Bar Rev 1038.

Lasser, Mitchel de S.-O.-l'E. *Judicial Deliberations: A Comparative Analysis of Judicial Transparency and Legitimacy* (Oxford: Oxford University Press, 2009).

LeBourdais, Isabel. *The Trial of Steven Truscott* (Toronto: McClelland and Stewart, 1966).

Lerner, Ralph. "The Supreme Court as Republican Schoolmaster" (1967) Sup Ct Rev 127.

L'Heureux-Dubé, Claire. "The Dissenting Opinion: Voice of the Future?" (2000) 38 Osgoode Hall LJ 495.

–. "The Length and Plurality of Supreme Court of Canada Decisions" (1990) 28 Alta L Rev 581.

Lynch, Andrew. "The Gleeson Court on Constitutional Law: An Empirical Analysis of Its First Five Years" (2003) 26 UNSWLJ 32.

MacCharles, Tonda. "Chief Justice Beverley McLachlin Ready to Write New Chapter with Novel." *Toronto Star* (June 15, 2017).

MacIntyre, J.M. "The Use of American Cases in Canadian Courts" (1966) 2 UBC L Rev 478.

Maltzman, Forrest, James F. Spriggs II, and Paul Wahlbeck. *Crafting Law on the Supreme Court: The Collegial Game* (Cambridge: Cambridge University Press, 2000).

Mathen, Carissima. "The Shadow of Absurdity and the Challenge of Easy Cases: Looking Back on the *Supreme Court Act Reference*" (2015) 71 Osgoode Hall LJ 161.

Maveety, Nancy. *Queen's Court: Judicial Power in the Rehnquist Era* (Lawrence: University Press of Kansas, 2008).

McConnell, W.H. "The Judicial Review of Prime Minister Bennett's 'New Deal'" (1968) 6 Osgoode Hall LJ 39.

McCormick, Peter. "American Citations and the McLachlin Court: An Empirical Study" (2009) 47 Osgoode Hall LJ 83.

–. "Assessing Leadership on the Supreme Court of Canada: Toward a Typology of Chief Justice Performance" (1993) 4 Sup Ct L Rev (2d ser.) 409.

–. "'By the Court' – the Untold Story of a Canadian Judicial Innovation" (2016) 53 Osgoode Hall LJ 1048.

–. "The Choral Court: Separate Concurrences on the McLachlin Court 2000–2004" (2005–06) 37 Ottawa LJ 1.

–. "Do Judges Read Books, Too? Academic Citations by the Supreme Court of Canada" (1998) 9 Sup Ct L Rev (2d ser.) 463.

–. "Duets, Not Solos: The McLachlin Court's Co-authorship Legacy" (2018) 41 Dal LJ 479.

–. *The End of the Charter Revolution: Looking Back from the New Normal* (Toronto: University of Toronto Press, 2015).

–. "Judgment and Opportunity: Decision Assignment on the McLachlin Court" (2015) 38 Dal LJ 271.

–. "Judicial Councils for Provincial Judges in Canada" (1986) 6 Windsor YB Access Just 160.

–. *Judicial Independence and Judicial Governance in the Provincial Courts* (Toronto: Canadian Association of Provincial Court Judges, 2004).

–. "New Questions about an Old Concept: The Supreme Court of Canada's Judicial Independence Jurisprudence" (2004) 37 Can J Political Science 839.

–. "*Nom de Plume:* Who Writes the Supreme Court's 'By the Court' Judgments?" (2016) 39 Dal LJ 77.

–. "The Political Jurisprudence of Hot Potatoes: A Comparison of the *Secession Reference* and *Bush v Gore*" (2002) 13 NJCL 271.

–. "Precedent by the Numbers: The Laskin Court" (Paper presented at the Midwest Political Science Association Annual Meeting, Chicago, April 2012).

–. "Second Thoughts: Supreme Court Citations of Dissents and Separate Concurrences, 1949–1996" (2001) 81 Can Bar Rev 369.

–. "Sharing the Spotlight: Co-authored Reasons on the Modern Supreme Court of Canada" (2011) 34 Dal LJ 165.

–. "Standing Apart: Separate Concurrence and the Supreme Court of Canada 1984–2006" (2008) 53 McGill LJ 137.

–. "Structures of Judgment: How the Modern Supreme Court of Canada Organizes Its Reasons" (2009) 32 Dal LJ 35.

–. "'Was It Something I Said?' Losing the Majority on the Modern Supreme Court of Canada, 1984–2011" (2012) 50 Osgoode Hall LJ 93.

–. "What Supreme Court Cases Does the Supreme Court Cite?" (1996) 7 Sup Ct L Rev (2d ser.) 452.

McCormick, Peter, and Marc Zanoni. "The First 'By the Court' Decisions: The Emergence of a Practice on the Supreme Court of Canada" (2014) 38 Man L Rev 1.

McEvoy, John. "Refusing to Answer: The Supreme Court and the Reference Power Revisited" (2005) 29 UNBLJ 29.

–. "Separation of Powers and the Reference Power: Is There a Right to Refuse?" (1988) 10 Sup Ct L Rev 429.

Moisidis, Cosmas. "Achieving the World's Best Practice in the Writing of Appellate Judgments" (2001) 66 L Inst J 30.

Morton, F.L., ed. *Law, Politics and the Judicial Process in Canada.* 1st ed. (Calgary: University of Calgary Press, 1984).

Motley, Constance Baker. "*Brown v. Board of Education* and Its Legacy" (1992) 61 Fordham L Rev 1.

Murchison, Kenneth M. "Four Terms of the Kennedy Court: Projecting the Future of Constitutional Doctrine" (2009–10) 39 U Balt L Rev 1.

Paterson, Alan. *Final Judgment: The Last Law Lords and the Supreme Court* (Oxford: Hart, 2013).

Popkin, William D. *Evolution of the Judicial Opinion: Institutional and Individual Styles* (New York: New York University Press, 2007).

Posner, Richard A. "What Do Judges and Justices Maximize?" (1993) 3 Sup Ct Econ Rev 1.

Puddister, Kate. *Inviting Judicial Review: A Comprehensive Analysis of Canadian Appellate Reference Cases* (PhD dissertation, McGill University, 2015). Online: McGill Library, http://digitool.library.mcgill.ca/.

Raffaelli, Rosa. *Dissenting Opinions in the Supreme Courts of the Member States* (Brussels: European Parliament/Policy Department, 2012). Online: European Parliament, www.europarl.europa.edu.

Ray, Laura Krugman. "Circumstance and Strategy: Jointly Authored Supreme Court Opinions" (2012) 12 Nev LJ 727.

–. "The Road to *Bush v Gore:* The History of the Supreme Court's Use of the Per Curiam Opinion" (2000) 79 Neb L Rev 518.

Robbins, Ira P. "Hiding Behind the Cloak of Invisibility: The Supreme Court and Per Curiam Opinions" (2012) 86 Tul L Rev 1215.

–. "The Supreme Court's Misuse of Per Curiam Opinions" (October 5, 2012). *SCOTUSblog* (blog). Online: www.scotusblog.com.

Robinson, Nick. "Structure Matters" (2013) 61 Am J Comp L 173.

Robinson, Zoe. "A Comparative Analysis of the Doctrinal Consequences of Interpretive Disagreement for Implied Constitutional Rights" (2012) 11 Wash U Global Studies L Rev 97.

Roland, Anne. "Official Law Reporting in Canada" (Paper presented at the Second International Symposium in Official Law Reporting, New York City, 2004).

Saywell, John. *The Lawmakers: Judicial Power and the Shaping of Canadian Federalism* (Toronto: University of Toronto Press, 2002).

Scalia, Antonin. "The Dissenting Opinion" (1994) 19 J Sup Ct History 33.

Schneiderman, David. "Haldane Unrevealed" (2012) 57 McGill LJ 597.

Shapiro, David L. "In Defense of Judicial Candor" (1987) 100 Harv L Rev 731.

Sharpe, Robert, and Kent Roach. *Brian Dickson: A Judge's Journey* (Toronto: University of Toronto Press, 2003).

Sheehan, Reginald S., Rebecca D. Gill, and Kirk A. Randazzo. *Judicialization of Politics: The Interplay of Institutional Structure, Legal Doctrine and Politics on the High Court of Australia* (Durham, NC: Carolina Academic Press, 2012).

Sirota, Leonid. "Judges in Masks" (February 1, 2017). *Double Aspect* (law blog). Online: http://doubleaspect.blog.

–. "Says Who?" (July 4, 2013). *Double Aspect* (law blog). Online: http://www.doubleaspect.blog.

–. "Says Who, Again?" (January 10, 2017). *Double Aspect* (law blog). Online: http://doubleaspect.blog.

Slaughter, Anne-Marie. "A Global Community of Courts" (2001) 44 Harv Int'l LJ 191.

–. "Judicial Globalization" (2000) 40 Va J Int'l L 1103.

Snell, James G., and Frederick Vaughan. *The Supreme Court of Canada: History of the Institution* (Toronto: University of Toronto Press, 1985).

Snyder, Eloise C. "The Supreme Court as a Small Group" (1958) 36 Social Forces 232.

Sunstein, Cass R. *One Case at a Time: Judicial Minimalism on the Supreme Court*. Rev. ed. (Cambridge, MA: Harvard University Press, 2001).

Tushnet, Mark. "Policy Distortion and Democratic Debilitation: Comparative Illustration of the Countermajoritarian Difficulty" (1995) 94 Mich L Rev 245.

–. "Style and the Supreme Court's Educational Role in Government" (1994–95) 11 Const Commentary 215.

–. *Weak Courts, Strong Rights: Judicial Review and Social Welfare Rights in Comparative Constitutional Law* (Princeton, NJ: Princeton University Press, 2009).

VanDam, Jeff. "The Per Curiam Cases: How the Post-Brown Court Changed America in Eleven Words or Less." Online: Social Science Research Network, http:ssrn.com/abstract=2264397.

Vaughan, Frederick. *Aggressive in Pursuit: The Life of Justice Emmett Hall* (Toronto: University of Toronto Press, 2004).

–. *Viscount Haldane: "The Wicked Step-Father of the Canadian Constitution"* (Toronto: Osgoode Society for Canadian Legal History/University of Toronto Press, 2010).

Virelli, Louis. *Disqualifying the High Court: Supreme Court Recusal and the Constitution* (Lawrence: University Press of Kansas, 2016).

Waitzer, Edward, and Johnny Jaswal. "Peoples, BCE and the Good Corporate 'Citizen'" (2009) 47 Osgoode Hall LJ 439.

Wasby, Stephen L., Steven Peterson, James Schubert, and Glendon Schubert. "The Per Curiam Opinions: Its Nature and Functions" (1992) 76 Judicature 29.

Weiler, Paul. *In the Last Resort: A Critical Study of the Supreme Court of Canada* (Toronto: Carswell, 1974).

Williams, John M. "Advisory Opinions 'A Well Covered Harbor'" (2010) 22 Bond L Rev 169.

–. "Re-thinking Advisory Opinions" (1996) 7 Pub L Rev 205.

Woolley, Alice. "The Problem of Judicial Arrogance" (October 20, 2016). *Slaw* (blog). Online: www.slaw.ca.

Zanoni, Marc. *An Early History of the "By the Court" Decisions on the Supreme Court of Canada* (MA thesis, University of Lethbridge, 2015). Online: University of Lethbridge, http://www.uleth.ca.

Index

Note: "(f)" after a page number indicates a figure or table